THE CONVERSATION CODE

How to Upgrade Your Social Skills and Your Life

Geoffrey "Gregory" Peart, M.Ed.

Aurelius books

Aurelius Books
P.O. Box 5171
Brighton, MI 48116
contact@aureliusbooks.com

Book Cover Design and Layout ©2016 Geoffrey Peart
Book Illustrations ©2016 Geoffrey Peart

The conversation code: how to upgrade your social skills and your life / Geoffrey "Gregory" Peart —1st ed.
ISBN 978-0-9898904-0-3

To my Dad, who inspires me to dream.
To my Mom, who inspires me to create.
To my Wife, who inspires me to persist.
To my Sons, who inspire me to play.
And to every friend I met along the way.

Without the herculean efforts of my editing team, this book would not exist in its current form. A giant thanks to Maureen Linnell, Katherine Hempel, and Patricia Banker. Also, a special thanks to Isaac Attia for encouraging me from the beginning. Thank you to everyone else who provided any feedback throughout the entire process.

CONTENTS

HABIT 4: SHARE

HABIT 5: ASSEMBLE

HABIT 6: CONNECT

PREFACE

"Hi, how have you been?"

So, remember that indoor children's play center I was telling you about? Well, normally, we only venture there to escape the house and help my son release his inner chimpanzee. But this last time was different. Out of nowhere, five-year-old Kaerigan asked me how he could make more friends. I wasn't sure what to say at first. But then the teacher in me decided that he was ready to learn his first major social skill: *initiating*.

Right away, we encountered a little girl about his age. And as usual, Kaerigan stood silently in place, as if his internal operating system lacked a program for social interactions. She, too, stood motionless.

She waited. Kaerigan waited. They were stuck playing a game of Shy Chicken.

I couldn't take it any longer. I bent down and whispered into Kaerigan's ear, "Say 'Hi'." He did. She did too. Then I advised, "Ask her what her name is." He asked, and she in turn responded, "Kate." Then I whispered, "Tell her your name now." Then, "Ask how old she is." She responded with her age. I felt like a modern day Cyrano De Bergerac for kids (see Steve Martin's character in *Roxanne* – it's a classic!).

And then it happened. I blinked, and they were gone. They ran off together and disappeared into the distant recesses of the climbing structure. My son had spoken just a few words and *Presto!* – he had a new friend. I was able to relax with my medium-roast coffee and watch my son and his new BFF play for the next hour.

Kaerigan left the play center that day not only with new social confidence, but with the knowledge that he possesses control over his social destiny. That one tiny realization is the key to a better social future. I was proud. I felt like I actually deserved my "World's Greatest Dad" coffee mug he bought me last Christmas.

Did I mention that my son was recently diagnosed as being somewhere on the autism spectrum? Although he is extremely bright and enjoys people and new experiences, I'm predicting we will have many more learning opportunities like the one we had that day.

This book began as a sort of manifesto to a younger version of myself. However, as the process of writing this book and the process of raising my son intermingled, I have come to realize that I have been writing it just as much for my son as well as for people like me.

Unlike many "communication experts," I know firsthand what it means to be truly shy and fearful of social experiences. At age 15, my best social skill was my ability to laugh on command at others' witty (and sometimes non-witty) comments. I always felt like an "extra" in the movie of life. I only felt socially comfortable with my closest friends. But unlike my son, I am not on any autistic spectrum. I don't really have an excuse. I just sucked at conversation. And telling stories. Or cracking jokes. I realized early on that I was programmed to be a shy introvert and my brain was not wired for exceptional communication.

It sounds absurd to think about now, but I couldn't even call and order pizza or go down to the drugstore without feeling anxiety about the impending social interaction. On one occasion, while sitting at a table in my high school art class, a girl next to me advised that I "should try to find a personality." I took her advice to heart, but where does someone *find* a personality? I didn't see any available on Amazon.com.

I started to realize that if I wanted to accomplish my goals, knowing how to converse effectively with others would likely be a prerequisite. This concept really hit home when I was dating a girl in college. My close friend at the time started dating her behind my back. He was an exceptional conversationalist. He was quick with a joke or to light up your smoke (or however that Billy Joel song goes). He was a deft storyteller. I didn't stand a chance. I was heart-broken. Sucker punched. I became painfully aware of how important conversation skills would be if I wanted any happiness in my life.

I decided to do something about it.

I scoured the libraries, bookstores, and academic journals. I read over 100 social skills books. Sadly, I never found the help I was seeking. I never found a book that helped me discover the secrets of great conversation. Too many authors were content offering generic opinions like, "People like jokes – *just say something funny!*" I needed a book that actually outlined steps for *how* to be interesting or *how* to initiate a conversation. I needed step-by-step, real-life, examples.

I eventually realized that I was looking for a book that didn't exist. Until now. I knew I was not the only one who felt trapped in a social cage (or worse: bullied, depressed, or abused). In fact, nearly 40% of the population considers themselves shy to some degree. I devoted the next 15 years to breaking out of the shyness cage and recording my research.

The content found in these pages helped me pursue my goals fearlessly. I went from "shy guy" to business manager, to star salesman, to landing the job of my dreams. I met my beautiful wife by approaching her at a 70's disco bar. I no longer fear confronting any social situation.

Today, instead of *fearing* interactions, I actually *look forward* to them.

When my son is old enough, I hope this book is on his bookshelf (or maybe on his Kindle 23?). I hope it provides him a roadmap for taking his conversational skills to the next level and the confidence to go after his ideal life. Sorry, I was blabbering about my son so much that I almost forgot: *I hope this book helps you too.*

INTRODUCTION

Think about the last conversation you had. Did you briefly chat with your spouse about dinner plans? Did you recommend a great movie to a friend? Did you make small talk about the weather with a stranger? Did you make someone laugh?

What made you choose those words? Why did you respond a certain way? Could you have been funnier? Could you have told a better story? Did you regret not saying more, or less?

Now think about the last time someone made *you* laugh. Or the last time someone regaled *you* with an entertaining story. Or the last time someone made *you* feel like they truly understood you. Who was this person?

You may have been in the presence of an exceptional conversationalist.

You already know who the exceptional conversationalists are. They can converse with anyone about anything. They can captivate entire crowds with a single word or glance. They seem to have an unlimited supply of entertaining stories and witty lines. They're invited to the best parties. They leave a trail of friends wherever they go. Like Neo from The Matrix, they possess a super-awareness of the underpinnings of conversation.

In fact, we all are capable of moments of exceptional conversation. However, some people are *consistently* exceptional. It's easy to be envious of another's social prowess and seemingly magical conversation skills. The fact is, exceptional conversationalists can't explain how they do it. (Trust me, I have asked quite a few!) You might as well ask a bottlenose dolphin how it learned to swim so well.

This book unravels the mystery behind the success of exceptional conversationalists, and what they do differently than most people. This book is based on a simple principle: Success in life comes from your ability to interact with a variety of people across all strata of society, in every common situation. By studying (and practicing) the habits of the best conversationalists, you'll become socially flexible and confident.

The good news is that no one is born speaking effectively. After all, I've never met a baby who could hold a conversation or tell a good joke! Over your lifetime, you have developed behaviors and patterns that continually underpin your social interactions.

For instance, if someone tells you they lost their phone, how might you respond? Would you choose one of the following comments?

SYMPATHIZE: Oh, I'm sorry, that's horrible!

SEEK INFORMATION: Really, what kind of phone was it?

OFFER ENCOURAGEMENT: At least this means you can finally get a new one, right?

SHARE AN EXPERIENCE: Really? I lost my phone a few years ago and I felt so useless without it!

You have been exposed to hundreds of thousands of conversations over your lifetime: some good, some bad, and some exceptional. You have heard thousands of witty one-liners, engaging stories, and friendly banter. With every social exposure and interaction, you form new neural connections or strengthen old ones. Up until this very moment, it has been a fairly random process. You may have picked up some great phrase structures, and you probably missed a few too. If your goal is to take control of the skills and habits you acquire, this book will serve as your guide. If you desire to achieve more exceptional conversational moments, this book will help you with that too.

What this book won't do is magically transform you into Jimmy Fallon, Tina Fey, Jennifer Lawrence, or Conan O'Brien. If it could, I would be a far richer man than I am today! You could dedicate your life to learning basketball, but you'd never be LeBron James either. And that's okay, because you'd probably end up being a pretty darn good basketball player!

Mind the Gap

The gap between poor and exceptional conversationalists is fascinating. Why are some people naturally comfortable with conversation, even from a young age? What did they know that their peers did not? How do effective responses come to them so quickly? How could the rest of us learn to communicate like they do?

There are many reasons for shyness, social skill deficits, or social anxiety. And there are an equal number of books that try to pathologize social differences. If you wanted, you could read the DSM IV (*Diagnostic and Statistical Manual of Mental Disorders*) to find out just how crazy you really are! My background is in Psychology and Human Performance, and I realized a long time ago that every one of us could be classified as "abnormal" in some way. Maybe you have *Lexical Deficit Disorder* or *Semantic Pragmatic Deficit Disorder* or *Expressive Language Disorder?* The good news is that this book makes no such attempt at a psychological diagnosis.

In fact, let's have a light-hearted look at our mental structures. We all have a little part of our brain responsible for learning social skills. Some of us are hard-wired and pre-disposed to pick up social skills easily and eventually metamorphose into a social butterfly. The rest of us? Not so lucky. I like to label someone's proclivity for learning social skills as either being like that of a *Verbal Sponge* or *Verbal Stone.*

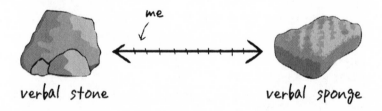

I posit that everyone sits somewhere on the spectrum between Verbal Stone and Verbal Sponge. My younger brother has always been a pure Verbal Sponge. He soaks up social expressions with ease. He actively seeks social interactions, and as a consequence, polishes his skills exponentially more. He is a year younger, but we both started speaking at the same time. In fact, he quickly overtook me. He has always been gregarious and popular. I have always been the opposite. Yet, our upbringings were essentially identical. Regarding the ability to learn, process, and retain conversation skills, we could not have been farther apart on the spectrum.

Verbal Stones were never wired for exceptional conversation. Stones tend to learn just enough to get by, relying on few options for conversation. Their brains often focus on other things. Because of their lack of social skills early on, they usually have experienced many more negative or awkward social situations, making them more hesitant to engage in future social interactions. Subsequently, they fall further and further behind their Verbal Sponge counterparts.

The Research

Finding studies based on *authentic* conversations is like finding needles in haystacks – there's not much useful information available. I realized quickly that research deconstructing great conversationalists was severely lacking. I knew I had to conduct my own research.

Over 17,500 conversations and interactions were studied over a period of 15 years (from age 20 to 35). I unabashedly collected data through face-to-face interactions and observations of participants in their true habitat (some may refer to this method as "purposeful eavesdropping," but I digress). Every effective comment or technique was recorded. And of course all identifying information was changed to protect everyone's privacy. (Except for my own family – because calling any of them some other name would just be weird.)

Only the best material was extracted and transcribed, coded, and organized to determine major themes and patterns. I started unraveling the mystery that escaped me for so many years. My analysis uncovered hundreds of behaviors that exceptional conversationalists consistently demonstrated. And the differences between the poor conversationalists and exceptional conversationalists became very apparent.

While you may consider yourself shy or introverted, socially anxious or happily withdrawn, for the sake of simplicity, I refer to everyone who may have gaps in their social skills, as *Poor Conversationalists*. And because I don't feel like typing it out a thousand times, Poor Conversationalists will be referred to as "PCs" and Exceptional Conversationalists as "ECs." I make this distinction simply to clarify certain points in the book. However, my assumption is that most people reading this book fall on a spectrum between being a PC and an EC.

The Seven Habits of Exceptional Conversationalists

Seven habits persistently presented themselves in my research. *Wait a minute!* Weren't there only six? Okay it's time I come clean – there are actually seven primary habits. This book covers the first six habits in depth, and occasionally weaves in the seventh, which I call "Play." The reason for this is simple: The seventh habit is so vast and ubiquitous to exceptional conversation, it requires its own book. I debated making this book 500+ pages, but my editors weren't fans of that idea!

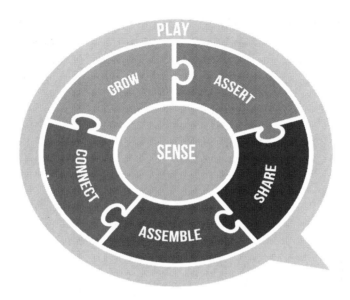

ECs demonstrate proficiency, and in some cases mastery, of each habit. Your goal should be proficiency in at least the first six habits, for one weak link can sabotage the whole! As you read about each habit, consider whether you're falling behind on any of them. The Play habit is more advanced and not necessary to achieve effective conversation.

In fact, you are reading this book because you may struggle with one or more of the habits. A major deficit with even one habit may be sabotaging your conversations.

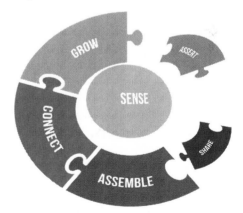

Do You Have Any Weak Links?

1. Are you completely aware of how you come across to others? Do you have a strong sense of self and a sense of life direction?
2. Are you consistently growing a collection of facts, experiences, and stories? Do you have a strong personality?
3. Are you able to consistently initiate conversation? Are you able to control the flow of conversation?
4. Do you frequently and effortlessly share your thoughts, feelings, and opinions?
5. Do people find your comments interesting and your conversation engaging?
6. Are you able to consistently maintain a conversation for as long as you desire?
7. Are you able to initiate playful and fun conversations?

The aforementioned questions correlate to one of the seven habits:

1. **SENSE.** ECs have a strong sense of self, advanced awareness of how they come across to others, and a strong sense of how conversations flow. ECs focus on strengthening the *core* of who they are: their personality, goals, and non-verbal traits.

2. **GROW.** ECs are constantly growing and developing themselves. They also focus on retaining information specifically for future conversations. The depth of experiences, stories, knowledge, and vocabulary are all critical to being able to contribute to conversations.

3. **ASSERT.** ECs assert themselves and control their conversations. They choose the topics. They initiate. They determine their own success.

4. **SHARE.** ECs know that sharing thoughts, feelings, observations, and opinions on topics is critical to maintaining engaging and interesting conversations. Self-disclosure is

critical to balancing conversations and building rapport. Sharing is also the root of small talk success.

5. **ASSEMBLE.** ECs have developed effective techniques for expressing their thoughts in interesting and engaging ways.

6. **CONNECT.** ECs know how to connect with people and to conversation topics. They are experts at maintaining and growing conversations.

7. **PLAY.** ECs add an element of play to half of what they say and do. Playfulness touches all areas, and it's the secret ingredient behind the EC's charm, wit, and humor.

As you read through this book, think about the people you know who perform well in most or all seven habits. Think about people who could become exceptional, but fall short in one or two habits. Maybe you're one of those people? For example, a poor sense of self and ineffective non-verbal skills, like frequent mumbling or low energy, would handicap every single social encounter.

A Few Last Thoughts about Acquiring Social Skills

Confident and likeable conversationalists are no different than everyone else. They are just closer to reaching their potential "selves". They are in touch with their authentic self and subsequently find it easier to initiate and maintain genuine relationships.

Learning the habits of exceptional conversationalists will equip you with the tools to help you reach the top and realize your entire "self." By understanding the conversation code, you can unlock any social shackles holding you down.

Imagine if Leonardo Da Vinci never had access to paints or pencils? What would Bill Gates or Steve Jobs have done 100 years ago before they had access to computer technology? We are all lucky benefactors of their talents and willingness to take advantage of the tools they were given in order to fully realize their potential.

Most of your dreams and desires cannot be achieved without going through, and working with, other people. Lacking sufficient social skills is expensive and the cost of not improving your social skills immeasurable. It's impossible to calculate the number of missed opportunities and experiences in your life, career, or relationships that are traced back to poor social skills or shyness. The real world demands a certain level of sociability if you desire to achieve anything of consequence. Countless studies have shown that people with better social skills and higher emotional intelligence fair better in the workplace than their counterparts with higher grades and standard intelligence scores.

Your authentic, true self, may be hidden behind many layers of fear and anxiety. But with more tools comes more confidence and ability. If you asked me to play a game of badminton, I would gladly join you. Why? Because I'm a highly skilled and seasoned badminton player. (You may have heard of some of my aliases: the *Bad Boy of Badminton* or the *Badminton Banshee*.) But I wasn't always so skilled. As a child, I refused to play the game with friends because I lacked any skills to keep up. Over time, I developed skills and experienced more positive outcomes. More skills = more confidence. Less skills = fear and avoidance. Okay moving on.

A major source of frustration stems from the attitude that you can't change the situation you are in or the person you are. You may experience a lot of self-doubt and guilt: "I'm so stupid," or "No one really likes me." If you desire real change, it's time to move away from a victim role and decide how you will take action. Everything can be improved. Your personality is *never* complete. Your habits and interests aren't finite. You're always changing – but only you decide the direction. Are you moving forward or backward? Are you going to be better today than you were yesterday?

Many people would argue that trying to be anything but themselves is a futile task and only results in artificial behavior. Some say that acting or speaking like anyone else can never last, or is deceitful in some way. It's tempting to excuse your actions by saying to yourself, "That's just who I am." I completely disagree. And unless you challenge those thoughts early in life, they may grow stronger with age.

Am I different than who I was fifteen years ago? You're damn right I am! Did it feel awkward or artificial to force myself to develop new habits sometimes? It sure did! But I am the person I am today because of those experiences and efforts. And I feel much more myself than ever.

Growing up as an introvert, I learned to develop an "on-off switch" that I could adjust depending on the situation. Turning my social skills "on" right before a work function or a presentation didn't always feel natural, but the more I did it, the easier it became, and the less it felt unnatural. In fact, I would consider myself more of an "ambivert" now (Someone with traits of both introverts and extroverts).

Be the best "you" you can be. Copy, imitate, learn from, but don't try to be exactly like someone else. Aim for the best version of "you." Enhance the good traits, and improve upon the bad. If you're stuck at 25% of your social potential, you may not be very likeable or successful, but the 82% "you" may have plenty of life successes and exceptional conversations. I once heard a quote that sent chills down my spine: "Hell is meeting the person you could have been, living the life you could have had."

Happiness stems in large part from feeling you are making progress in life. It comes from being able to control your personal direction – whether in a momentary conversation or a professional career.

Let's be honest: You're not going to remember everything you read in this book. Instead, your goal should be to focus and re-read (and practice!) specific areas you desire to improve.

People spend thousands of dollars on improving their lives – hoping it will bear the fruit of happiness. New cars, houses, plastic surgery, clothes – these are usually temporary fixes. True happiness is not possible without meaningful relationships and a sense of connectedness to others. Upgrading your social skills can be more enduring and beneficial than *anything* money can buy.

Let's get started!

Important Note

The examples found herein come from 100% certified organic free-range conversations. I highly recommend reading some of them aloud for a more authentic experience. Some may come across as awkward because I am unable to provide the entire context – but trust me, the examples were highly effective at the time. Due to their purely colloquial nature, some examples contain crass elements not be suitable for all audiences. This book is rated PG.

HABIT ONE

SENSE

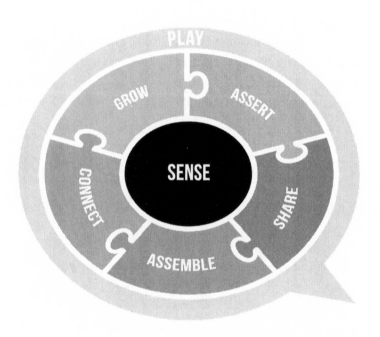

Preview: *We begin with the very foundation of verbal conversation – your voice. Your words won't travel far without the weight and energy of effective non-verbal delivery. It's also critical to develop awareness of how you come across to others. Improving this area first offers the best bang for your buck!*

[CHAPTER 1]

FIRST, LISTEN TO YOURSELF

Why would I start a book on verbal conversation with a chapter about non-verbal skills? Two reasons:

1. Non-verbal skills are the most important communication skills you can develop – and the easiest to overlook. They are the foundation of everything you do and say.

2. Non-verbal skills are the easiest to change and improve. You can dramatically enhance every future conversation by tweaking a little non-verbal behavior today.

What's the easiest and quickest way to express confidence? *Surprise!* Through your non-verbal communication. For example, the simple act of deliberately slowing down a few words and inserting a pregnant pause signals that you're in control and confident. On the flip side, what's the easiest and quickest way to project poor confidence? Poor non-verbal skills: bad posture, fidgety hands, mumbled rapid speech, etc. If you're someone who talks too softly, you may lack much "presence" within the social situation. Other dominant conversationalists may verbally step over/on you, cut you off, and generally not respect or react to what you say.

3....2....1....*Speak!* Your spoken words are tiny rockets blasting off into communication space. Your every word, expression, and social interaction is reliant on the non-verbal fuel you supply. Are you providing enough non-verbal fuel for them to reach their mission? Should you add extra energy? Volume? Enthusiasm?

Want to know a secret? Half the stuff so called "interesting people" say isn't that interesting! But they *say it* like it's interesting – their words *sound* interesting. It's often that simple. The opposite is true too – you may utter interesting comments, but if you express the words like they aren't interesting, don't be surprised if others view the words as uninteresting also.

The simplest statements (e.g. "That was awesome!" or "I like that.") can be very effective in conjunction with fantastic non-verbal skills. Many well-liked and popular people are not particularly great wordsmiths, yet conversationally thrive due to exceptional non-verbal skills.

This is the first chapter because it is designed to force you to step back for a minute before jumping gung-ho into learning any new verbal communication skills. Upgrading your non-verbal skills will instantly revitalize your current collection of comments, making you more engaging and interesting by simply saying the same things you've always been saying. Frankly, it's impossible to offer interesting remarks to everyone all the time. Unless you're a pirate, we don't live lives that exciting. We go to the grocery store. We watch movies. We clean kitchens and take out the garbage (Well, some of us do!).

 Quick Practice: Let's pause for a quick exercise. Go grab your phone, find your voice recorder app or download a free one. Record yourself telling me a quick (under 1 minute) story about an event from your childhood (Don't just read text – this recording needs to be natural). Record in your normal everyday voice. Save the recording, we'll get to it later.

Countless studies indicate people who have better non-verbal communication skills, simply come across as more interesting and likeable. You probably know a person or two you could just listen to forever, simply because their voice is so mesmerizing. They could be bloviating at length about thermodynamic laws – it wouldn't matter. I listen to podcasts every day, and it's often the podcasts with great voices that keep me coming back – even if the content is only average.

A lot of research suggests that your tone of voice can give the impression that you're more intelligent or successful than someone who has a weaker voice. Don't let a weak voice hold you back. Think about it: If people don't enjoy your voice, then how can you expect them to enjoy your conversation? Have you ever talked to someone with a bad case of the mumbles? Or someone who was so quiet it was hard to hear every word? It can be an incredibly frustrating experience. Next time someone says, "What?" or misunderstands your message, your voice could be at fault.

I was born with a soft voice and I never realized how frustrating it was for other people to listen to me until my wife pointed it out (on multiple occasions!). My soft voice partially explained why I didn't receive the reactions I expected over the years. Luckily I was able to cure my disease by forcing out a little volume and energy.

Remember that time you felt socially embarrassed or ineffective? (For many of you I'm sure this is a daily angst.) You may have obsessed for hours over your word choices and whether you said the wrong thing. The problem may stem from *how* those words were spoken. And an important component of how you speak is *energy*.

Are You an Energy Donor or Energy Vampire?

Energy is the effort you put into your words. Energy isn't simply acting excited or speaking in loud, high-pitched tones. It is passion; enthusiasm; conviction; feeling; concern; and a whole lot more. Talk like you care about what you're saying. Because if you don't care, why should the other person?

Exceptional conversations thrive on *energy*. If you aren't adding energy, you're unintentionally sucking it from others. Don't be an energy vampire! No one likes talking to energy vampires. People only like conversing with vampires in the movies – especially if the vampires look like Brad Pitt or Robert Pattinson. (*They* never have to worry about vocal variation.)

Have you ever experienced that moment where you suddenly get the feeling no one is listening anymore? That you're boring the other person? I'm not here to flatter you – you may in fact have been boring. People are impatient. People require stimulation. People want to see movement and feel energy. Good non-verbal communication keeps the audience stimulated in case your words aren't interesting enough.

Try this experiment next time you get a chance: During a plain everyday interaction, add more energy than normal into a few statements, and see if you notice the other person adding more energy into their responses. Energy begets energy.

Speak Like a Roller Coaster

A *roller coaster?* How exactly does a roller coaster talk? What does that mean? How can you apply it to the way you talk? Should you try to sound like a cheerleader all day? Please don't! Should you shout a lot? No thanks!

From now on, think of your voice as a roller coaster ride. When you speak, you're giving your audience an auditory ride – whether you plan to or not. Are you forcing your audience to ride on a flat, boring, monotonous ride? If you are, you can't be surprised if no one is pushing and shoving to get back in line for your next ride.

Additionally, people from all corners of the world, prefer tonal variance when listening to another person speak. Some people are born with melodious voices, but no one is born a singer, professional speaker, or book narrator. It takes training to fully control vocal modulation and rhythms. Many people, born with unfortunate voices, learn to improve the quality and pitch of their sounds.

Compare the roller coaster rides in the illustration. If your voice is a roller coaster, which ride do you think people would prefer?

Although you may view the third roller coaster as being the most fun, when it comes to how you talk, you should aim for something like the middle roller coaster. The first ride is probably too mild and monotonous. And the third ride may sound more like a restless teenager after downing three Red Bull energy drinks.

We could delve deeper into terms like *timbre* and *resonance*, but knowing the terminology is not the point. If I played a recording of five people speaking, you would instinctively recognize who sounds pleasing and who doesn't. The good news is that your voice is very easy to control with practice and effort. It doesn't have to be perfect. Simply try to vary the inflection in your voice: change your volume, pitch, and your speed/tempo. In general, deeper/lower pitches tend to be more pleasing. You can also vary the energy on a single phrase or even a single word for extra emphasis.

 Quick Practice: Go grab your phone again for another recording. Tell the same childhood story you told from the last practice, but this time deliberately maintain a very flat, monotone voice the entire time. Then record the story again, but vary your voice wildly (to the point you feel silly recording it!). Go up, go down, pause for a few seconds, vary your pitch, speed, lower your voice, add emphasis on certain words, etc. Have fun! Save both recordings.

Insecure people often do one of three things with their voice:

1. Lose energy/volume and trail off at the end of their statements.
2. Talk quietly.
3. Pronounce statements as if they were questions (AKA "uptalk").

On the contrary, people in positions of power have a certain method of speaking with energy and conviction all the way through to the end. Also, listen carefully to journalists and news anchors. They are masters at controlling their voices and therefore come off as very confident – even if deep down they are petrified. They slow a word down or stretch it out at will. It's as if they are saying, "I'm going to take up more time and space with this word, because I'm in control." They deliberately pause to add tension – as if taking you to the peak of the ride before moving again.

Some of my favorite examples of vocal modulation and non-verbal habits come from comedians like Aziz Ansari. The secret of humor doesn't necessarily stem from what he says as much as how he sounds. He has perfected the art of varying his voice and taking his listeners on a tremendous auditory ride. His timing and emphasis on certain words is the secret to his magic.

A key tactic for most comedians is the strategic use of emphasis; they wait until the perfect series of words to add extra emphasis. I have a few very funny friends who similarly have learned to add an extra punch of energy and enthusiasm to the keywords or punchline of their statement – it doesn't have to be only during jokes! Some people offer an observation or tell a story and hold the extra emphasis for when they're describing their reaction. For example, "She finally turned around to look at me and I thought she was wearing some kind of zombie mask, but she really wasn't – I was like, *Whoa! I'm getting outta here!*" If the reaction, in italics, was said with extra emphasis, it would come off as much more entertaining. You could go one step further and show the look of horror in your facial expressions, acting out the reaction as if you were truly scared. How would you sound? Try dramatizing it for fun.

There are a few sports commentators who follow very predictable – but effective speech patterns. These guys will state their point, and then rephrase what they just said, but more succinctly and with jolt of power and enthusiasm. For example, "The way he runs with the ball, he's one of the best in the league right now – *ONE OF THE BEST!*" It's a very simple but effective technique.

Speak in Chunky Phrases

Insecurities often manifest in the voice. Shy people, when they actually open up, tend to communicate quickly and softly; often stringing every phrase together without any breaks. Too much attention and too many staring eyes are intimidating. Unfortunately, it's hard for anyone listening to completely process everything.

From this point on, mentally focus on chunking each main point or phrase. Deliberately pause between each point. Chunking helps you add variance to your voice, keeping it interesting. If we continue the awesome roller coaster analogy – it's akin to pausing at the top of the hill before the next drop. Every time you pause before your next set of statements, you're allowing them to mentally break and process what you said before the ride picks up steam again. The act of deliberately pausing is an incredibly simple but powerful act; it says you are in control and you are comfortable with silence for a few seconds.

Chunking will instantly do five things for you:

1. You will have extra time to think about what to say next and how to present yourself verbally.
2. You will have a mental break, so you can inject more energy into the next phrase.
3. You will be able to take a breath and relax more.
4. You will gain a sense of control instead of feeling like your words are running away from you.
5. You will sound more interesting, confident, and likeable.

Initially, it may feel unnatural and difficult to always remind yourself to speak in chunks – especially if you're feeling too much pressure. Luckily, forcing your brain to think and talk in chunks becomes habitual over time; your brain will start formulating phrases in chunks automatically.

So far we've covered improving your non-verbal skills so everything you say sounds and looks better. After practicing, you should have a good sense of how you come across to others, and how you *want* to come across to others. At the end of each chapter is a challenge activity affectionately titled "Use It or Lose It." Put these techniques into practice if you desire to see any significant improvement!

CHAPTER 1: USE IT OR LOSE IT

Pull out your phone and play all three of the recordings you created from the practice exercises in this chapter. Compare your "normal" recording with the subsequent recordings. What did you notice? Did the wild version sound as wild as you felt it was when you recorded it? Was the monotone version painful to listen to? Did you hear any poor habits like mumbling? Is your pitch too high? Do you lose energy at the end of your comments?

Let's do one more recording. This time tell the same childhood story or choose another story. Remember, it's important to tell a story for this exercise because during the process of recalling events, you may notice some poor conversation habits creep in. During this recording, see if you can improve upon your "normal" vocal habits and create something even more interesting. Then listen to your new recording, how did you do?

Extra credit exercise: Find a YouTube clip of a popular talk show host or news reporter. Watch them four or five times. After repeatedly watching the same clip, it will become easier to listen to their vocal mannerisms because you won't be distracted by the content of their message anymore. What did you notice?

CHAPTER 1: REVIEW

Before this chapter:
- ✓ The Seven Habits: Sense, Grow, Assert, Share, Assemble, Connect, and Play
- ✓ Start working towards improving any weak links

From this chapter:
- ✓ Don't be an energy vampire
- ✓ Vary your voice
- ✓ Speak in more chunks

Key takeaway from this chapter:
Poor non-verbal habits sabotage your communication. Practice listening to your voice until you become keenly aware of how you come across. Find and fix any bad vocal habits.

Coming up next:

We'll continue examining how to improve your non-verbal skills with a focus on visual communication.

Preview: *Improving how you communicate visually is a critical part of the non-verbal foundation. It's important to develop awareness of how you appear, add effective behaviors, and fix any behaviors holding back your conversations.*

[CHAPTER 2]

WATCH YOURSELF

Your Movie is Always Playing

Aside from when you're alone, you're always communicating something non-verbally! If someone can hear or see you, then you're serving as a visual or auditory stimulus to that person. In other words, you are a form of entertainment, and the movie called (insert your name here) has a running length of – *forever*.

Many people shutter at the thought of being watched or listened to by so many people. But luckily for the self-conscious, there's so much stimuli in the world, 99.9% of what you do and say won't be remembered for very long. It's time to embrace the fact you're a form of entertainment. You can't escape it, so you might as well put on a good show! Make your movie interesting. Give people something to enjoy.

Ask yourself a few questions: What kind of movie are you showing? Do you barely move when you talk? Does your head shift a little? Do you add gestures? Do your eyes dart around? (I used to always have trouble with that one!) Do you forget to smile? (I *still* have trouble with this one!)

Many people talk like robots or statues – barely moving their faces. You can try to be funny or light-hearted, but you won't get the reaction you seek if you deliver the lines wearing a solemn face. You can tell an amazing story, but if you have a monotone voice and no facial or body expressions, your audience will still lose interest. It's not enough to *tell* them that you were "shocked," sometimes it helps to *show* them. Just a subtle glimpse of what you looked like when you were surprised, increases your box office appeal. Let them *hear* the shock in your voice. Let them *see* the dismay on your face.

Without non-verbal additives, conversations would proceed more like email exchanges – where most of the human-ness is replaced with objective text messages. If given the option, people prefer consuming the entire movie and feeling the stimulation of the auditory *and* the visual senses.

Many experts agree that the *majority* of what you're communicating to the other person is non-verbal. Don't forget, this includes your overall appearance and clothing. A little effort towards your looks and sense of style goes a long way. Dress like a successful, confident person, and you'll start feeling more confident. Don't let an old pair of shoes and a hash brown-stained T-shirt be your downfall!

If you struggle with your non-verbal expressions, then definitely take the practice section seriously for this chapter. You'll notice huge gains with just a little effort. Don't forget to have fun with gestures. I have always been amazed at how well even a quick dramatic head-turn can hold someone's attention for a few moments.

 Quick Practice: Go on YouTube and search for a comedian or talk show host. Watch a few of the videos with the volume muted. Study their visual communication skills only. What do you notice? *Successful communicators regularly move their bodies and animate their faces.*

Don't Forget about Gestures

Gestures inject life into your expressions. Too many speakers feel that their words alone will carry the weight of a conversation, then struggle to keep their audience engaged, because they are too rigid. The opposite also exists – someone expressing the most boring content may appear very interesting and engaging simply by employing fantastic gestures and energy. With practice, gestures are easy to incorporate into your daily conversational habits.

Your descriptions and stories become twice as vivid when you act them out in subtle ways. Describing an incident with a statement like, "I looked over and he had his hands up," is much more effective if you actually show how is hands went up.

Animating your hands or body is another method of obtaining some control over your conversation. Control is a key to confidence, especially in social situations. The more in control you feel, the more confident you appear, and the less you appear nervous and tense.

You know that dreaded feeling that overtakes you when everyone's eyes are focused like lasers on your face? Gestures provide the audience with something else to focus on rather than your eyes and face, which for many people, can be a very insecure and vulnerable experience. Gestures act as your psychological shield, redirecting those intimidating gazes.

As a bonus, gestures have been found to aid in memory recall, and if you're like me and need all the help you can get, you might as well try it!

This chapter is brief because the concepts are simple, however; the work required is demanding. Dedicate significant time to practicing better non-verbal skills and you'll be one step closer to maximizing your social potential. Become completely aware of how others see you, and stop relying on how you *think* you appear.

CHAPTER 2: USE IT OR LOSE IT

Record a video of yourself telling a story. Any story will do. Then record the same story again but deliberately add more movement, energy, facial expressions, and gestures. Go out of your comfort zone!

Watch both versions and compare the new behaviors with your existing behaviors. What did you notice? Is one more entertaining than the other? Does the more demonstrative version look as silly as it felt while you were recording it?

CHAPTER 2: REVIEW

Before this chapter:
- ✓ The Seven Habits: Sense, Grow, Assert, Share, Assemble, Connect, and Play
- ✓ Start working towards improving any weak links
- ✓ Add energy and variety to your voice

From this chapter:
- ✓ Show a better movie
- ✓ Take advantage of the power of gestures

Key takeaway from this chapter:
Poor non-verbal habits sabotage your communication. Expressive visual communication is a key part of your package of non-verbal skills.

Coming up next:
Next, we'll examine the underlying building blocks of conversation, and improve your conversational awareness. It's important to deconstruct conversations down to the basic parts before diving into the details of how to put them together in more effective ways.

Preview: *Developing your conversational intelligence is the next step towards improving social skills. We'll examine the underlying structures of conversation so you improve your conversational awareness (or "sixth sense").*

[CHAPTER 3]

INCREASE YOUR CONVERSATIONAL AWARENESS

A generation ago a psychotherapist named *Eliza* achieved momentary fame. Eliza was not the greatest conversationalist – but she had a good excuse: She was a computer program (an early "chat bot"). The funny thing is, many people who "conversed" with her actually believed she was real for a while. She was simply following coded scripts. Her conversations with humans would proceed like this:

ELIZA: How are you today?
HUMAN: Good, how are you?
ELIZA: Good, thanks. Where are you from?
HUMAN: Detroit.
ELIZA: That's nice, what do you do for a living?
HUMAN: I'm a writer.
ELIZA: That sounds interesting.
HUMAN: What do you do?
ELIZA: I'm a therapist. Do you like your job?

Many human interactions really sound like this. Do your conversations? Eliza was programmed to follow a basic script. Like many chat bots, they fare well in the beginning of a new social interaction because meeting someone for the first time often follows predictable social scripts. She was coded to ask a few good initial "getting to know you" questions, and she knew how to answer some commonly asked questions as well. Historically, chat bots start failing miserably when the conversation ventures into more substantive and ambiguous areas.

If you want more interesting conversations, you'll have to do much better than a computer program.

Are You Following a Script?

In some ways, we humans are similar to computers. Computers can only do what they are programmed to do. Likewise, humans tend to act in very predictable ways. Throughout our lives, we have all become aware of hundreds of scripts to help us navigate the complex world of conversation and social interaction. Being aware of social scripts help determine and guide where we can insert the words and phrases we have stored away. Scripts help guide your thoughts and reduce the cognitive load on your brain. The more you're in-tune to social scripts, the more you've practiced them, the smoother and more confident your conversations will proceed.

Cognitive psychologists discovered long ago that we all need to form mental models (often referred to as "schemas") to help us understand and process all the information we're exposed to on a daily basis. Our brains are constantly trying to make sense of every experience. Anxiety can often be attributed to simply not possessing the proper script of how to act and what to say. In other words, we may lack enough data to finish the mental model, so to speak.

Children are often anxious in new situations because they have no idea how to proceed correctly. As a teenager, my anxiety over ordering pizza was not because I was afraid of "people" or "talking," I simply didn't feel comfortable with the *pizza ordering script*. I had a general sense of how to call and place an order, but part of me worried the conversation may get off track and then I'd be stuck. We sometimes assume a conversation can be as simple as, "Give me a pepperoni pizza." But in reality it's not always that simple. A script as simple as ordering dinner may include a variety of small talk comments. Most conversations are infinitely more complex.

Let's look at an example of a very common script. At a birthday, baby shower, or holiday, when someone gives someone else a present, there is a very predictable, culturally ingrained exchange. Think about the last time you were handed a gift – what did you say? Did you stick to something similar to the following script?

GIFT RECEIVER'S SCRIPT
1. STATE APPRECIATION: Thank you.
2. DESCRIBE GIFT: A *reading light*, this is great!
3. STATE BENEFIT: I can read my books at night now.
4. SHOW APPRECIATION: Thank you, Pat.

GIFT GIVER'S SCRIPT
1. ACKNOWLEDGE APPRECIATION: You're welcome.
2. PROVIDE AN EXPLANATION: I was thinking you could use one of those since you're always reading so much.

Does this scenario sound familiar? You've probably heard or followed a similar script hundreds of times in your life. The aforementioned script may seem obvious and second nature to you, but there was a point in your life where you didn't quite follow it yet, where you were still learning the correct order of things, the correct placement of certain phrases. Now consider an interaction you still feel anxious about – it's likely that you aren't comfortable enough with the script of how it is supposed to play out.

What scenario is really challenging for most people? *Confrontation.* The following scripts excel at handling confrontations, but don't worry about memorizing every step. Simply rehearsing scripts a few times can do wonders.

One of my favorite simple scripts is the *I feel, When You, Because* script. It's incredibly helping for minor confrontations and communicating something that's bothering you. For example, "**I feel** really frustrated **when you** don't finish the work on time **because** it prevents me from finishing my own work." For more complex confrontations, a script below might be in order:

CONFRONTATION SCRIPT
1. SETUP THE CONVERSATION: Hey Steve, I need to talk to you about something.
2. DESCRIBE THE PROBLEM BEHAVIOR/ACTION: Remember when you said you were going to have that project finished on time, and it was a week late?
3. DESCRIBE THE CONSEQUENCES OF THE ACTION/BEHAVIOR: Well, because it was late, I got in big trouble with Carl.
4. STATE YOUR FEELINGS: I didn't appreciate how you didn't give us any warning.
5. ACKNOWLEDGE THEIR PERSPECTIVE: I realize that you had a rough week that week, but...
6. STATE DESIRED ACTION OR OUTCOME: Next time, I need you to at least let me know ahead of time if you think you're going to get behind.
7. STATE APPRECIATION: I know you didn't want to hurt our project, so thanks for hearing me out on this.

The master of rhetoric, Aristotle, introduced a classic guideline for speeches, but it applies to many other situations as well. Essentially, *tell them what you're going to tell them, then tell them, then tell them what you just told them.* Sound silly? It's not. Look at the following series of statements common in business interactions:

TELL THEM OVERVIEW: Hey, I just wanted to touch base about my feelings on the X project.
TELL THEM DETAILS: I was thinking it needs more _____, and maybe less _____. Also...

TELL THEM SUMMARY: So basically I think we should do
_____ with the X project. I just wanted to touch base and
make sure we're on the same page.

Of course, the other person would be involved with the interaction, but you could stick to the Aristotle script in a general sense in order to keep your thoughts focused and clear.

 Quick Practice: Do you know that ending a conversation often follows very predictable scripts? Imagine you need to wrap up a conversation with Chatty Cathy, how would you proceed? Write on the following line what you would say to end the conversation (or just think about it for a minute).

Were you able to think of how you end conversations? A good script for ending a substantive conversation goes something like this:

ENDING A CONVERSATION SCRIPT

1. STATE REASON: Well, I have to go see/do/finish _____.
2. POSITIVE WORDS: It was great chatting/seeing/doing
   _____ with you.
3. REFERENCE POSSIBLE FUTURE EVENT: We should do
   _____ sometime. / Good luck with the _____, I'm sure
   you'll do great!

Some conversations may require a *2B.*, which summarizes or recaps any important point from the conversation. "Your ideas about _____ were really interesting." Or "So I think we concluded that _____ should never _____, right?"

You might be wondering how to go about learning more scripts. There's isn't room in this book for many more, but I encourage you to start listening to social interactions like a social scientist and develop your conversational sixth sense. One of the best ways to analyze the structure of a conversation is by listening multiple times. Hearing something multiple times allows your brain to focus on underlying structures and nuances. Find a few podcasts with natural banter and social interactions, like the *Stuff You Should Know* podcast with Josh and Chuck, and listen to the same show three or four times, you'll see what I mean. The same goes for any other type of social skill. For example, if you want to learn more about humor, listen to a comedian's show four or five times. You'll start seeing patterns emerge. The act of deliberately listening to structures will automatically improve your social skills, even if you don't think you learned anything specific.

Successful professionals from all walks of life – pro athletes, sales people, etc. – have mental strategies to prepare for big, important events. Like what, you ask? They often find a quiet place, and mentally walk through the potential events, scripts, or dialogue numerous times. They prime their brains to be ready for specific events or dialogue. Many life events contain predictable structures. For example, I've always said you can plan for at least 75% of a job interview beforehand. You should mentally walk through meeting the hiring manager, making small talk, and answering the questions you know they are likely to ask. A little online research will tell you most of the questions being asked of the position.

Deconstructing the Conversation

Let's open up conversation and take a look inside. Check out the following diagram. Pretty basic right?

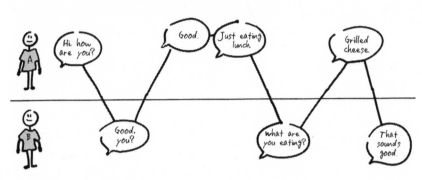

Every conversation you have ever had or will ever have can fit into a diagram like this. Conversations are simply a series of connections and not some nebulous uncontrollable entity. Conversations are very controllable and sometimes predictable. They often start and end in a similar fashion. The body of a conversation consists of connected statements and questions. Each speech bubble in the diagram represents one statement or question.

In the previous diagram, Person A initiated the conversation by calling and asking "Hi, how are you?" The comments go back and forth until the conversation ends.

Look at the next conversation diagram and see if you can speculate anything about the conversation or people involved, without knowing anything about the spoken words. What can you tell about this conversation and the participants without knowing anything about their words? Who is probably the exceptional conversationalist in the diagram?

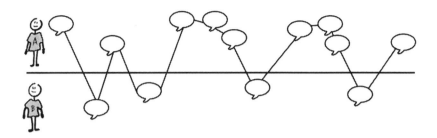

Person A initiated the conversation. Person A said more. Person A also closed the conversation. Person A is more likely to be an exceptional conversationalist. Person B looks like s/he was merely responding to Person A the entire time.

Every comment or question opens the door to multiple connections, additional comments, or questions. For any given comment, your brain is tasked with the job of finding a suitable connection. After finding an appropriate comment to connect with, the comment is verbalized and the conversation continues. The process of searching and sorting through all possible options is tremendously complex, but the brain is well equipped for the task. You may have realized that your brain may not be as proficient or skilled at generating good comments as the exceptional conversationalists. That's possibly because you lack the number of acceptable comments an EC has available in their brain's conversation storage tank.

Let's examine the different ways an EC and PC respond. Someone starts a conversation topic by asking, "Have you seen _____ yet? We just started watching it." Assuming a PC and an EC haven't seen the show, let's compare comments.

A PC may only think of two fairly limited options to choose from in that moment:

No, I haven't seen it.
No, I haven't. Is it good?

An EC's brain may be wired to scan many more – and better – options before making a selection:

No, I haven't seen it.
No, I'm really into _____ right now. Have you seen that?
No, but I bet Maureen would love that. She's crazy about crime dramas. One time she binged on the entire season of ____ in one weekend!
No, I'm more of a science fiction kind of guy. If Star Trek is ever on, I drop everything to watch it.

Conversations can grow infinitely complex very quickly. At every turn, ECs often have more – and better – options than PCs. A PC may do fine during a more structured and simpler environment like playing Monopoly or working on a group project, but falter during a less scripted, more complex, and ambiguous conversation. By the end of this book you'll be exposed to enough habits that coming up with something effective to say should never be a problem again.

Your brain is a powerful machine, but left untrained, it won't function as efficiently as it could. It's time you start training your brain to achieve better results. As you work through this book, take the practice sections seriously and work on training your brain to develop better habits. Remember, an untrained brain picks and chooses random information. You can train it to choose better responses, form better connections, and remember more interesting information.

CHAPTER 3: USE IT OR LOSE IT

Turn to the last *Use It or Lose It* of this book in Chapter 18: *Listen and Grow the Conversation Together.* You'll find a few authentic conversation samples borrowed from exceptional conversations. It's important to study great conversations in their entirety, and not just single comments out of context. Choose one example case study and read every line. Read it again, but add some additional enthusiasm and energy, as if you were really there, playing the part of each person talking. Read it aloud a third time. Read it a few more times if you can. Reading it over and over encodes the scripts and comment structures in your memory – even if you don't realize it. If you feel like you struggle with the flow of conversation and want to improve your awareness, then dedicate significant time to this exercise.

CHAPTER 3: REVIEW

Before this chapter:

- ✓ The Seven Habits: Sense, Grow, Assert, Share, Assemble, Connect, and Play
- ✓ Start working towards improving any weak links
- ✓ Add energy and variety to your voice
- ✓ Pay attention to the movie you're showing people

From this chapter:

- ✓ Scripts are everywhere, start paying more attention
- ✓ The *I Feel, When You, Because* is a classic script to remember

Key takeaway from this chapter:

Study more scripts so you become more comfortable with the structure and flow of conversations.

Coming up next:

Social interactions loosely follow underlying scripts, but for the most part, people don't follow anything exactly the same way every time. It's important to become more aware of what guides the words that come out of your mouth. We're examining your core personality traits next.

Preview: *Social scripts may provide general direction, but your personality is what determines which comments you ultimately verbalize. It's important to improve upon any negative traits or poor habits.*

[CHAPTER 4]

AIM TO BE MORE LIKEABLE

Everyday conversations follow some patterns, but the majority are still challenging to predict with any degree of accuracy. When you're faced with social ambiguity, your personality guides which comments come out of your mouth. You may know thousands of interesting pieces of information and have thousands of comments ready to go, but your personality makes the final judgment call as to what you communicate. Be careful: All the training in the world won't help if you're a jerk!

Before venturing any further, it's important to take a detour to chat about your personality. You're probably not a jerk, but you have to be careful of acting in certain ways that annoy your conversation partner(s) and decrease your social effectiveness. And on the flipside, emulating the best and most likeable personalities will reap instant benefits.

We have all developed a Conversation Style. Some people love to listen and offer statements of sympathy. Some people love to entertain. Some people frequently offer opinions and observations. Some people often introduce new information and cultural references to the conversation. Part of solidifying your inner core is truly understanding who you are and how you fit into conversations with other people.

I was at a social event recently where a woman was telling story after story – she was really captivating the group. However, when I tried to discuss something with her one-on-one, she was a terrible listener, and immediately shifted the conversation back to another personal anecdote. I was turned off immediately. Naturally, she got along swimmingly with a few people who loved to listen. They made a good match. As you read through all the habits, try to analyze your own habits and behaviors as they compare to exceptional conversationalists.

Likeable personalities are generally effective in any type of environment or conversation, scripted or unscripted. Below are the seven most likeable personality traits (and their unlikeable counterparts). Whatever your conversation style, try to incorporate these seven traits into your personality if you don't already. Falling on the side of an unlikeable trait may be to blame for many of your past negative social experiences.

The Seven Most Likeable Traits

1. BE HUMBLE

Admit your mistakes and don't brag. Give others credit. Embracing your flaws is disarming; People will warm up to you quickly and more easily identify with you. *Don't be arrogant.*

He's an amazing artist. I still struggle drawing triangles!

2. BE CARING AND UNSELFISH

Care about others and what they are saying, doing, and feeling. Ask follow-up questions, and reference something they said in the past. Share and relate to their feelings. *Don't be cold or self-centered.*

You mentioned last month you were thinking of _____, did you end up doing that?

3. BE POSITIVE

Not many people enjoy hanging out with *Debbie Downer* or *Eeyore*. You increase your odds of being likeable by generally remaining optimistic and looking for the good in life. You will see more good in things simply by *trying* to see more good. Avoid complaining too much. *Don't be too cynical, negative, or bitter.*

At least we were able to _____.

4. BE ENTHUSIASTIC

Give your words and expressions some *life*! You don't have to be a cheerleader, but if someone tells you some good news, be excited for them. Put some feeling and energy in your voice. Remember, if you aren't adding energy, you may be unintentionally subtracting from it. *Don't be an Energy Vampire.*

I *love* your kitchen...it reminds me of _____.

5. BE GOAL-ORIENTED AND PASSIONATE

Have direction in life and be able to share your goals. Working towards goals will increase your inner confidence. People are drawn to success and passion. Develop hobbies and passions. Talk about them. *Don't be overly lazy and uninspiring.*

This weekend, I'm volunteering for _____ / running a _____ / trying to build a _____.

6. BE PLAYFUL

Lighten up! Humor and playfulness are critical to exceptional conversation, but also the hardest to achieve. But don't worry, humor and play are covered thoroughly in my next book. *For now, don't be too serious all the time.*

Even if I miss the game, I avoid everyone until I can watch it. I'm actually good at avoiding everyone. If there was a career for professional avoiders, I'd be a very wealthy man by now!

7. BE FLEXIBLE

Adapt to changing environments. Don't turn cranky when something doesn't go your way. Being flexible means being easy-going and going with the flow of conversation instead of stopping it. Play along with silly jokes. *Don't be rigid or defensive with friends.*

It's closed? That's okay, I bet we can find some cool _____ over at _____ too!

How Do You Make Others Feel?

The essence of being likeable is how you make others feel when they are around you. Your efforts spent improving your financial situation, career, appearance, accomplishments, etc., don't equate to likeability if the other person doesn't feel good when they're around you.

Imagine I created flashcards containing a photo of someone you know on each card. If I showed you one card at a time, and measured your physical and mental reaction, we'd discover how each person made you feel. Some people would elicit joy, sorrow, anger, jealousy, etc.

I'm not advocating that you obsesses about what others think about you – I'm simply suggesting you watch out for any negative habits preventing others from feeling good around you. What are those behaviors? Many are the unlikeable traits listed previously. For example, being too negative, selfish, or arrogant.

How someone feels around you is connected to their desires. Be cognizant of the **two primary levels of human desire**:

1. SHALLOW
2. DEEP

On a **shallow** level, people want to relax, learn, play, laugh, be entertained, and generally enjoy themselves. The **deep** level is the heavier stuff – the average person wants to feel loved, respected, valued, and listened to. They want to feel like their opinions matter. Start becoming hyper aware of how you make others feel on both levels – are you providing value on a shallow level? Do you own a house everyone enjoys visiting? Do you keep people informed of the latest news? Do you tell entertaining stories? Do you add some energy? Do you know how to joke around? Or do you make people feel uneasy or tense? Do you get defensive too easily? Maybe your value is more with the deeper levels. Maybe you offer deep friendship. Maybe you're the person who listens well and always supports your friends when they need you.

Ask yourself if your actions, behaviors, thoughts, and words are contributing to the other person's positive feelings or reducing them? ECs are dynamic. They offer value across both levels. They offer excitement, energy, and positive attitudes. They look toward the future, they inspire, they uplift others around them, they offer entertainment value, they seek to help others, and fulfill desires by being a good listener. PCs may not subtract from any desire, but they may not appeal to any desire either.

CHAPTER 4: USE IT OR LOSE IT

Which one of the Seven Most Likeable Traits could you improve immediately? Pick one and do something today that moves you closer to being more likeable.

CHAPTER 4: REVIEW

Before this chapter:

- ✓ The Seven Habits: Sense, Grow, Assert, Share, Assemble, Connect, and Play
- ✓ Add energy and variety to your voice
- ✓ Pay attention to the movie you're showing people
- ✓ Scripts are everywhere, start paying more attention

From this chapter:

- ✓ The Seven Most Likeable Traits: Be Humble, Caring, Positive, Enthusiastic, Goal-Oriented, Playful, and Flexible
- ✓ Pay attention to how you make others feel on a shallow and deep level

Key takeaway from this chapter:

No social encounter is truly predictable and controllable, but by sticking to likeable traits, you'll help yourself succeed in any situation.

Coming up next:

The Grow habit is next. It's critical that you grow your mental capacity for exceptional conversation.

HABIT TWO

GROW

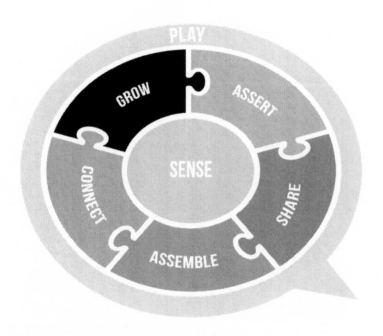

Preview: *Developing yourself, retaining conversational nuggets, and improving your conversational memory are key parts of the Grow habit. This chapter explores why you are sometimes at a loss for words, how to contribute more to conversation, and how to grow into a better conversationalist.*

[CHAPTER 5]

FILL UP YOUR CONVERSATION STORAGE TANK

"I Never Know What to Say!"

Why do you struggle coming up with responses? Why do your conversations stall? This is one of the most common challenges to conversationalists everywhere.

I teach classes on improving interviewing skills. The first question I ask my students is based on an ancient Chinese proverb.

> ME: When is the best time to plant a tree?
> STUDENT: I don't know.
> ME: 20 years ago. When is the second best time to plant a tree?
> STUDENT: I don't know.
> ME: Now.

The interview itself is the last part of what determines if you will land the job. Everything you did up until the interview is far more important. Did you gain valuable experiences in your field you can reference? A strong portfolio you can draw on? Have you learned the appropriate vernacular for the role? The interview is a lesson in long-term preparation.

Just like during an interview, it's very difficult to fake a good conversation. The conversation itself can only be as good as the content it pulls from. No self-help book is capable of telling you exactly what to say in every conversation. It takes time and effort – there are no "get rich quick" strategies.

Imagine being stuck in an elevator with a stranger for one hour. There's nothing to see or observe besides the elevator. It's incredibly boring. This is a very challenging scenario for PCs. ECs would still thrive. Why? ECs dedicate time to remembering thousands of effective comments, facts, opinions, and stories for use in a myriad of situations. We all have a part of our memory dedicated to information we can reference in conversation; I refer to this part of our brain as the *conversation storage tank.*

Your storage tank is always with you – even in a dark, stalled elevator. An EC could tell stories for hours if given the opportunity. Adding to your conversation storage tank now, will help you avoid the dreaded awkward silences later.

Become an Information Hunter

When you watch a movie, let's say *Attack of the Zombie Squirrels* (it's a classic!), you may think to yourself, "Wow, I like this John Smith actor, he's really funny," or "The ending could have been much better, they should have driven the motorcycle off the building."

Actively processing information shifts the information to a more accessible place in your memory. You're literally assembling random pieces of information into coherent, usable thoughts. Many of these thoughts can be used later in conversation. If someone brings up Attack of the Zombie Squirrels, you may refer to how much you like that John Smith actor. **That's conversational information.**

So what *isn't* conversational information? Unusable information includes information you wouldn't typically share in a conversation. For example: highly personal details, esoteric science facts, etc. It all depends on the people involved and the context.

You may have a great personality, but if everyone in the group is talking about the latest TV series, or about the time they met their significant other, or about their favorite place to visit in Chicago – your odds of contributing increase substantially if you *also* follow some similar TV series, or have a story about how you met your significant other, or can describe your favorite places in Chicago.

Great Conversations Cannot Be Built without Proper Materials

The house builder requires quality wood, the artist requires a good selection of paint, and the conversationalist requires useful conversational information. This chapter is about training your brain to fill up your conversation storage tanks with useful and interesting conversational information; information your brain can draw from for conversational purposes. If you think about it, most information you encounter over your life wouldn't translate to effective conversation material.

On a daily basis, our brains are passively absorbing and filtering out millions and millions of bytes of data. We only actively think about a small percentage of that vast amount of information. Once the new information is placed in your memory, it's available to process and assemble into useful comments. You may combine the new information with existing information. Either way, the ultimate objective is to assemble these thoughts into nice little packages you can employ at a moment's notice.

Maybe you have a story about that time you threw-up after band practice. Or maybe you have a strong opinion about climate change. Or maybe you memorized a great line from your favorite movie. Your brain has assembled many of your random thoughts into coherent comments already. I call these *previously assembled thoughts:* **PATs.** Remember the name Pat, because Pat is your best friend when it comes to efficient and effective conversation. Exceptional conversationalists store thousands of PATs.

> **REMEMBER:** People with more pre-assembled thoughts fare better, they have more to say, and can think of comments faster.

PATs are the secret to speedier responses; rather than digging around your mental closet for articles of clothing to create an outfit, PATs are like pre-assembled outfits, ready to wear. So how can you collect more of these PATs? I'm glad you asked! Some common – and important – PATs can be organized by the following categories: **Comments, Knowledge, Opinions**, and **Autobiographical**.

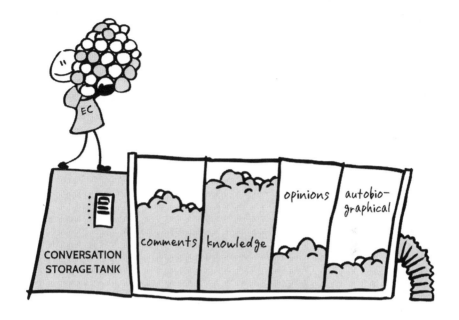

Exceptional conversationalists relentlessly hunt for information they can convert to PATs. Let's get to know the four best PATs in more detail.

PAT 1: Comments

Remember Eliza the chat bot? Chat bots, as of this writing, are loaded with useful *words* and *comments*. As we know, chat bots have to follow previously defined scripts and communicate with previously defined words and comments. A human may type "Hi, how are you?" and the chat bot is programmed to output "Good, how are you?" in return. How can you add more and better words and comments into your conversation storage?

Do you feel like your comment options are too limited? Are there phrases you tend to over-use? I worked with someone many years ago whose default response to almost any opinion was "I like that" or "I don't know if I like that." I also know someone who often ends their phrases with "I'm not kidding." *I'm not kidding.* You probably know someone like that as well. Or maybe that someone else is you. I'm not kidding. Like, for real. I mean it. Seriously.

Let me tell you a quick story. Last year I decided to officially grow a beard for the first time. That single act sparked countless conversations. The beard became a trigger for a very specific conversation. Almost every friend I encountered felt the urge to comment on my new facial hair experiment, and they all said a variation of the same simple observation: "Hey, I see you're growing a beard." It was becoming a social script that played out again and again.

The first time someone made that comment, my brain sluggishly gathered and sorted some acceptable and possibly interesting response options. Now after a few of these exchanges about my beard, I discovered what phrases worked well and what phrases did not. After a few more "beard comments," do you really think my brain had to work that hard to find a response? Nope.

When the topic of "beards" came up, I was prepared, and responded with lightning fast comments. And not only that, but I was already planning my next move while the other person was focusing on how to respond to one of my pre-assembled thoughts:

> Well hey, winter's coming, I have to stay warm!
> This is my new hipster beard - I'm trying really hard to fit in.
> Yeah, guys don't have many options for our hair styles, it's either grow facial hair or no facial hair - I don't think HR would allow much more than that!

How to Add Better Words and Comments

Every common situation loosely follows cultural scripts. People are supposed to act in certain ways. But there are so many types of comments available within a given social interaction, it would be a fool's errand to try to memorize every comment for every script and situation. Instead, start noticing useful and interesting comments. Start hunting them, and mentally filing them away whenever you hear a good comment. Rehearse them in your head. Write them down. Focus on them.

Have you ever been bowling? A typical bowling event usually proceeds by following a scripted series of actions/events:

The Series of Events/Actions during Bowling

You arrive. You choose shoes and a ball. You find your lane. You form teams. Someone writes names on the board. Everyone takes turn bowling and one of four main outcomes usually occurs:

1. *Bowl a strike*
2. *Bowl a spare*
3. *Knock over less than eight pins*
4. *Miss entirely*

When people do well, they act excited. When they do poorly, they act disappointed. Eventually people eat food or drink. After a while some people become tired. At the end, the score is tallied, the winning team celebrates. Everyone goes home.

This pattern happens nearly every time, in bowling alleys everywhere. The only parts of the interaction left are *the comments in between the actions/events*. Because the events of bowling are so consistent, the next time you go bowling, try to remember any clever phrase someone utters – because you can borrow those exact phrases and apply them to the next time you bowl! And the time after that. And the time after that. Until suddenly you developed your own arsenal of bowling comments, ready to go at a moment's notice. Because I'm such a nice guy, I have collected some for you:

Event 1. You/They bowl a strike.

Did you see *that*?! I wanted to make sure you were watching.
WOW! I can't believe I actually knocked them all down!
I hope you took a picture of that! That should be on a poster.

Event 2. You/They start bowling poorly.

Maybe I should stick to darts/pool.
Hey, no one can say you're not consistent.
At least I'm good at hitting the right side.
I think it's time for another beer - I need to improve my focus.
If the goal was to knock over the right side pins, I'd be a
    champion.
I just got robbed…that was totally going in.
I don't think there's a strike in my future.

Event 3. The other player just finished their throw.

Good job!
Look out - we've got a pro bowler on the team.
You got robbed - you'll get it next time.
Don't worry, the floor's definitely not even - I think there's a
    bump on that side.

Event 4. People become tired of bowling.

Who said bowling wasn't a workout?
I think I'm getting too old for this.
My arm was not meant to throw heavy objects all night.
I think I pulled something - it feels like I pulled a hammy.
All those high school football injuries are starting to catch up to
    me.

Most environments contain re-usable phrases like this – we're just not usually conscious of when we hear or utilize them.

PATs can be very versatile and aren't always locked into one type of function. Often, what your brain is remembering, is the *structure* of the statement – then when the time comes to express the statement, your brain just fills in the blanks. The PAT statement, "That's how you know you're getting old; you get excited about _____," is able to be recycled in numerous ways. Check out the following examples utilizing the PAT:

SOMEONE SAYS: I'm so happy; I just saved a bunch of money on my insurance!

YOU: *That's how you know you're getting old; you get excited about* saving money on insurance.

SOMEONE SAYS: I'm so happy; we just refinanced and lowered our interest rate by a whole point!

YOU: *That's how you know you're getting old; you get excited about* saving money on interest rates.

The content just depends on the context of the conversation. Check out this example:

The statement "I love *cheesecake*, I'll never say 'No' to *cheesecake*," can be a fun PAT response anytime someone mentions cheesecake. But what if someone mentions M&Ms? Or Butterfingers? In this case, the underlying structure is: "I love _____, I'll never say 'No' to _____." It can be applied to many things. Can you think of any?

At every placed I've worked, the most popular question asked on Friday is: "Have any plans for the weekend?" If I don't know a good response, I fall back on a PAT I have used over 40 times to good effect:

I have no idea. My wife makes all the plans. I wake up on Saturday and she lets me know what we're doing for the day. It's a surprise every weekend!

I'm not kidding, I literally go to that response if I can't think of anything else. If nothing else, it keeps the conversation moving along until I can think of something more substantive.

The next important type of PAT to pre-assemble is factual information. Knowledge forms the foundation for substantive conversations.

PAT 2: **Knowledge**

Justin and Melissa are having a fun conversation about the movie *Top Gun*. Because of their *knowledge* of the movie, they can make many fun references to the movie within a single conversation:

MELISSA: You hear Top Gun is going to be in 3D?

JUSTIN: Really? Those air combat scenes should be sweet.

MELISSA: I'm probably not going to watch it.

JUSTIN: What? I thought for sure you would watch it - you're like the Queen of 80s movies; how can you not like Tom Cruise singing *You've Lost that Lovin' Feelin'*.

MELISSA: Slow down there, *Iceman*...I've never seen you get so excited over a movie before.

The small aforementioned conversation had four references to Top Gun in various forms, but without information about the movie, the conversation might have proceeded as follows:

MELISSA: You hear Top Gun is going to be in 3D?

JUSTIN: Yeah? It's been a while since I saw it - I don't really remember it.

MELISSA: Oh, well - you might like it.

JUSTIN: Yeah, maybe.

Millions of conversations a day meet a similar boring fate because one or both of the conversation partners can't (or won't) contribute more information. This is one of the primary reasons why conversations fall short and stall – one or both of the conversation partners lack easily-accessible knowledge to maintain the topic. Of course, I say "easily-accessible" because many people have the ability to recall knowledge if given enough time. But conversations are not patient beasts.

Conversations move quickly and end abruptly if not continuously fed content and information. Even if you have a poor memory for details, just remembering one or two tidbits of what the movie is about can go a long way towards maintaining dialogue.

Think about the last TV show you watched or article you read. Exceptional conversationalists don't just passively consume movies, shows, books, news, etc. *ECs remember the interesting parts.* They realize (sometimes subconsciously) that this knowledge may be useful for future conversation. And they don't just remember every fact they can – they hunt specifically for *conversational information* – information that may be interesting to other people.

It's not good enough that you can tell people that your favorite movie is Braveheart – you also need to keep it interesting. You may need to explain why it's your favorite, or re-tell an interesting line from the movie, state an interesting fact about an actor in the movie, etc. ECs look up additional information and read about fascinating stories to re-tell. In fact, many skilled conversationalists unabashedly steal content verbatim from comedians and journalists.

How to Add Better Facts and Knowledge: Just TAPP!

How can you increase your odds of always having conversation information to contribute to a conversation? By reviewing and studying the TAPP topics! The TAPP topics run the gamut of common conversation topics you're likely to encounter in any given social exchange. TAPP stands for *Things, Activities, People,* and *Places.* The TAPP topics function as a guideline to follow as you expand and add to your mental storage of facts, opinions, and experiences. TAPP also acts as a comprehensive list of ideas for conversation starters. Take a gander:

TAPP Topics

THINGS: Technology, Books, Clothes, Cars, Movies, TV Shows, Food, Drink, and Weather

ACTIVITIES: Hobbies, Volunteering, Sports, Fitness, Diets, Entertainment, Gaming, Education, Dating, Vacations, Shopping, and Careers

PEOPLE: Kids/Parenting, Family, Pets, Gossip, Relationships, Opposite Sex, You, Them, Culture, Common friends/Co-workers, Local/Global News, Appearance, and Human Behavior

PLACES: Surroundings, Cities, Landmarks, States, Restaurants, Festivals, Houses, and Stores

Can you add an interesting fact about each of the THINGS? Or PLACES? Becoming familiar with the topics is the easy part; coming up with something interesting to say about each one is much harder. At the very least, develop a solid portfolio of comments in certain areas so you can confidently steer the conversation towards your strengths.

One of the TAPP topics is "Education." Maybe your son's school requires silly neon green school uniforms; that's an interesting fact. If you collect interesting tidbits related to education, the second the conversation turns to something related to education, you may have your exceptional conversationalist moment!

By no means should you try to memorize this list. But being very familiar with TAPP topics gives you building blocks for great conversations with a wide and diverse audience. ECs are able to converse with a diverse crowd because they know a little about a lot.

 Quick Practice: Let's try a TAPP exercise right now. The topic is *Food*. Can you think of an interesting food fact? Once you think of a fact, see if you can think of another fact to connect to the first fact. For example, "Did you know that almost half the world's food is thrown away every year?" Second fact, "And grocery stores have to throw food out if it reaches its expiration date, even though it could be perfectly safe." It doesn't have to be deep – the fact that *Tony's Tacos* down the street serves burritoes until 11pm is pretty awesome too!

Factual information isn't always interesting on its own. Offering your own opinion or feelings on a certain piece of knowledge is invariably more interesting. The next type of PAT (Opinions) adds the pizzazz to existing knowledge and facts.

PAT 3: Opinions

Did you see that time a computer named Watson kicked-butt on Jeopardy? Newer chat bots are being programmed with factual knowledge about the world. Obviously computers have no problem storing and retrieving facts. Unfortunately for Watson and chat bots, they typically don't go beyond fact retrieval and scripted comments. In addition, the type of facts they learn are usually limited to just the external world, and rarely contain facts about their "inner world"; for example, how they're feeling, or what they've experienced.

Exceptional conversationalists are experts on themselves. They have already formed interesting opinions and views about the facts in the world. They are in tune with their preferences and feelings. *Do you think you're already an expert on yourself?* Hmmmm? Being an expert on yourself means that you can do more than just ace a test on YOU. It means that you can ace the test while only having *three seconds per question*. It means that when you're put on the spot, you're able to recall a myriad of personal opinions and insights. And unfortunately, in most conversations, you only have a few seconds. Many smart people have difficulty communicating their opinions effectively and efficiently.

 Quick Practice: See if you can answer each question in the following **Opinion Speed Test** without hesitating for more than three seconds (you may be surprised by the results!):

Opinion Speed Test

1. *What is one of your favorite desserts?*
2. *What's your biggest pet peeve?*
3. *If you could only read one more book, what would it be?*
4. *What new technology would you like to see?*
5. *What's your favorite car?*
6. *Who would make a great president?*
7. *What's the best place to visit in your town?*

Be honest, could you answer those seven questions without thinking more than a few second per question? I'm betting you couldn't. Don't worry, most people can't. Only people who have already previously assembled their thoughts on those topics could. Answering five of the seven is still very good.

Let's talk more about preferences and opinions. What are your thoughts concerning college education? The Middle East crisis? Justin Bieber's hair cut? Can you tell me your political views? *Why* do you believe what you do? What are your goals? Hopes? Fears? Can you tell me about your favorite places to visit? *Why* are those your favorite?

It's ideal to collect a catalogue of useful opinions for common topics, but don't be afraid to communicate facts about your interests or hobbies that stick out from the norm. Do you have a secret love for 1960's comedies? Are you obsessed with baking pies? These quirky traits can be endearing and help enforce your uniqueness.

Develop a *signature* something. What is your signature drink? Do you have a unique watch or pair of glasses you always wear? Signature things also help jump-start conversation. I'm an American and British citizen. Disclosing that I'm also a British citizen has sparked at a least a hundred engaging and *jolly good* conversations over the years! Take advantage of your uniqueness.

Quick Practice: Look back at TAPP again and see if you can go beyond plain facts about each topic. Pick a few topics and add a personal take. For example, if the topic is *Technology*, rather than just sticking to facts with a question like, "Have you tried the new XYZ app?" Add your own views and feelings towards it. "It does everything I need – I can even _____!"

How to Add More Conversational Opinions

Besides reading opinions of experts in magazines and listening to podcasts, etc., it's important to take some time to analyze your own thoughts and opinions on a variety of TAPP topics. That's why I created this handy dandy **Opinion Inventory Worksheet**. It's slightly more specific than TAPP, and whether you do it now or later, this will help you add more opinion-based PATs to your conversation storage tank. Don't worry if you can't answer everything right now – merely attempting the worksheet will boost your natural propensity to form opinions.

Opinion Inventory Worksheet

List THREE FAVORITES and ONE LEAST FAVORITE
(when applicable)

For example, my three favorite *dinners:*
1.Corned Beef & Cabbage, 2. Pizza, 3. BBQ Pulled Pork
Lease favorite dinner: Greek Salad.

Dinner:
Books:
Authors:
Phone Apps:
Technological Devices:
Clothing Brand/Store:

Cars:

Movies:

Movie Lines:

Actors/Actresses:

Current TV shows:

Older TV shows:

Hobbies:

Artists:

Sports Teams:

Athletes:

Stores:

Games:

Desserts:

Drinks:

Breakfast:

Fast Food:

Current Bands:

Older Bands:

Musicians:

Motivational Songs:

Sad Songs:

Fun Songs:

Pets:

Vacation Spots:

Restaurants:

Bars:

Plants:

Junk Food:

Radio Station:

Local Attractions:

Political Leaders:

Newsworthy Figures:

Historical Figures:

Historical Events:
Friends:
Celebrity Crushes:
Days:
Websites:
Gifts Received:
Fictional Characters:
Daytime Activities:
Nighttime Activities:
Parties:
Advice:
Hypothetical occupations:
Places to live:
Human behaviors:
Physical traits (self):
Physical traits (attracted to in others):

Bonus Section: *Things*

Three things I despise:
Three things I love:
Three things I'm good at:
Three things I'm bad at:
Three things I wish I could do:
Three scariest things:
Three coolest things:
Three funniest things:
Three grossest things:

Extra challenge 1. Go back and explain WHY they are your favorite or least favorite!

Extra challenge 2. Go back and think of superlatives for each – think of the best, biggest, longest, tastiest, coolest, most frustrating, most enjoyable, etc.

Opinions Galore!

Unfortunately, a lot of opinions aren't easily categorized into nice lists. Opinions about other people and the nuances of human behavior constitute a large area ripe for opinions. For example:

> I think all kids should join at least one sport.
> Aunt Betty has a crazy laugh.
> The project at work should be managed by Bill instead of Bob
> I think my girlfriend should keep her hair long.
> Justin's probably going to be late.
> Your cat is not going to enjoy getting his flea medicine.
> You always make the best cookies.
> You're going to love the new coffee they have now.

We'll be revisiting how to offer better opinions later in the book, but for now, start paying attention to how often you offer opinions.

PAT 4: Autobiographical

Information Hunters not only remember general knowledge and opinions, but they also make a point to remember all of those funny, zany, unusual, interesting life moments and events. Start paying more attention to interesting personal information worth sharing.

Can you easily conjure up stories about school, work, family, pets, significant others, adventures, mistakes, embarrassments, etc.? If you kept track, you would have stories for nearly every major topic that could come up in an average conversation. Stories don't have to be long elaborate tales of adventure. For example: "When I turned 30, my Uncle Steve told me I was going to gain five pounds a year – I was like, 'Thanks for the vote of confidence Uncle Steve!'"

The goal is to focus on adding personal nuggets with wide appeal – Focus on *relatable* stories, anecdotes, and events. Always remain cognizant of what your audience would be interested in hearing.

You may lack the memory power of a chat bot, but you will always maintain an advantage over artificial intelligence because you are able to experience life events. Chat bots often sound artificial because they lack any experiences to reference or draw from. They can't tell you much about themselves, what they've done, where they've been, or what they possess. They lack a human "timeline" so to speak, and don't have a past, present, or future to discuss.

One summer my family lost power for four days and we were forced to stay with our in-laws. We went out to dinner the first night and my mother-in-law asked what we did with our food to prevent it from spoiling.

My wife, Maureen, answered, "One of my friends let us use the fridge in their garage. We spilled a few things, but we managed to save all of the food, at least."

My mother-in-law responded, "Oh, that's good."

My wife left out a few "minor" details, however, and I was not about to allow a good story go to waste. Transferring the food was actually a *giant* fiasco, so I chimed in before the conversation moved on. I'll spare you the details, but it involved a loose Pitbull, the house alarm going off, and fish juice spilling all over my wife. I proceeded to tell the entire story of what happened and the story was an absolute hit!

My wife and I shared the same experience. However, she didn't see value in the story like I did. I deliberately filed away the interesting parts, because I knew it was useful conversation information. And by re-telling the story, the interesting parts became cemented even further in my brain.

Let's pretend you went on a trip last week to Tampa to visit your family. This event may naturally surface in a conversation upon your return (unless you live by yourself in a cave).

FRIEND: How was Tampa?
YOU: It was good. Really hot.
FRIEND: Yeah, I bet.

By not offering much information, the conversation becomes stilted and your conversation partner is forced to maintain the conversation for you. Many people won't bother inquiring, and will instead steer the conversation elsewhere (or to someone else). A few hours later, in a different conversation, the topic re-surfaces. But this time, you've already thought of an interesting nugget to share.

FRIEND: How was Tampa?
YOU: Yeah, it was really neat, and oh my gosh, I couldn't believe how many alligators were around. Everywhere we walked we saw alligators like 10 feet away. It was kind of scary but kind of exciting too. My brother even tried to touch one!

This type of interesting nugget can be formed long before that particular moment in the conversation. You could have thought about that incident on the beach, or how scary the Sunshine Skyway Bridge is to drive over, or how...*you get the point.* It just requires a little foresight. Of course the exact words don't need to be planned out, but if the general idea or thought crossed your mind before you engaged in the conversation, you would be one step ahead.

It also comes down to your habits. For ECs, information hunting is a part of their life. They remember that funny event that happened last week and think about which parts would make a good story. The event may not have been interesting on the surface, but after careful examination, a few interesting nuggets could be extracted. It's a very active, deliberate process. And it's a process that converts random thoughts and data into conversational nuggets for faster retrieval later.

I was doing some spring cleaning the other day and happened upon some old photos from my childhood experiences at my great Aunt Alice's farm in Virginia. Until that moment, I had forgotten about all those interesting stories involving ghosts in the attic, giant snakes, chasing off turkey hunters, and many more. After seeing those photos and reliving the events in my mind, those stories moved back into my conversational storage tank. If I don't purposely try to remember tidbits like those, they become lost forever in the dark cavities of my brain, never to be referenced again.

Of course you can't know and remember everything. If you haven't discovered it already, the sheer act of trying harder to remember will help you remember more. Your brain processes millions of pieces of information a day. It won't just automatically remember everything – it's necessary to direct it and focus on certain details and topics. Sometimes you have to rehearse or mentally go back over details to refresh your memory.

Part of training your brain to reference more personal anecdotes involves adding better statement structures to your vernacular. Memorize the following statements and make a conscious effort to incorporate statements like these into your conversations:

That reminds me of when _____
That's kind of like the time I/s/he/John _____
That makes me think of _____

I was recently at a wedding for one of my friends and I knew going in that I would run into many acquaintances. Social climatologists predicted a 100% chance of small talk. I came in armed with a story that happened to me recently. Everywhere I went, you better believe that story came with me. *I was socially armed.* I probably told the core of the story five times throughout the course of one evening! And it was entertaining to everyone I told it to. Some people added to it, sometimes I added or subtracted from it. Either way, one good pre-assembled story contained a lot of value!

Of course, unless you're Oprah, you'll probably lack knowledge in certain areas. Mocking your lack of knowledge in that area is at least better than nothing.

How to Add More Autobiographical Information

Brace yourself, another exercise cometh. I call this exercise, "Tell me about a time." Pretend for a moment you're on a date with Stacy Story. As her name implies, she only wants to hear stories. Act like she's asking you questions from the following list. How many can you answer? Of course, you may not have time to answer them all now, but I encourage you to revisit this exercise when you have some time.

Tell Me About a Time Worksheet

Best childhood memory?
Scariest childhood memory?
Happiest childhood memory?
Best place to visit as a child?
A story about your favorite place to visit as an adult?
A story about someone you'd call an enemy / adversary?
A funny story from high school?
A funny story from college?
Ever won a prize?
Ever moved far away?
An interesting / funny story about a relative?
A sad story about a relative?
A funny story that occurred in the past week or month?
An interesting story from the past week or month?
An interesting story about one of your hobbies?
A story about a time you got in trouble?
A story about a time you were late for a major event?
An embarrassing / regretful event?
A story about how you won something?
A story about how you lost something?
A story about an animal / pet?
A story about how you were really sick?
An interesting / funny story about a friend?

Something unusual from your childhood?
Something unusual about your childhood home?
Something unusual about where you lived as a teen / young adult?
Something unusual about a friend?
An interesting / funny story related to food / eating?
An interesting / funny story about a music or sporting event?
A story about a time you were embarrassed?
A story where you overcame some challenge?
A story about an injury?
Ever been or hosted a great / horrible party?
Have you had any life-changing moments?
Have you ever had an alien / ghost encounter?
A story about your first / worst date?
A time you regretted buying something?
A time you made a costly mistake?
A time you got lost?
A time you really lucked out?

Stacy decides she is sick of hearing your stories. She wants to know other personal information. Can you continue answering her questions?

What's your oldest / most sacred possession?
What's your favorite possession?
What do you want to own?
What is something you're embarrassed to tell most people?
What's something you want to accomplish in the next year, five years, and ten years?
What are you most proud of?
What would you write a book about?
If you had a million dollars to spend, what would you spend it on?
Something interesting you did last week? Yesterday? Today?
Something interesting you're planning on doing this month? Year?

I strongly encourage you to start a *story journal*. Fill it with every kind of story, but also try to maintain a log of stories as they occur. Just jot down a few sentences to remind you of the interesting details. It's a great habit to get into for more effective storytelling during conversations. On a side note, Winston Churchill was famous for keeping a journal of interesting lines, anecdotes, and more. His journals helped him remember and deliver some of the greatest speeches of all time.

Don't forget to share information about the variety of *events* in your life. If you talk about a future event, you may be asked about the event after it occurs also. Are you going to an interesting concert in a few days? Are you excited about seeing your cousin next week? Are you training for a marathon? Events turn into stories later. Communicating information about the events in our lives – past, present, and future – help shape our social autobiography.

Turbo Charge Your Thinking Speed

You know that moment where you think of the perfect response two minutes after the conversation already moved on!? Frustrating isn't it? Speed is an essential ingredient to exceptional conversation.

Thoughts are more likely to be remembered quickly if you have built a road leading to them instead of a path. Think about your favorite story to tell. Before the first time you told that story – it was simply a memory amongst millions of other thoughts and memories in the giant unkempt wilderness of your mind. As you mentally reconstructed the story and told it for the first time, you moved the thoughts from the primordial soup of your innermost memory regions into the light of your executive vantage point. Your brain kept track of how to find that story by creating a narrow mental trail through the wilderness leading directly to the story. Then you told the story again; the trail to the story widened. Then you told the story again; the trail became a dirt road. Then you typed the story in an email to someone; the dirt road became a paved road. Then again; the paved road became a highway! With each re-telling, the neural pathway to the story became stronger and your brain is able to access the story with greater and greater speed and efficiency.

So what's the EC's secret to speedy comments? They recycle the same thoughts – *a lot.*

One of my favorite stories will help illustrate this point. I title it *Bijou and the Bat*:

> We have an orange tabby cat named Bijou. He is a lover, and a ruthless killer. He is very complex. If I let him stay out at night, it's guaranteed I'll receive a present in the morning in the form of a dead animal. One day my in-laws were complaining of a bat that managed to fly into their house. They couldn't catch it. They didn't want to pay a service to come out and remove it, so they asked if Bijou was available. Bijou's schedule was pretty open that day so we drove up to their house and let him inside. Within minutes he was on their kitchen counter. Like a heat seeking missile, he pounced - and in mid-air - caught the bat between his two front paws. He brought the bat to the floor, looked up at my father-in-law and said, 'Was that all?'

Now I'm not a naturally good story teller – I never have been. But I have built a conversation superhighway to that story and it's a hit with every re-telling. I've built side streets off of it depending on where I want to take the conversation. Sometimes I embellish a little. Sometimes I expand. Sometimes I change up the ending to add something about requiring two bags of catnip as payment. Sometimes people add ideas about how I could run a side company that offers *natural pest control.*

The best part is that my house contains a reliable trigger for initiating the story – Bijou himself. Why? Because without fail, Bijou will appear, jump on the couch or counter next to the guest, and proceed to rub against them. Without fail, the guest comments about how friendly Bijou is. And without fail again, I quickly and easily travel down my mental highway to pick up my *Bijou and The Bat* story. I barely think about it anymore – it's like going on auto-pilot for a minute.

You can't always predict conversation topics, but what you can do is think more about autobiographical information in preparation for when you do encounter a trigger. How do you know what triggers to plan for? You don't, but you can make very good educated guesses as to what topics will come up in conversations with your friends. Focus on autobiographical information that's more likely to be relevant to your social circles.

 Quick Tip: Want to remember more PATs in general? Every time you hear, think, see, or experience something interesting, share it with someone *as soon as possible*. "I just saw the funniest thing on the way here..." It will stick longer that way.

CHAPTER 5: USE IT OR LOSE IT

A practice exercise after making you answer all those lists of questions?! I'm not that mean – there isn't a Use It or Lose It exercise this time.

CHAPTER 5: REVIEW

Before this chapter:
- ✓ Add energy and variety to your voice
- ✓ Pay attention to the movie you're showing people
- ✓ Scripts are everywhere, start paying more attention
- ✓ The Seven Most Likeable Traits: Be Humble, Caring, Positive, Enthusiastic, Goal-Oriented, Playful, and Flexible

From this chapter:
- ✓ The four primary PATs: Comments, Knowledge, Opinions, and Autobiographical stuff
- ✓ The TAPP topics: Things, Activities, People, and Places
- ✓ Practice your opinions and stories in order to increase your recall speed

Key takeaway from this chapter:
Hunting conversational information and storing previously assembled thoughts (PATs), is critical to your ability to communicate quickly and effectively.

Coming up next:
We're going to continue looking at what it means to grow.

Preview: *This short chapter covers a few critical steps for achieving successful growth, including how to convert flaws into strengths.*

[CHAPTER 6]

KEEP GROWING

Are You Adding New Types of Material?

You may be a Lepidopterist and have amazing conversations with other Lepidopterists. But alas, not everyone wishes to discuss butterfly and moth species. I'm a firm believer that expanding your horizons and improving yourself is a primary source of happiness. Not only that, but when you take risks and expand your "self," you'll find new opportunities, new friends, and new facets of your personality. If you currently find your life feeling stagnant, try finding another hobby or interest. Join a club or group with people who have similar interests. The *act* of expanding your borders or comfort zone can improve your conversation in and of itself. Conversation doors will open up by simply telling someone how you're trying something new. You can describe your fears, hopes, and discoveries related to the new hobby.

Do you ever wonder why conversation with friends is so much easier than with other people? Obviously if you have similar interests and hobbies, you'll naturally connect more easily. But there's something else at play too. Over the years, you have collected a set of PETs and habits that work well with your friends. Your friends also understand what works well with you. You understand each other and the conversation flows easily and comfortably. Just as importantly, you know what thoughts and comments your friends won't like. However, conversing with people beyond your close set of friends will naturally expand your collection of thoughts and PATs.

Accept, Know, and Grow Who You Are

Socrates once said, "Know thyself: for the unexamined life isn't worth living." Socrates was a pretty smart guy, so I figure it doesn't hurt to include his advice here. Deep self-knowledge and awareness is freedom. Knowing who you truly are will make your conversations easier and more natural. If you have a better sense of who you are, you'll have a more defined way of behaving in social settings. What do you value? What's important to you? What are you consistent with? People with strong views also tend to have strong character. *If you try to be everything to everybody you'll have a hard time.* Figure out what role(s) suit you best. Maybe you're the guy who tells the good stories. Maybe you're the nice guy who always gives compliments and helps people. Maybe you're the girl who always shares the latest news events. And maybe you're comfortable in multiple roles. Having a definite identity will help you be more resolute in your decisions and opinions and increase your sense of confidence. Shaky conversations are usually built on shaky foundations. People without a strong sense of self-identity and self-worth often express vague or hesitant statements; they tend not to express any strong preferences or opinions.

This is a good place to note that you simply can't have exceptional conversations with everyone. There are certain people your personality will not jive with – no matter what! Just focus on getting along with most types of people across common situations. When you hit an outlier – don't worry about it!

Self-esteem is partially based on your abilities and your goals. Do you feel your life progressing and moving towards something positive? Are you trying to become a great artist? An amazing programmer? Do you want to open your own restaurant? Graduate law school? Without actively pursuing goals, you're merely floating through life, never forming a solid self-identity.

You have to get in touch with *you* and decide who you are: what you are good at and what you are bad at; what you are aiming for and what you'll never aim for; what you want and what you need. Be proud of your strengths and accepting of your weaknesses. We're all dealt different hands. Everyone – even seemingly perfect people – face challenges and self-doubts. However, ECs turn challenges, doubts, mistakes, insecurities, and fears into conversational advantages. How, you ask? Keep reading.

Take Advantages of Your Flaws

"Once you've accepted your flaws, no one can use them against you."

—Tyrion Lannister, played by Peter Dinklage, in *Game of Thrones* (written by George R. R. Martin).

Think about the person or people who make you feel comfortable. Likeable and easy-going people are usually comfortable in their own skin and have embraced their character flaws. They are okay being a little vulnerable. These likeable people are the first to admit that they aren't perfect and are happy to laugh at their personal quirks. They use their flaws to their advantage.

Think about that for a minute.

Exceptional conversationalists realize their weaknesses and insecurities can actually make some interesting conversation material. Not many people desire to listen to a braggart rave about how well he did on a test or how many new sports cars he owns. But everyone enjoys hearing about the time you made a fool of yourself at that party – especially if you can laugh about it after the fact. Your flaws subconsciously make others feel better about themselves, as well. The end result is that people will often like you *more* after you expose an inner flaw or embarrassing experience.

REMEMBER: If you're not taking advantage of flaws, and only discussing your good traits and behaviors, you're shortchanging some of the best aspects of your personality.

Think about your favorite comedian – there's a 75% chance that he/she relies on a heavy dose of self-deprecating humor. It's one of the most common comedic techniques. A few years ago I was riding in a car with my new boss, and she asked me how to find our destination. I responded rather bluntly, "I'll be honest, I'm *navigationally impaired*...I'm probably the worst person to ask for directions. If I say turn 'left', you're probably better off turning 'right'!" She quickly admitted that she, too, was horrible at navigating, and we both had a few laughs over who was worse! It was a good bonding experience.

When you leverage mistakes instead of fear them, mistakes can often lead to fun and engaging tangents rather than awkward moments. As a bonus, being accepting of yourself is also the best protection against feeling anxious after making a mistake or being verbally bullied. Nothing steals the power from an awkward situation or dulls the sharp barbs of a bully better than being the first to point out your mistake or flaw. Many statements can turn an anxious situation into a light-hearted event. True confidence comes from accepting one's flaws:

> I can't believe I just did that! I'm so scatterbrained today.
> Trust me, you don't want to see my drawing...a five year old could probably draw better.
> Maybe I need more coffee!
> We shouldn't take my car - it will probably break down on the way there!
> Sorry, I've just been on auto-pilot this morning.
> I just completely butchered that expression didn't I?

One time a colleague of mine committed a small error by misspelling some simple word on a report. When it was pointed out to her, she handled it brilliantly. She quickly acknowledged her mistake and then exaggeratingly mocked herself. "Oh yeah, I added an extra 'T'. *Apparently I don't know how to write or spell anymore!*" Everyone chuckled and the conversation moved on.

Over the years, many colleagues have made lemonade out of lemons. Another colleague, Beth, didn't see a mistake that was obvious to everyone else. "Oooh, now I see it! That was my 'duh!' moment for the day. I'm glad I got that over with, now I can be smart for a while."

Next time you say something weird, dumb, or off-putting, try this gem: "That's just the first thing that popped into my head...*I don't know why!*" For extra effect, add "...I need to work on my internal filters."

One of the reasons most people don't embark on more social interactions is because they're afraid of saying something "stupid" or making a mistake. But when you come to terms with your imperfections, and you realize how to capitalize on mistakes, you no longer feel that fear. You take more chances and you experience more social interactions. You go forth with extra confidence.

One of the beautiful side effects of conversation is that the more you communicate, the more you learn not only about others, but about yourself. Conversation is more than just exchanging phrases: it's about sharing – and personal growth. Internally processing a thought is very different from actually sharing the thought with someone else. Some years ago, I thought my book was great. I thought it was ready to be published and I was excited to share it with everyone. Until I asked someone to read it, and learned how wrong I was. When you're forced to explain something to someone, it can change how you perceive and process that thought. You grow and evolve with every new conversation.

Grow Better Mental Instructions

Deliberately collecting PATs is smart. Unfortunately, it's impossible for anyone to collect PATs for every social situation. It's still necessary to teach your brain better techniques and mental instructions for constructing comments on the fly. Growing your capacity for conversation includes growing your ability to improvise. That's why the remainder of this book focuses more on providing you, dear reader, with instructions and techniques for assembling your own effective comments when you don't have a comment ready to go.

Let's check out a simple example highlighting different mental instructions. Your friend starts a dialogue by asking:

Have you seen that new Killer Squirrel show yet?

You haven't seen it. So how do you respond?

Perhaps you follow a simple mental instruction:
No, I haven't.

Perhaps your mental instructions suggest maintaining the conversation by asking a follow-up question:
No, I haven't. Is it any good?

However, some people would apply the "self-label" technique also:
No, I haven't. I'm more of a History-show kind of guy. Is it any good?

Each of the aforementioned three options are all acceptable. However, the third is superior and is a more accurate reflection of what an EC may say, as opposed to the first one being what a PC may say.

Since you were born, you've been picking up good and bad habits, techniques, and mental instructions. This is your chance to change yourself for the better. While reading this book, try to deliberately focus, practice, and learn more good habits and mental instructions so your bad habits and instructions eventually deteriorate.

CHAPTER 6: USE IT OR LOSE IT

1. Look for and do an activity outside of your comfort zone.
2. During a conversation today or tomorrow, try to mention (or mock!) a personal flaw or weakness.

CHAPTER 6: REVIEW

Before this chapter:
   ✓ Add energy and variety to your voice

- ✓ Pay attention to the movie you're showing people
- ✓ Scripts are everywhere, start paying more attention
- ✓ The Seven Most Likeable Traits: Be Humble, Caring, Positive, Enthusiastic, Goal-Oriented, Playful, and Flexible
- ✓ The four primary PATs: Comments, Knowledge, Opinions, and Autobiographical stuff
- ✓ The TAPP topics: Things, Activities, People, and Places

From this chapter:
- ✓ Keep learning and trying things outside of your comfort zone
- ✓ Take advantage of your flaws
- ✓ PATs are not realistic for every situation – learning better mental instructions and techniques are just as valuable

Key takeaway from this chapter:
Deep self-knowledge and awareness is freedom. Knowing who you truly – and accepting of your faults as well as your strengths – will make your conversations easier and more natural.

Coming up next:
Next, you're going to grow your ability to form more interesting words and descriptions for things.

Preview: *In this chapter, you'll learn the art and science of describing things. You'll also grow your ability to offer more interesting and colorful descriptions.*

[CHAPTER 7]

EXPAND YOUR WORD CHOICES

"So avoid using the word 'very' because it's lazy. A man is not very tired, he is *exhausted*. Don't use very sad, use morose. Language was invented for one reason, boys – to woo women – and, in that endeavor, laziness will not do."

– John Keating, played by Robin Williams, in *Dead Poets Society* (written by N.H. Kleinbaum).

Danger: Boring Words May Lead to Boring Conversation

The quality of your conversation relies upon your ability to describe "things" – your environment, yourself, other people, abstract concepts, etc. All of your amazing thoughts and insightful opinions are limited by the words stored in your personal lexicon. It's critical you learn instructions and techniques for improving your word choices.

One of the most commonly shared experiences for a new parent is changing dirty diapers. But even something as mundane and unpleasant as changing a dirty diaper contains moments of levity and fun if you play with your descriptions. There is an entire range of experiences, from the easy-clean-up to the total nuclear disaster; the more extreme, the more options are available for colorful descriptions. You could say little Rowan let loose a *torrential flood of toxic waste. 100% liquid. Flammable liquid. Napalm.* Have fun with your words.

Some words are inherently more interesting than others. Saying "His breath smelled *bad*" isn't nearly as funny as saying "His breath smelled like *beef stroganoff.*" Regardless of the meaning, the name "beef stroganoff" just sounds funny by itself. You could substitute "beef stroganoff" with "gorgonzola cheese" and it would probably still work. Pay attention to what your circle of friends think is funny and sprinkle those words into your vernacular.

Have you ever wondered why someone else can say the same basic thing you did earlier, but receive a much better reaction? Sometimes, one or two words can make or break a phrase, joke, or story. You may think that is obvious, but poor conversationalists often underestimate the power of words. Let's look at some useful techniques.

Notice Your Boring Words

Not all statements and comments are created equal. Do you find yourself relying on the same trite phrases like "That's crazy" or "That's really cool" far too often? Focus on making your comments more descriptive, and they (and you!) will instantly be more interesting. Try to become more mindful of the boring words in your vocabulary and seek to upgrade them when appropriate.

The following are three ways to describe a good-looking person:

He was very good-looking.
He was definitely a *runway model*.
He was like *Brad Pitt-level* good looking.

Notice how the second and third options were more interesting because the average description, "good-looking," is replaced with more descriptive words.

The following three statements are all in response to a friend complaining about a jerk boyfriend. They all say basically the same thing, except for one difference.

Does he think you're going to make him *food* every morning too?
Does he think you're going to make him *breakfast* every morning too?
Does he think you're going to make him *banana-nut pancakes* every morning too?

In conversation, the third version of the aforementioned examples will always be more interesting than the first version. Why? It's more descriptive. And obviously it's not poetic verse either – adding even one detail is often sufficient.

 Quick Practice: If I told you about a recent event I attended, which of the following statements is the *least* interesting?

There were a lot of people there.
It was jammed from wall-to-wall with people. I could barely move.

It was like a mob scene.

It was like *Woodstock* all over again, with less drugs and mud.

They all express essentially the same point, but the latter three express the concept more colorfully than the first option. All it takes is one or two words to trigger an emotion or memory.

There are no right or wrong statements – just more interesting statements. Your word choices color your personality and communicate a lot about who you are. Look at the following statements, can you envision the type of people who would choose these specific words?

I *created* some of these...

I *formulated* some of these...

I *whipped up* some of these...

I *kind of tried to make* some of these...

I *done tried to make* some of these...

This chapter requires a disclaimer: Everything you say doesn't need to be colorful or bursting with flavor. The goal is to strike a balance between a few boring words and too many detailed words. You never want to go all Shakespearean and overload someone with too many details. Many good statements consist of very ordinary words, but can still be packed with emotion, feeling, or meaning. For example, expressing a feeling statement like "I think this is going to be fun," doesn't contain interesting words, yet still has potential to be interesting if you say it in an interesting way. Remember, a lot depends on *how* you say it. Bottom line: Try new approaches and see what works best for you.

Aim for Figurative Over Literal

It's natural to stick to literal language. Think about when someone asks a question like, "What do you do?" You would probably feel inclined to answer literally and directly. "I'm a substitute teacher." Instead of saying "I'm a substitute teacher," try "I baby-sit rooms full of little monsters."

Instead of lamenting that you're bad at math, you could disclose, "I'm algebraically challenged." Or "As some of you know, math and I are not best friends."

Try New Combinations of Words

You're a parent at an event with other parents and kids. The kids are making crafts in a room and the parents are at the side, sitting in chairs watching. You could walk to the section with the parents and state "This must be the *parent's lounge*." The words "parent" and "lounge" are not found together in the wild, but it's certainly more interesting than saying something like "This must be where parents sit." Experiment more and interesting descriptions will organically emerge.

 Quick Practice: Imagine I drove you and some of our mutual friends to the movies. I accidentally left the child safety lock on so you were trapped in the backseat and needed help opening your door. What is a fun and novel way to describe either the situation or my action? Think of synonyms for "child" and also think of new ways to describe being trapped or being stuck in something.

The aforementioned event occurred recently to my friend, and he offered the following funny comment: "Oh, you have it on *kid prison mode!*" He took a potentially boring statement about a child safety lock, and added a little extra flair and meaning to it by combining a few simple – but normally unassociated – words. Did you think of anything yourself?

Switch Nouns and Objects with Verbs or Adjectives

Instead of stating your frustration as "I almost honked at him!" You could try "He almost got the *honk!*"

Tweak Normal Expressions

Instead of the standard "How are you?" try "How the HECK are ya?" or "How's life in your world?" Instead of saying "I'm good," try "I'm peachy" or "I'm still alive" or "Just livin' the dream..." People usually don't expect much variation with common sayings, so when you do go off the beaten path, it's often appreciated and elicits a smile or two.

Reach into the past (or other cultures) and introduce some old expressions.

That tickles my fancy.
You know what really grinds my gears?
Oh, bollocks!
Quit lollygagging and get over here!

Talk About the Choice of Words

Exceptional conversationalists have fun with the conversation and take joy in thinking and commenting *about the conversation*. In fact, some of the best conversationalists will make comments about their word choices. For example, "I just sounded like someone's mom didn't I?" Sometimes ECs play and debate the choice of words. For example:

TYLER: That looks like you're carrying a purse!
JACK: It's not a purse, it's a *travel wallet*!
ISAAC: It's not a purse - it's a *murse*! Totally different.

Paint a Colorful Picture

People prefer visual imagery and emotionally packed words. Advertisers and good writers know that incorporating visual imagery, analogies, and emotive words are among the fastest ways to your heart (and wallet). That's why most sports broadcasts have "color commentators." Fans don't just want the facts. They want the emotions that go along with the game. They desire the colorful descriptions! If I described a woman as "grumpy," it would be sufficient. You'd get it. But what if I painted a picture with something descriptive and relatable. "She had this grumpy, just drank apple cider vinegar look." Can you visualize her a little better now?

 Quick Practice: Let's say I call you right now and ask how you're doing. For this exercise, pretend it's winter and you're outside, so you're *very* cold. Rather than just telling me you're very cold – try painting a more colorful picture. *Can you think of anything?* Try to do better than just synonyms like "freezing" or "frigid."

Saying "I'm so cold I can hardly feel my fingers anymore," or "I think icycles are starting to grow on my ears," creates more vivid imagery.

Examine the evolution of the following statement:

I had to make sure my beard looked okay.
I had to make sure my beard didn't look unkempt.
I had to make sure there wasn't a piece of toast stuck in my beard.

The second and third aforementioned comments were superior to the first. Here's why: The second comment employed a more interesting adjective ("unkempt") than the first. The third comment was the most colorful and visual. Check out some more examples of painting a picture:

INSTEAD OF: The wedding is so expensive.
PAINT A PICTURE: The wedding is going to make my wallet start crying soon.

INSTEAD OF: Because you're older than me.
PAINT A PICTURE: Because you've got more gray hairs than me.

In the right situations, it's entertaining to paint an entire scene (with a few sentences or less). Maybe you encounter a situation where you need to sit in tiny chairs. "I feel like I'm in Kindergarten again. I better check to see if there's gum or peanut butter anywhere before I sit down." Maybe you overhear someone blasting country music. "I feel like I should be line-dancing at a bar next to some cornfields right now."

Have Some Fun and Exaggerate

Four people offer a comment about their coffee.

> JOE: This coffee might keep me up for a while.
>
> PAT: This coffee's going to keep me up all night.
>
> JUSTIN: This coffee's going to keep me up until next Tuesday!
>
> RANDAL: This coffee's going to keep me up until I'm 62.

Of the four people above, who is the least interesting? Most people would say Joe sounds the least interesting. Can you see why? Could it be because Pat, Justin, and Randal all exaggerated the effects of the coffee? (Although Randal may have taken it too far!)

One of the most alluring aspects of exaggeration is simply making a situation more interesting than it really is. Everyone knows and understands that the coffee won't keep anyone up for a week. You won't go to jail if you exaggerate. Our culture allows for such artistic license, and in fact, prefers it.

Describing your dad as "old" is boring. "Ancient" is better. Referencing how he "fought in the Civil War," is just plain fun!

Next time you eat too much of Aunt Alice's BBQ pork or that giant bowl of Cincinnati chili, exaggerate the consequences. "I could barely move afterwards." Or "I think my stomach is still recovering." Overstated figures, hyperbole, and distortions signal to the audience, "*Hey, I'm only joking.*" Of course you may want to refrain from exaggeration when your credibility is at stake.

Check out the following simple exchange between Jen and Brian:

> JEN: You don't like mushrooms on your pizza?
>
> BRIAN: *I never eat anything squishy and brown.* It's served me well so far!

Of course Brian may eat squishy or brown things occasionally, but definitively stating he never does is much more interesting and fun.

Try exaggerating your own words or escalating someone else's to new levels. Simply describing something in a new or more exaggerated way commonly serves as a good response to someone else's comment. Look at the progression below:

JOE: I never knew he could make such a good sandwich.

JUSTIN: That's because he's a sandwich visionary.

RANDAL: He's actually a culinary icon.

PAT: A global icon in the sandwich community.

Here's another escalation describing sales:

JOE: They're selling like hot cakes.

JUSTIN: They're sweeping the nation.

RANDAL: They're going to turn this economy around!

REMEMBER: You're more likely to spark a positive emotional connection with exaggerations. Literal or factual comments will never be as visual, emotional, or dramatic as exaggerated comments. It's the documentary vs the drama. More people prefer to watch a drama than a documentary. Just don't position your exaggeration so far outside the realm of possibility that it morphs into nonsense.

Superlatives are the Best

Joe runs up to you and says, "Hey, I just saw something over there." Before you can respond, Libby runs up to you and says, "Hey, I just saw the *craziest* thing over there."

Who do you intuitively prefer to follow up with? Probably Libby, right? We are drawn to superlatives in life, and naturally, in conversation.

The biggest, best, longest, etc. Superlatives make everything more dramatic and interesting. Use them. Love them. They'll undoubtedly help you steer your stories in the right direction. Don't rely on them constantly or you'll lose credibility, but don't forget their power either.

Feel free to add some commentary after the superlative, also. For example, "He may have the worst serve in the history of men's tennis – *I think my three-year-old nephew can hit the ball better!*"

You're at an ice cream shop and they ask if you want one more scoop. A fun response? "Sure, let's make it as gratuitous and fattening as possible!" This response also lends credence to the idea that you have an exaggerated appetite. Exaggerated idiosyncrasies and quirks are usually very entertaining and should be taken advantage of (unless you're the vampire Goth guy with face tattoos).

The Labeling Technique

JEN: I'm more of a *hippy, crunchy granola* person.

BRIAN: Yeah well I'm more of a *greasy bacon kind of guy*.

People love labels. You can label anything! Put it in a category and you'll probably spark some interesting or humorous conversation. Labels already come pre-loaded with meanings, memories, and feelings. People love to put complex things (people or situations) in nice little packages and compartments. You can even label actions or intentions. Labels and references can also help improve your exaggerations. You may disclose: "I haven't gotten a pedicure in quite a while." But you could exaggerate the severity by saying: "It looks like a crime scene down there! CSI might be showing up soon."

A teacher was complaining about teacher appreciation week. Instead of just saying she didn't like it, she said, "It's teacher appreciation week...but it should be called *shove donuts in your face week*. That's all I get all week – and it's not helping my diet."

You're at a carnival. Your friend wants to ride the Tilt-a-Whirl ride, but you think it's too extreme. Instead of a boring "No," or "I can't handle that," you could state, "No way. It looks more like a Tilt-a-*Hurl*!"

Instead of saying "It's basically a station-wagon," try "It's so cheaply constructed; we call it our *plastic-wagon.*" Or "We barely use it; we call it our *grocery-getter.*"

Your coworker says he's just eating Raman noodles for lunch. You could label his food choice by commenting, "Going with the *old college special,* huh?"

Holding the door open for someone at a party? Now you can playfully refer to yourself as the "Greeter" or "Doorman." Do you walk up and down the stairs every day at work? Call it your "corporate aerobics." Does your daughter take care of visiting wildlife in the backyard? You could refer to her as the "Squirrel Whisperer."

Many labels and descriptions reference common knowledge.

INSTEAD OF SAYING: I can't get past his monotone voice.
TRY: I can't get past his *Dracula* voice.

INSTEAD OF SAYING: He thinks he's so cool.
TRY: He thinks he's *James Bond* or something.

If you (or someone else) add a successful label to a conversation, feel free to expand on it, explain why the label fits or does not fit, etc. For example:

JUSTIN: You always have to keep *everything* don't you? You're such a *hoarder.*
MELISSA: I'm not a *hoarder* - I'm more like a *collector,* but definitely not a *hoarder.*

The Marvelous Metaphor

Metaphors are the epitome of non-literal, figurative communication. They help us make sense of the world and serve as a very effective and fun communication tool. Corporate buzzwords often get a bad rap, but they are popular for good reason; they are colorful and meaningful phrases packaged as a single sound bite. Look at the following list of common buzzwords (I hear at least three buzzwords or phrases spoken in every meeting I attend at work!):

> It's the final piece of the puzzle.
> I'd like to take a deeper dive and see what we discover.
> I'm trying to wrap my brain around this whole thing.
> We can put that in Jill's bucket for now.
> Well that muddies the waters a little.
> Why do I feel like I'm walking into a minefield here?
> Jim's got an ace up his sleeve.
> I don't want it to fall through the cracks.

Metaphors help you create more interesting statements. Instead of stating the literal "I'm feeling tired," try "My brain is shutting down. I think its battery needs recharging."

The technical support guy at my work, let's call him Metaphor Mike, loves his metaphors. After apologizing for not knowing about something, he said, "Sorry, I'm usually the last grape on the grapevine." When I wanted to keep old software, but install the new operating system, he said, "Well you can't go halfway. You're either in the water or you're sitting on the beach getting a tan."

The other day one of my colleagues landed a good joke at my expense after I made a mistake. His follow up comment was a classic: "I couldn't resist – you put the ball on a tee and I took a swing at it!" Let's look at some other sports metaphors:

> You don't need to try to hit a home run.
> They hit it out into left field.
> Close? No, we're still on the 50 yard line.

Once a metaphor is introduced, see if you can twist, bend, and squeeze it into something else. Play with it! How could you have even more fun with one of the sports metaphors? How about "I was trying to hit a home run, but I couldn't even manage to get a walk."

You continue the metaphor with, "Maybe you should spend more time in the batters cage." Or "Next time you could go for a bunt and see what happens."

Play with the Cliché

Unfortunately for the metaphor, when it becomes too popular, it may be demoted to a "cliché." Many communication experts argue that clichés are over-used and should be avoided like the plague. However, a good cliché is still better than a boring statement, and can go a long way towards making your conversation more colorful and interesting. Clichés, maxims, adages, idioms, metaphors, and proverbs should all be part of your conversation arsenal.

I was in a meeting once where someone swiftly denounced a new project idea by stating one line: "Yeah, well you can put lipstick on a pig, but it's still a pig." The meaning was understood by everyone and no one dared challenge such a simple and powerful accusation.

I thanked someone at work for helping me with something and he responded with the classic: "No problem, ask and ye shall receive." Which is fine on its own, but he didn't stop there. He simply tweaked his own cliché and it was pretty funny: "...except on Fridays, or the weekends. Don't expect to receive anything those days."

Have fun with clichés. Clichés create opportunities for humor because they predictably follow a well-known path, which means you have a chance to contort them into something *unpredictable*, and therefore unexpected. Try twisting and tweaking normal everyday phrases in your own way. Add descriptive words to clichés to make them more interesting. Play with them. Debate the accuracy of the cliché or metaphor. Pretend to take them literally. Talk about the cliché as if it had a real consequence or effect on you or some situation. Here are some examples of playing with clichés:

THEM: You just derailed my train of thought.

YOU: I hope it can get back on the tracks!

THEM: In fact, I think it crashed - and the passengers are jumping out the windows.

YOU: I think I'm going crazy.

THEM: No, you're not going crazy - you're already *at* crazy. You *were* going crazy, but now you've arrived at your destination.

THEM: I just finished that project - I can finally take it off the back burner.

YOU: Now you just have to clear out the front burners - and the microwave!

CHAPTER 7: USE IT OR LOSE IT

Over the course of your next few conversations, try the following challenges:

1. Exaggerate something more than you normally would.
2. Try labeling something.
3. Use a superlative.
4. Play with a cliché.

CHAPTER 7: REVIEW

Before this chapter:

- ✓ Pay attention to the movie you're showing people
- ✓ Add energy and variety to your voice
- ✓ Scripts are everywhere, start paying more attention
- ✓ The Seven Most Likeable Traits: Be Humble, Caring, Positive, Enthusiastic, Goal-Oriented, Playful, and Flexible
- ✓ The four primary PATs: Comments, Knowledge, Opinions, and Autobiographical stuff
- ✓ The TAPP topics: Things, Activities, People, and Places
- ✓ Take advantage of your flaws

From this chapter:

- ✓ Focus on making your words more interesting, descriptive, and colorful
- ✓ Don't forget to exaggerate and also utilize superlatives more
- ✓ Play with more clichés and metaphors

Key takeaway from this chapter:

Experiment with more colorful words and word combinations more often – you may be surprised by the results!

Coming up next:

The Assert habit is next. Initiating, expressing yourself, and controlling the conversation direction are vitally important skills for achieving social success.

HABIT THREE

ASSERT

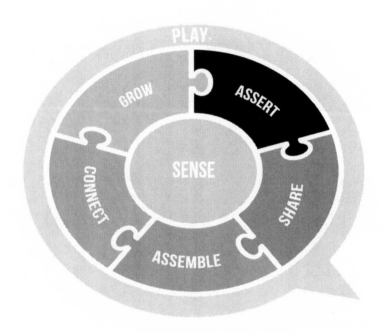

Preview: *A critical aspect of the Assert habit is starting conversations. This chapter focuses primarily on the psychological aspects of initiating and how to improve your confidence.*

[CHAPTER 8]

ADAPT THE ACTIVE MINDSET AND INITIATE WITH ANYONE

What is your biggest social fear? I bet initiating a conversation with a stranger ranks near the top. It's a valid concern; fear of embarrassment from saying the wrong thing is very real. Most people, even ECs, have similar fears. The difference is, some people are overwhelmed by them and some people realize the fears almost never actualize. Positive thinking helps a little. However, the only way to truly allay those fears is by creating more positive social experiences and proving your doubts wrong. Easier said than done right? I personally hate when a self-help book advises to just "go out there and talk to people."

Everyone reading this book is at a different conversational level. The best strategy for developing positive experiences is to *start at your level and incrementally challenge yourself.* Start with simple challenges in safe environments. Practice new techniques with friends or family. Initiate with a cashier. Practice with a restaurant server. Practice a story on your hair dresser. Systematically desensitize yourself to the fears by starting slowly and in small doses.

Uninhibited social freedom is a feeling not many people experience. It took many years of taking social risks and countless mental and emotional battles to dramatically reduce my social fears, but the sense of freedom I have now is incredible. I'm not at the late Robin Williams level yet (check out his late night interviews if you haven't seen them yet!), but I feel confident talking with anyone. If you haven't experienced it yet, I hope you can achieve social freedom one day as well!

Adapt the Active Mindset

Five years ago I attended a small gathering at a neighbor's house. Before long, I found myself standing in a group of four guys whom I just met at the party. One of the guys was talking about his occupation – automobile engineering. Another guy was very interested because he too, was an auto engineer. The third guy knew a lot about car design so he was engaged as well.

My knowledge of auto engineering is about as great as my knowledge of the history of cheese – barely non-existent. All the guys went back and forth in rapid-fire succession. I found myself quietly listening, nodding my head, and feigning interest for at least 10 minutes. Then it hit me, I was subtly being nudged out of the circle. I could have just walked away, but I wanted to get to know them. I wanted to be social. However, I couldn't get a word in edgewise. I also didn't want to appear too naïve before they knew anything about me.

And then it happened. I saw an opening. One of the guys transitioned from engineering, to the design of the house he just purchased. I know a lot about real estate, so that was my open window to jump through. I decided to take control of the conversation, and asked when he bought the house. Then I transitioned to the local housing market. Another guy was interested in selling his house. Then I talked about mortgage rates and the best time to sell. I was contributing. I suddenly found myself in the driver's seat. They were playing in *my* sandbox.

If you're reading this book, you've probably wondered how exceptional conversationalists always know what to say. You may have asked, "Why don't they ever struggle? Why do I take longer to respond than they do?"

The answer is: They aren't any smarter than you – they just put themselves in positions to succeed. No one – not even ECs – can always have a good response ready for any topic. But ECs understand one very simple concept – if you're in the position of responding to someone else's question or topic, *you're at their mercy.* (At least during that moment in the conversation.) Conversationalists who initiate the conversation topic *always have the advantage* over people on the receiving end.

If you and I are friends, and I called you on the phone right now – right this very minute – I can guarantee myself a major advantage from a conversational perspective. I would plan on telling you my plans to go *sailing* this weekend. How is that an advantage you may wonder?

By introducing sailing, I'm taking control and kicking off the conversation with one of my own topics, forcing you into a more passive position. You will have to respond and make a connection to my topic, and to my statements. It's not easy for your brain to sort through sailing related memories in a matter of seconds. Especially if you don't have much to offer on the topic, or were thinking about or doing something else totally unrelated. However, I may have had minutes, hours, days, or weeks to think about what and how I wanted to initiate that conversation with you! I may, in fact, be a professional sailor! I may have had many previous conversations about sailing that helped me develop a giant arsenal of sailing anecdotes, facts, and opinions ready to "float" into any conversation.

The comfort level I have with the topic will manifest itself as confidence. Because you have to react and exert energy searching for related material on the spot, you will naturally be at a disadvantage and may project a lack of confidence.

Pay close attention next time an EC converses with you; *they are probably initiating most of the topics!* ECs usually direct the show! They aren't caught off guard or left without anything to say. In those rare cases where they are speechless, they can still ask poignant questions and eventually steer the conversation ship back to where they want it to go.

Gain Confidence by Going First

We all desire more confidence. A short-cut to immediate confidence is simple: *go first.*

Be the first to ask "Hi, how are you?" Be the first to ask a question, raise your hand, speak up in class, or take action. Acting first, in any situation, instantly boosts how confident you appear to others, and in turn, boosts your feeling of confidence also. Poor conversationalists are normally *reactive*, as opposed to *proactive*. PCs wait for something to happen to them. ECs go after what they want.

When you see a colleague in the hallway, ask them how their day is going before they ask you. When you sit down with someone for lunch, ask them questions first. Do you have to meet with someone? Go to them and initiate the meeting first, rather than hoping that they eventually ask you to meet. During a conversation, try to ask more questions than they do. Steer the conversation more times than they steer it.

Make it a game! When you go first, you win a point. When they go first, you lose a point! It took me years to realize how often I instinctively waited for the other person to go first – as if I was not allowed to dictate the conversation.

After taking that initial step of acting first, not only will you feel an extra boost of confidence, but you'll feel an infusion of happiness. Why, you say? When you act first and control the conversational direction, you feel a *sense of control*. And people who feel in control of their lives are happier. If you're someone who always waits for something to happen to you, you'll find it very difficult to find happiness. Good things usually don't just fall out of trees and hit you on the head. Shifting from a *passive* to an *active* mindset can truly change your world.

Of course action comes with risk; staying passive is much safer and easier. Most people spend time deliberating over the negative possibilities of a potential action. Be careful, because too much deliberation leads to over-thinking and *paralysis by analysis*! Many more good things come from trying *something*, as opposed to trying *nothing*. (Insert inspirational quote here about missing 100% of the shots you don't take, etc.) If you currently lead a passive lifestyle, you may feel like you lack control over your fate, and that life happens *to* you, instead of *because of* you.

Quickly Reduce Your Initial Anxiety in Three Steps

1. Accept some anxiety. The first step to reducing anxiety is understanding the reality that you'll never completely rid yourself of it. Stop trying to obtain a Zen-like perfect state of mind. It's okay to feel anxiety; everyone does to a certain extent.

2. Don't forget they're human. If you peer inside the mind of the average person, you'd discover they are more preoccupied with thinking about how they come across to you and other people, than about anything concerning you. They may temporarily make a quick judgment about you, but most of their mental energy will be expended on their own issues and concerns. Remember that next time you interact with someone not very familiar to you – their eyes may be looking at you, but their thoughts are focused more inwardly than outwardly.

Force yourself to realize – no matter how perfect someone may seem to you – that they're really just a normal person with normal fears, desires, and habits. Be careful of artificially putting someone on a pedestal capable of making or breaking your ego. Bring the person back down to earth by visualizing the person doing very ordinary things – brushing their teeth, combing their messy hair – even going to the bathroom!

3. Lower your expectations. When initiating with strangers and new acquaintances, let go of focusing on the outcome. Many things in life are out of your control. Focus on establishing a friendly relationship without any more expectations. Remove the pressure to perform. Your criteria for success shouldn't be "Did I get her to laugh?" or "Did I get her phone number?" Lower your expectations. Did you initiate dialogue? Then bravo, many people can't even work up the courage to do that.

Activity Breeds Interesting Conversation

The simple act of *doing* creates interesting conversation. In fact, simply taking action, even by mistake, can magically spark conversation. Let's look at an example to illustrate this point:

> Jack and Jill are on their first date. They are both shy. They exchange greetings and sit down. Then an awkward silence takes over. They wait. And wait. Then Jack stands up to take off his jacket and accidently knocks over his water! Jill laughs. Jack laughs. Jill makes a comment. Jack slips in a joke about his clumsiness. Conversation ensues. Jack references his clumsy mistake again later in the conversation. Jill laughs again.

You get the idea? There is magic in action – even unintentional action. Many people I've talked to about social skills express the same frustrations: "I don't have any interesting stories to tell or anything interesting to talk about." My father lives by the proverb, "All work and no play make Jack a dull boy." He was raised in a strict English boarding school but still emerged with a terrific sense of adventure and curiosity. He can tell stories for days. He has experienced enough of life to write an autobiographical series. If you find yourself struggling to think of entertaining stories or interesting observations, you may need to get out more. I'd like to contribute another proverb, "All day on the couch with no activity makes Jack a dull conversationalist." Join a new group, sign up for a new class, or drive to a new city. You're bound to find something interesting if you look. But what if your car breaks down on the way? Great, you've got yourself an interesting story! Going on a date? Pick an interesting venue – a place where neither of you has been so there will be plenty to observe and experience. Experiences create the memories that your brain draws on during future conversations.

"Life begins at the edge of your comfort zone."

– Neale Donald Walsch

If you look back on your life, you may discover a single moment or decision that altered your life forever. I can distinctly remember five actions in 2006 that led to who I am today. At each major point during the six month period, I had a clear choice between doing something new and risky, and staying the course. The first major action occurred late one afternoon while I was working a dead-end job at a boring company. Out of the blue, a salesman stopped by the office asking if anyone wanted a few free tickets to a Tiger's baseball game that night. I debated even going. I was tired. I would be forced to mingle with strangers. But I decided to convince my friend Paul to go with me. He agreed, and we went. That was the first action. It was at that Tiger's game that we met Zack, one of Paul's friends. Zack worked at a rival company to ours. He convinced us to check out his company and guaranteed he could set up an interview for us. I took a risk, and decided to interview. That was action two. Paul and I landed jobs at the new company a month later. Fast forward a few more actions, and I'm at a disco bar one night. I see a beautiful woman dancing with her friends. I had to make a choice between standing in my spot or approaching her. You can probably guess what action I took!

The woman at the disco bar would eventually become my wife. My wife, coincidently, later ended up helping me land my dream job. So technically, I wouldn't have my family or dream career if I didn't leave my comfort zone and go to that Tiger's baseball game that night. Crazy how life works, isn't it?

Taking an active approach will open many more doors in your conversations, and your life. Even commenting on the actions you took or plan to take is a great technique. For example, "I signed up for _____ this week, and I'm kind of nervous about it."

Become an Interest Hunter

How much easier would initiating be if everyone just wore a sign around their neck listing everything they wanted to talk about? You may be ready to initiate and adapt an active mindset, but if you don't talk about something the other party is interested in, you still may have trouble with conversation.

You wish to discuss fashion trends of 17th century European Royalty, but the other person is obsessed with talking about how cute their Pugs are. What to do? You could focus on their dogs the entire time, right? Nope. Good conversation is never one-sided. Even the most selfish people want to hear about your opinions, thoughts, and interests (sometimes).

ECs are constantly searching for where their interests and their conversational partner's interests intersect. Think *Venn diagram*. (Who said Venn diagrams wouldn't come in handy one day?) When you find these intersections of interest, keep the conversation honed in on those topics. Try to conversationally synchronize your shared interests, if you will (and I think you will). That's why my previous conversation about houses, from the beginning of this chapter, flowed so well – all the members of that conversation had an active interest in the same topic. If the topics of Pugs and European Royalty don't intersect, keep searching.

Look at the following Venn diagram. If you become an interest hunter, I guarantee you'll find a few areas where you have something in common with practically anyone (even your cantankerous old neighbor, Mr. Fossilowicz).

Everyone has "hot button" issues, interests, and passions. Find these and you'll find the potential for great conversation. Notice their energy during each topic – which topics did they seem more interested in? Focus on those or find a way to circle back to a related topic when you have the chance.

In addition to interests, look out for shared experiences, views, and beliefs. If you and someone else share parallel experiences, it can spark an instant connection and bond. One similar unique experience can communicate that both people have a shared understanding of each other without ever having interacted before. Richly textured experiences can provide a treasure chest of connections.

My mom was raised strict Catholic and taught by nuns. When she meets someone with a similar background, she forms an instant bond with the other person. My mom always has a specific example about how they treated her and a funny story about how she misbehaved. Commonality is often a shortcut to achieving rapport. Having said all that, I'm obligated to state that of course you can still experience incredible conversations with someone who has wildly different experiences and interests – but it's often more challenging.

Be Genuinely Interested in Them

As the great Dale Carnegie suggested in *How to Make Friends and Influence People*, the secret to making more friends is by being interested in other people.

Showing interest goes beyond just listening to the other person's long story about the time they went camping in the mountains of Virginia. It's about asking follow-up questions based on previous discussions. It's about being excited for the other person when they share good news. Sympathize with them when they tell you they just lost their wallet. Offer to help if they could use a hand. Try to learn something new about them. Be interested in what is happening in *their* life. Let your curiosity take over. Remember, curiosity only kills cats – not conversations.

Your conversation partner's favorite word (besides their name) will always be "you." Dale Carnegie hit the nail on the head when he said "Talk to someone about themselves, and they'll listen for hours." Check out some examples focused on the other person:

> *You* always have the cutest shoes – where did you get those?
> Really? That surprises me, I thought *you* would want to _____.
> That's like the time *you* went to _____.
> Do *you* like _____?
> *You* have to drive all the way to _____ every day? That's a hike!
> *You* have the new _____? Can I see that? I'm so jealous. Can I borrow it sometime?

REMEMBER: Revolving the conversation around the other person works well, but balance is still key to exceptional conversation. Real friends still have interest in hearing about *you* also.

How to Initiate Conversation with Strangers

Your smartphone probably displays a few pieces of information on the lock screen – the date, missed phone calls, etc. This information is readily available to anyone looking at your phone. In a public environment, we often act like our smartphones: We display a little information, but before we are open to engaging in authentic conversation, someone needs to know the correct password.

For many strangers you encounter, a simple, innocent comment like "It looks like the rain will be here any minute," or "Do you know if the internet is working here?" or "I hope this line starts moving soon," is usually all it takes to unlock their social self and start a dialogue.

In general, the bar is set very low; be careful not to artificially raise the bar for yourself. Don't over-think it. Don't try to be a comedian. Just stick to the basics. Putting too much pressure on yourself will sabotage your confidence before you even start. Finding the courage to initiate a conversation and say the first few words, is the real challenge because most of us fear the unknown. If you maintain the view that you need to act like the leading role in a movie and approach with a James Bond one-liner – then you'll never initiate. You'll convince yourself that nothing you could say would ever be "good enough."

If you don't receive a warm reception, that's okay too. Some passwords are harder to crack. To me it has never been worth trying too hard – if someone is socially unavailable, then I move on. (Additionally, your personality may not "click" with someone else's, no matter how hard you try.) The odds improve substantially if you are at a place with like-minded folk, like at a convention or cocktail party.

Be on the lookout for clues that indicate what comments may unlock their password. For example, if the stranger is wearing a *Denison University* hat, I would attempt the following:

ME: Hey, did you go to Denison?
THEM: Yes, I did.
ME: So did I! I don't meet many alums around here.

THEM: What year did you graduate?

Presto! The person opened up to having a conversation with me.

Body language is the key to deciphering how open someone is to conversation and how easy their password will be to crack. Unfortunately, if your breath smells or you look like a serial killer, none of your passwords will work, no matter how accurate they are! On the flip side, something about the way you look or act may be very appealing to the other person, and they may automatically open up to you without much effort on your part.

Keep in mind that most people are not completely comfortable meeting strangers. Next time you're at some event where people are supposed to socialize, rest assured you won't be the only one feeling self-conscious or nervous. When you walk into a room full of people, do you instantly feel like they are all looking at you or judging you? If this sounds familiar, it's time to change your focus. That *inwardly* focused mindset places too much pressure on yourself and your performance. ECs understand that the vast majority of people are more concerned with themselves than anything you're doing or saying. ECs focus *outwardly* on other people, and look to actively make connections with people. Instead of focusing on whether you're saying the right things or looking good enough, focus on helping other people start and maintain conversations. Starting a conversation with someone else looking for a friend improves the nerves of two people – you and them – at the same time!

How to Form the Quick Connection

Establishing a personal connection requires a certain degree of commonality and trust. To form a connection, two people must relate and understand each other on some level.

Many initiating techniques share a common tactic – demonstrating similarities. Underneath, we all have a primal desire to know if the other person could be a *friend* or *foe*, bring joy or pain, and provide safety or danger. Show them that you could qualify as a member of their "tribe" and not an "enemy."

One time at work, I had to meet with a new executive in his office. I saw a Michigan State mascot on his desk. But I never attended Michigan State – and it didn't matter. I simply initiated the conversation with a comment about Michigan State in general. I could have talked about the previous game, an upcoming game, or maybe about how many of my friends attended the school. I could have even said I *almost* went there but I decided to go to a school out of state. Either way it jump-started a connection between us.

Maybe you're at Joe's party, but only know Joe? Then you already have a connection to everyone – you just haven't capitalized on it yet. You can always keep this gem up your sleeve for any point in the conversation: "So how do you know Joe?" / "So what's your connection to Joe?"

Your efforts should move you towards revealing your commonality. Prove that you have common desires, interests, thoughts, experiences, etc.:

COMMON FRIENDS: You're a friend of Jenny's right?

COMMON INTERESTS: Do you know which quarterback is starting today?

COMMON THOUGHTS: This dessert is great, isn't it?

COMMON POSSESSIONS OR CONCERNS: Is your internet connection working okay?

COMMON ENVIRONMENTS: Do you know if it's supposed to snow later today? (*I had to include a weather example!*)

CHAPTER 8: USE IT OR LOSE IT

Over the next few days:

1. Be the first to say "Hi, how are you?" to every friend or coworker you encounter.
2. Find something in common with someone.

CHAPTER 8: REVIEW

Before this chapter:

- ✓ Pay attention to the movie you're showing people
- ✓ Add energy and variety to your voice
- ✓ Scripts are everywhere, start paying more attention
- ✓ The Seven Most Likeable Traits: Be Humble, Caring, Positive, Enthusiastic, Goal-Oriented, Playful, and Flexible
- ✓ The four primary PATs: Comments, Knowledge, Opinions, and Autobiographical stuff
- ✓ The TAPP topics: Things, Activities, People, and Places
- ✓ Take advantage of your flaws
- ✓ Focus on making your words more interesting, descriptive, exaggerated, and colorful

From this chapter:

- ✓ Gain confidence by going first
- ✓ Become an Interest Hunter and seek out commonalities

Key takeaway from this chapter:

Moving from a passive to an active mindset will immediately upgrade your social skills and send you on a new trajectory of personal growth.

Coming up next:

In the next chapter, we'll examine some of the most useful techniques and tools for starting conversations.

Preview: *Adapting an active mindset won't help much if you don't know some useful techniques for starting conversations. This chapter focuses on some of the best methods for initiating conversations with anyone.*

[CHAPTER 9]

INITIATE WITH FEELER STATEMENTS

What's the best type of comment for initiating conversation? Technically, anything can initiate a conversation. I've seen a single burp initiate a decent conversation! However, the **Feeler Statements** are some of the best low-risk options for cracking people's social passwords. "Feelers" are simple observations or questions that kick-start conversations. They also help you gauge if the other person is receptive to talking. Expressing a feeler also lets other people know you are open as well.

I liken feeler statements to sweeping back and forth over the sand with a metal detector. Sometimes you'll receive nothing but a "...beep...beep...beep," but sometimes you'll hit on something interesting. Then you would start to dig. Initiating conversation, especially with unfamiliar people, often follows the same process.

Because initiating a conversation can be daunting, I attempted to simplify the options by lumping feelers into the following three categories:

YOU: your behavior/appearance/thoughts
ENVIRONMENT: mutual surroundings/other people
THEM: their behavior/appearance/thoughts

Feelers are relied on heavily by casual acquaintances – like neighbors. I have moved many times in my life, and the dynamic among neighbors has always fascinated me. For the most part, neighbors are forced to talk to each other once in a while. In fact, I would guess a million miniscule social pleasantries are exchanged between neighbors every day. Conversations often proceed like the following, and include various feeler categories:

ENVIRONMENT: Nice day for some gardening/walking/car washing, huh?
YOU: Yeah, I figured I should rake the leaves/clean the cars before it gets too cold out.
YOU: I'm hoping I can get _____ done before _____ happens.
ENVIRONMENT: Looks like we'll need umbrellas later today.

THEM: I never knew you had so many flowers growing over there. What kind are those?

There are probably 10,000 neighbors – right this very minute – talking about their lawns. And 50,000 talking about pets or kids. And at least a million talking about the upcoming weather! These simple observations and questions serve as excellent social lubricant to start a conversation if both parties are interested. If your attempt at initiating a conversation hits a brick wall, *half the time it has nothing to do with you.* (Perhaps they're running late to a Yoga class or maybe Jimmy's famous chili isn't cooperating with their stomach.) Even I, an individual with an unhealthy obsession with conversations, don't always feel like engaging in conversation with someone, no matter how friendly or interesting they seem! You could always try a different feeler, or depending on their behavior, press the abort button.

Feelers serve as valuable phrases for introducing new topics and engaging in small talk. Even the most important and serious business meetings never start out talking about the business matter itself. It's standard business etiquette to grease the pan a little bit before cooking anything significant. I had a boss who, every December, always recycled the same line about being late for Christmas shopping as part of her pre-meeting small talk. It impressed me how often she recycled it during our meetings with various executives.

 Quick Tip: Start small and simple, no matter what. Try not to ever over-explain. If you're talking about something esoteric or intellectual, cover the bare minimum first. Let the other person indicate if they are interested in hearing more.

Studying the following feeler categories will prepare your brain with a better framework for initiating conversations. Poor conversationalists enter new social situations without any idea or regard for the type of statements they'll communicate with. You'll never be able to predict exactly what someone will say in every situation, but if your brain is familiar with the three main feeler statements types, and you're expecting to use some, you'll be one step ahead.

The following section dives deeper into each type of feeler statement. I tried to stick to examples for initiating with strangers, but most of them could be used for friends or acquaintances too. *Disclaimer: Many feelers combine aspects of the environment, you, or the other person. I did the best I could to divide them into categories that made sense.*

Feeler Category 1. You

Regardless of the social setting you find yourself in, you will always have the ability to mention simple comments about your own behavior, appearance, thoughts, expectations, or plans. In fact, many ECs go into new situations with a few *You* feelers in mind. For example, an EC who chooses to wear a classy sports coat to the bar, may go into the situation prepared with a few comments about their coat. When the moment arrives, they'll say something like, "I figured I'd get a little dressed up for once." The feeler statement about the coat would work in any situation, regardless of who else shows up, etc.

Mentioning expectations is another easy feeler to start with. For example, "I didn't expect it to be this big/nice/classy/etc." Feelings regarding what is currently happening is very common for ECs as well. "I'm loving the big crowds in here, this place is really hopping tonight."

Going on a date or business dinner carries extra pressure to maintain good conversation. Notice the following example feelers mostly involve a preference, hope, expectation, or concern:

> *I don't know* about you, but *I love* Italian food.
> *I don't know* which appetizer to choose - they all look so good.
> *I was worried* that I picked the hardest restaurant in the world
>   to find. Did you find the place okay?
> *I was hoping* I would get here earlier so you wouldn't think I was a
>   perpetually late person, but I guess it's too late for that!

Did you notice anything about the previous examples? I'll let you in on a little secret: **Any of the previous feeler statements could have been thought of beforehand.** What about the feeler about the appetizers? How in the world could someone have known what appetizers are available? They wouldn't have known. But I guarantee you, at a nice restaurant, they serve nice appetizers. If for some reason they don't serve many options, you could have just mentioned how you couldn't decide between two or three options that look very good – the feeler remains basically the same.

Want to approach someone at a bar, coffee shop, or bookstore? Don't over-think it; just state your intentions out-loud. For example, "Hey, how are you? I just wanted to come over and say 'Hi.'" Or "Hi, how are you? I thought you looked friendly so I wanted to come say 'Hi.'" The following comment stands out at a bar where a lot of people start with pick-up lines: "Hey, I don't know any good pick-up lines; I just wanted to say 'Hi.'" If you receive a warm reception, introduce yourself, ask their name, and throw out a few more feelers to keep it going, like, "I was hoping I would find at least one cool person to talk to here." (Which, again, could have been thought of beforehand). If your attempt at initiating epically fails, no worries, at least you can say you tried. Most people can't even say that.

Feeler Category 2. The Environment

Observations and questions about the environment, and other people, should focus on what stands out. Point out something unique or interesting. A little playfulness and sarcasm works well if you feel confident enough to try.

I was in an elevator at a conference with a bunch of strangers. We all stood in silence for at least 30 seconds. Then the elevator suddenly made a loud screeching sound. Someone sarcastically observed, "Well, that sounds *safe*." Everyone chuckled and it broke the tension. People felt comfortable talking from that point on.

Comments about the environment are typically very safe (unless you start criticizing other people, for example). Not to mention, environment feelers are sometimes more relatable than the *You* feeler type because the environment is something you both share. Here are a few environment examples:

> This place is packed - I've never seen this many people here before.
> Wow - that cake looks like a major sugar rush.
> It must have cost them a fortune to decorate this place.

Feeler Category 3. Them

There is a reason this option appears third on the list. Commenting about the other person is the riskiest type of feeler statement unless you stick to something positive, flattering, or helpful (or unless you know them well already). Every day I hear women compliment each other's attire/hair as a way of starting the conversation on a positive note.

> I love those shoes - where did you get them?
> That's a great tattoo - where did you get it done?
> Nice watch - what kind is it?
> Do you need help carrying that in?

Occasionally, the other person will be adorned with clues as to what topics they'd be interested in talking about. For example, a sports team's jersey naturally invites comments about how the team is doing that year or something about a particular star on that team. What someone wears is almost always a tangible expression of their interests. It's safe to assume they enjoy talking about it and know enough to understand references to it.

> What did you think about the Lions game yesterday?
> So you think the Lions are going to win this weekend?
> Is that the new _____? How do you like it?

Notice how many aforementioned observations ended with a question. Many compliments receive only a "thanks," so be prepared to ask a follow-up question.

Get to Know the Problem Feelers

Let's face it, feeler categories about the environment, yourself, or the other person are very broad. You could think of many types of feelers within each category. One of the most useful feeler comments combines aspects of *You* and *Them*, which I affectionately term, *The Problem Feeler*: state a simple problem *you* have, that *they* may be able to fix. Asking for help or information is one of the best ways to initiate conversation with anyone. People inherently enjoy helping others, and asking for help often mitigates any potential awkwardness. Asking for help also masks any other intentions (e.g. maybe you plan on flirting or asking them out). You may not enjoy asking for help because your ego sits in the way or you don't want to inconvenience someone, so just keep your requests simple.

Even if you already know the answer, you can still employ this technique to break the ice. The next time you're at a coffee shop with your laptop, you can ask anyone near you the innocent question "Is your internet working? Mine seems really slow." You may have fast internet, or you may know very well why your internet connection is slow, but that's not the point. Regardless of your true internet speed, it still comes off as a very honest and normal question, and tests to see if anyone is open to conversing. (A tiny white lie – *in the name of conversation and friendship* – never hurt anyone!)

Remember, these questions should be easy enough for the other person to answer, but not simple enough where you come off like a complete dimwit! If the person is interested in talking with you, you'll know. If they respond with a grunt or growl, then you may want to sit next to someone else. If you receive a warm reception – even if they do not know the answer – you have successfully broken the ice and can follow up. "Yours is? Hmmm – maybe it's a problem with my computer. I really need to buy a new one. Do you like your Toshiba?" You get the idea.

Here are a few more problem feelers that work well: (Remember, you may know the answer, but that's beside the point!)

Do you know if this teacher/class is hard/any good?
I wonder what's going on down there?

Are they supposed to serve any food/drinks at this event?
Is that any good? I was thinking about trying that.
There are just too many options - I don't know how I'm going to
decide. What do you recommend?

You can think of many feelers as just spoken out-loud thoughts and observations that aren't directed at anyone in particular (although ideally someone takes the bait and responds). Inner thoughts like "Wow it's cold in here," or "I have no idea what to pick," don't necessarily demand a response, so there isn't pressure for a conversation to start. But they open the door to conversation if anyone is up for it.

One time a stranger next to me let out an overly dramatic sigh, which signaled to me they were looking to possibly chat. Remember, people who aren't interested in talking typically don't draw attention to themselves. I took the bait and said, "Whatever you're working on sure sounds stressful." We then had a very natural conversation after that – all because of a single sigh.

Problem feelers allow you to place yourself in a more vulnerable position before you step over any boundary. You have the option to explain or provide a legitimate reason why you're approaching the other person. For example, "Is that any good? I just thought I'd ask since I saw you reading that," or "Were you going to this conference too? I'm curious if it's any good."

A while ago I was at an ice cream shop with my kids. The woman in front of me was asking the cashier what options existed for children with food allergies. I interjected that my son has a dairy allergy so we always opt for the mango sorbet. After paying for our ice cream, the woman found me again and asked if I knew of any other places catering to food allergies in the area. She had just moved to our town. The conversation easily flowed from there.

Also, a secret to diffusing the awkwardness of a situation is to simply point out something awkward about the situation. By pointing out a potential problem or difficulty, you can remove some of the tension and start an actual conversation. If you find yourself alone at an event, these gems work every time:

I don't know anyone - can I join you?
I don't know anyone here so I'd thought I'd come over here and say 'Hi'.
I'm looking for a table to join, can I join yours?
I don't want to sit at a table by myself and look lonely, can I join you guys?

Don't Forget Problem Feelers for Friends Too

Problem feelers are exceptional for starting conversations with friends and acquaintances too. Instead of stating simple problems related to losing your internet connection, for example, you could introduce more interesting dilemmas or scenarios that inherently encourage advice or opinions.

Try to stay away from the "death and disease" variety of problem, and stick with more everyday problems others may have some experience with. Let's look at some examples:

I'm almost done with my show - I need to find a new TV series to be addicted to soon!
I'm thinking about getting a dog/cat/snake/new car. Do you recommend _____?
I'm thinking of moving out of my apartment, but I'm not sure if I should do a condo or a house.
I don't know if I should call him back - he's nice and all but...
I need help. Do you guys know of any good places I can take Betty for our anniversary?

Even if you already know what you're going to do, it can be productive to seek others' input – you never know what you may learn. Sometimes you may receive great audience participation. Let's look at some real-life interactions:

Aimee introduces a light-hearted problem.

AIMEE: I have to bring something to my boyfriend's soccer game tonight - do you think it's okay if I bring cookies? Are those too girly? Would everyone make fun of him?

JEREMY: As long as they are manly cookies and not girly cookies with glitter frosting or anything.

LORAINE: What if you wrote the words, "I'm a bad-ass" on each one?

AIMEE: That's a good idea! Maybe I should.

TYLER: What about little milk cartons? He'd probably be totally embarrassed. But it would be so funny.

You don't always have to literally ask for advice. Sometimes just stating your predicament can invite friends to contribute.

LIZ: I don't know what to do about my son.

AKUA: What do you mean?

LIZ: Well, he keeps hitting kids at preschool. The other kids are calling him the "hitting boy" now.

AKUA: Have you tried _____?

Liz could have also initiated with "Guess what my son did this time?" or "My son is back in trouble again." Either would have invited Akua to inquire further and to eventually offer advice or opinions.

Of course, when you introduce a problem, don't hesitate to offer your own opinions and thoughts as well; the other person may need time to generate their opinions.

What if you can't think of any problems to introduce? Starting with a *plan of action* sometimes leads to problems arising organically. Do you need to plan a project? Do you want to see a movie or concert? Do you want to catch up? You'll have to figure out how to solve simple problems like who is going to drive, or what time is best to meet, etc. Great conversations start with talking about plans for something and naturally branch off from there. The action provides the reason, or backdrop, behind starting the conversation.

Tailor Your Feelers

Any time you can skip generic weather talk and tailor the feeler to the person or context, it's a good thing. Awhile back, I was at my son's kindergarten open house. There were many parents meandering about, and I didn't know a soul. But I wasn't afraid; I looked forward to it. Do you know why? You see, I already knew something about each person there – they all had a kindergartener. I already knew a lot about them because of that single shared experience. When you're part of an exclusive club/event/group, it's an opportunity to skip the generic feelers and tailor your feelers to the appropriate context. I already knew what these strangers would be open to and enjoy talking about. (It's almost like having a cheat code for a video game.) I knew that some of the thoughts and experiences I had would be mutually shared. We were in an environment ripe for targeted, tailored comments. Here are some examples:

YOU
I think I'm more nervous than my son is!

ENVIRONMENT
Isn't this room great? They even have a SMART board.

THEM
Looks like your daughter has already found her seat.

With friends or familiar associates, you typically skip any generic feelers and jump right into tailored feelers. When you get together with a friend you haven't seen in a few days or more, there's often a situation or context around the event. Are you both seeing a movie? Meeting for coffee? Think about a feeler before you arrive. Are you excited for the movie? Have you ever been to the place you're meeting at? Did you see something interesting on the way?

If you haven't see them in a while, there's probably something unique about them you can add: Did they change their hair style? Wear new shoes? Are they doing anything that sticks out? Are they always early? Did they just put up Christmas lights? Are they baking something that smells good?

Check out the following blend of *you, environment,* and *them* feelers. Notice how they are tailored to more specific or personal information than you typically would use with someone unfamiliar to you.

> I'm loving your short hair...it makes you look so cool.
> Well I'm looking forward to that pie I've been hearing all about.
> Wow, whatever you're cooking smells fantastic.
> I love your Christmas lights. You're making me feel bad - I only have a tree and a bush covered.
> Ready to watch the Lions lose today?
> Wow, they gave you some nice cabinets in your new office. I could use some like that for my kitchen at home!
> How did you beat me here? I swear I thought this time I would be more punctual than you!

These initial tailored feelers are critical to setting the mood for the remainder of the interaction. Depending on your level of familiarity with the other person, there's great potential for awkwardness or anxiety during the first few minutes while everyone is acclimating to the new situation. A poor opening exchange can set an awkward precedent.

Improve the Transition

As mentioned already, many of the previous examples could have been thought of before the interaction started. Some of them rely on your powers of observation, and some rely on a transition object. A **transition object** is something that helps you transition from one situation to the next, from the moments before the interaction to the moments after.

Bringing wine is a classic transition object utilized by people for centuries. As soon as you walk in, you can comment about it. You can position the focus of the conversation onto the object. In a way it absorbs any awkward energy and helps jump-start the conversation. It also helps absorb some of the anxiety you may be feeling, because a lot of anxiety stems from the thought of being in a social situation with nothing to say.

If you have a transition object, you can safely assume the conversation will start with a comment about it. Other transition object ideas include bringing a pet to the park to meet someone, or bringing donuts to a meeting.

The *reason* for the event should aid the transition as well. Maybe you're going to someone's Halloween party. A transition comment will naturally be something Halloween related. You'll probably have on a costume, or the host or host's child will. Comments you can think of right before the interaction may include something like, "I had no idea what I was going to be so I kept it simple and wore _____." Or "I decided to go all out this year and join the Avengers." Similarly, you can expect to comment about their costume or their child's costume with a useful comment like, "I love your _____, that's the best ____ I've seen in a while."

Sometimes outside elements aid with transitions if you know how to take advantage of them. Did you get rained on while walking to the place? Your wet coat is your transition object; you can comment about it first thing. "Well, I wasn't expecting that I'd be walking through a small hurricane today." Or "Of all times to forget an umbrella – I had to pick today!" Or "Gotta love that Michigan weather!" Or "Hey I needed a shower anyway, I was feeling kind of dirty." Was it difficult finding the place? Try "I was so lost coming here. I started to worry that I wasn't going to make it." You get the idea.

The Time Feeler

You may know the story, *A Christmas Carol*, by Charles Dickens. Essentially, three ghosts visited Ebenezer Scrooge one fateful night: the ghost of Christmas past, present, and future. Next time you're at a loss for words, try racking your brain for a statement related to *time*, specifically about the past, present, or future. The Time Feeler serves as a great guide for your brain the next time you feel overwhelmed by possibilities or frozen with fear. Examine the following time-related statements:

1. The recent past:

You'll never guess who I saw last week.

I never thought I would find this place, it's like a labyrinth back here.

I was driving over here and this guy...

2. The present moment:

I'm feeling like a nice white wine. I deserve it.

This place reminds of me of those ancient Roman temples.

Who would have thought we'd be here...sitting here next to the

_____...

3. The near future:

Do you think they'd look at me weird if I ordered every single appetizer?

When we get home tonight, we should...

I'm thinking about seeing that horror movie this weekend.

Try to eventually take this technique one step further and incorporate all three periods of time into your conversation – you'll be amazed at the results. This is one of those mental structures I highly suggest memorizing. Here's an example:

I've been healthy all week so I'm keeping it up until the weekend. I'm ordering the turkey wrap. But once Friday evening gets here, look out! I'm going crazy. An entire deep dish pizza is not out of the question.

Set Yourself Up for Success with Setup Statements

In general, exceptional conversationalists rarely jump right into their main point or thought. In any given conversation, before you launch into your main thought, it's sometimes important to *gain attention, establish your presence, warm up the crowd, or carefully introduce a complex or sensitive topic*. There's a very useful type of statement that often goes unheralded and unnoticed, I call the "Setup." If you heard the following statements in conversation, you may not even notice them:

> I would like to talk for a minute.
> I'll tell you what, this is what I'm going to do...
> Here's something you'll appreciate...

Setups have the very undistinguished job of setting up other, more important points. However, setups provide numerous benefits. They buy you a few extra seconds to formulate your thoughts. They also help project strength and confidence in the business world. Additionally, they can add clarity and structure to your statements, making them more persuasive and powerful. Check out the following:

> We need to do three things. First...
> Here are my thoughts about it...
> I'm in an uncomfortable position, because...
> I may come off as a jerk for saying this, but...
> So I have good and bad news...
> I appreciate your honesty, and I think that...

On the contrary, some setups serve to soften a message. For example, *"This is just my opinion,* but..." Utilizing setups may avoid coming across as brash or harsh.

PCs rarely take advantage of setups. On the surface they may not seem important enough to give much attention to. But I assure you they are worth incorporating into your everyday habits. They not only help you gain control of a conversation, but they help you *appear* in control.

In today's day and age, people are distracted easily, and in everyday conversation, you won't always have everyone's full attention. Setups are exceptional at attracting attention to your main message.

> It was so funny, yesterday I _____.
> That reminds me of this great deal.
> I saw the weirdest show yesterday...

Do you ever have trouble breaking into a fast paced, lively group banter? When a fortress appears impenetrable, medieval soldiers would turn to the strength of a battering ram. Some setups mimic verbal battering rams and help you force your way into the conversation.

You know what! I think we should...
Hold on a second!
That reminds me!
Speaking of dogs! I was...

Not only can setups project confidence and help you control the conversation, but setups can help add some playfulness to your statements as well. A guy could say, "I love a good manicure." But if he sets up his comment in one of the following ways, it's funnier: *"I'm not afraid to say it –* I love a good manicure." Or *"I don't usually admit this,* but I love a good manicure."

I've experienced hundreds of corporate meetings, and each time someone utilized one of the following setups, it elicited a positive reaction (and a few laughs).

Examine the following statements WITHOUT and WITH setups:

WITHOUT A SETUP: I think the entire company should purchase new tablets.
WITH A SETUP: *I may come off as a big nerd for saying this,* but I think the entire company should purchase new tablets.

WITHOUT A SETUP: I actually don't like the Dave Matthews Band.
WITH A SETUP: *Promise you won't break up with me if I tell you this,* but I actually don't like the Dave Mathews Band.

Keep in mind, ECs may employ two or more setups before they actually get to their main point. For example, "Okay listen. Here's the deal. What I want to talk about today is _____." (This example is also proof of how some phrases look ridiculous in print, but in the context of real conversation, sound completely normal.)

Quick Tip: Whether you employ feelers or setups to initiate, it's better to start *general and objective* and move towards *focused and subjective*. If you stated "I think we should sell XYZ and start developing a new line of products," you run the risk of an emotional backlash. You're better off warming up the crowd before launching into specifics. Initiating with "We should discuss XYZ sales," or "It's important to talk about XYZ sales at some point," instead.

Greet Friends and Acquaintances with Extra Energy

When Kramer from *Seinfeld* opens the door, he doesn't just open the door – he swings it open wildly as part of his grand entrance. He starts strong. In conversations with friends, colleagues, and acquaintances, focus on starting strong. Think of a few lines ahead of time. Make them count. Give them energy. Haven't seen your friend in a while? Act happy to see them.

How you speak in the beginning will echo throughout the rest of your conversation. Initial energy and confidence carries you a long way. Meekly saying "Hi" to your boss before a meeting sets a poor tone for the remainder of the conversation and gives a poor impression from the get-go.

This is where the whole "Fake it 'til you make it" saying works well. It's hard to fake confidence for an extended period of time – but even the shyest and mildest folks can inject confidence into the first few lines.

The Vegas Three-Step Technique for When You're Alone

Want to know my favorite strategy for breaking into an established "group" at an event? It's a two-step operation, but I'm including a bonus third step at the end. The first time I put it into action, I was at a Las Vegas conference (hence the name). And it worked to perfection.

Step One: Find another lonely person. There was a social hour planned after the conference activities concluded on the first day. I didn't know a soul. I walked in, ordered my beverage of choice, and walked around for a few minutes to survey the scene. Groups of two are the hardest to breach – three or more are a little easier, but a single lonely person? That's the best option. I found plenty of people in my same boat – they appeared like they came by themselves also. I walked up next to someone who looked interesting, stated, "I don't know anyone here so I figured I would come say 'Hi.'" He happily replied, "I don't either, that makes two of us!" And I replied, "Now we don't look so lonely!" And we talked for about ten minutes.

Keep in mind, my feeler was successful because it was a social hour and I knew that anyone standing around would be open to socializing. And because we were at the same conference, there were many good tailored feelers to consider ahead of time. Another solid opening would have been to ask the other person if they had been to the conference before. If *yes*, you can ask what they like or recommend, if *not*, you can ask why they chose to come, where they're from, what they do, what they're looking forward to, or give them some tips about the conference.

Step Two: Join a larger group. After some small talk, ask your new friend if they'd like to seek out a larger group to join. It introduces a fun problem to solve. It introduces some action. Your new friend will most likely be glad to help you join a larger group, and you can both have fun exploring the crowd and finding a group that looks like a good match. It's pretty easy from that point on – your friend may even prove to be a good social co-pilot.

Three good lines for breaking into a group with your new friend are:

Mind if we join?
We heard this was the fun/cool/popular group.
We're lonely; will you adopt us into your group?

Of course the mood of the event is important for how playfully your deliver your lines. Your non-verbal communication, like energy and tempo, should try to align with the situation.

Bonus Step: Initiate more. Do you want to know how things turned out after my social hour ended? I didn't just ask for business cards and conclude by saying my goodbyes. I ended up going out to dinner with the group – and guess who initiated the idea of going out to dinner? *This guy.* Yeah, me. It turned out to be a blast. We walked around Vegas the rest of the night. Then we all met up again each additional night we were there. I have five new friends because of three small actions: Approaching a lonely person, approaching a group, and then initiating further action.

That's what initiating is all about. William Butler Yeats has a perfect quote for this spot in the book: "There are no strangers here; only friends you haven't yet met."

 Quick Tip: Do you want to initiate an action more naturally? Start with a reason. For example, rather than stating, "Want to grab some coffee?" put the reason up front, "I'm really thirsty, want to go grab some coffee?" It's more natural that way.

CHAPTER 9: USE IT OR LOSE IT

Go back and read aloud all the feeler statements from this chapter (multiple times if possible). The long-term goal is to reach a point where feelers are an automatic part of your conversation repertoire.

Over the next few days:

1. Initiate a conversation with a You, Environment, or Them Feeler.
2. Initiate a conversation with a Problem Feeler.
3. Initiate a conversation with a Time Feeler.

CHAPTER 9: REVIEW

Before this chapter:

✓ Pay attention to the movie you're showing people
✓ Add energy and variety to your voice
✓ Scripts are everywhere, start paying more attention
✓ The four primary PATs: Comments, Knowledge, Opinions, and Autobiographical stuff

✓ The TAPP topics: Things, Activities, People, and Places
✓ Take advantage of your flaws
✓ Focus on making your words more interesting, descriptive, exaggerated, and colorful
✓ Gain confidence by going first
✓ Become an Interest Hunter and seek out commonalities

From this chapter:

✓ Become very familiar and comfortable with the three main types of Feeler statements: You, Environment, and Them
✓ Problem Feelers are incredibly effective at starting conversations with strangers and friends alike
✓ Initiate with comments related to Time: the past, present, and future
✓ Don't forget about the Setup statement for helping you introduce other comments

Key takeaway from this chapter:

Reviewing and practicing effective feeler statements will go a long way towards training your brain to automatically think of feelers when you need to initiate a conversation.

Coming up next:

Knowing how to initiate is a valuable and critical skill, but what happens after you start a conversation? Small talk. The next chapter looks at small talk in depth to help you continue the conversations you initiate.

Preview: *What happens after the conversation starts is just as important as starting the conversation in the first place – and no less challenging. Small talk is an inevitability of life. Millions of business deals have been made, millions of friendships have formed, and millions of relationships have turned to romance, all because of small talk. Either learn to become proficient in small talk, or get left behind.*

[CHAPTER 10]

START SMALL WITH SMALL TALK

"I hate small talk!" my wife exclaimed. "I'd rather just get to the interesting stuff." Do you have similar views toward small talk?

Why is small talk disliked by so many? I've certainly been guilty of harboring disdain for idle chit chat, but I've since changed my tune. (I've also been guilty of frequently switching metaphors, but we all have our quirks!). There are two primary reasons for the disdain:

1. It seems like it doesn't accomplish anything and wastes time.
2. It involves too much self-disclosure; private or introverted people are uncomfortable with sharing so much information.

Both are fair points. But to generalize small talk as only idle chit chat is selling it short. Small talk comes in a range of shapes and sizes. Exceptional conversationalists understand that it serves a few very important objectives. Primarily, small talk is what gets the conversation ball rolling. Without small talk, it's hard to reach meaningful conversations.

Much to the dismay of my children, most public pools post "No Diving!" signs. They would rather dive in to the deep area than have to walk through the shallow water first. Many adults have a similar view of conversation. Many people want to skip the shallow end of the pool and jump directly into deeper areas. Rather than rushing to the deep end, I hope this chapter persuades you to appreciate the shallower side of conversation.

A New Perspective on Small Talk

If you're not comfortable with small talk – and still harbor a general distaste for it – I'll present another case for why you should reevaluate your views. Besides being a means to an end, small talk is a form of collaborative story-telling. You and the other conversation participants are the characters in the story of life. And small talk is the means by which you're describing life as its happening, reflecting on what has happened, and discussing what's to come (no matter how trivial). If you recorded every word, you'd end up with a giant novel. In a way, you're not only a character, but you're also a narrator. As you narrate the story with someone else, you form a bond and a connection. Small talk is one of the most effective ways to achieving quick rapport with someone.

Talking about the sandwich you had for lunch, or the soccer game you're going to on Friday aren't overly exciting, by any means. But all the small events and happenings, represent the chapters in your life story. The opinions, thoughts, and dialogue you verbalize during those events fill in the pages of each chapter.

The story you tell may not be exciting or full of romance and adventure, but most novels aren't full of exciting events and poignant opinions on every page either. Most novels are chock-full of trivial details and regular dialogue – just like real life. Small talk just verbalizes those details.

Talk about what you just did, are doing, or want to do soon. For example, "I can't believe we made it here...this place is great...I'm so hungry...I could eat everything on the menu." Act as a narrator and talk about the talk itself, "Wow, I sound like I haven't eaten in two weeks, don't I? I need to control myself."

Describe your actions, problems, or how something affected you or someone else. For example, "I don't feel like eating lunch after seeing that." Or "He said he would be here around 11. I sure hope he makes it."

If you simply desire to carry out a plan or achieve an objective, you may need to wade through small talk before the meaningful discussions occur. In every business meeting I've ever attended, there is *always* small talk for a few minutes beforehand and afterwards (especially if you arrive early or stay late). Small talk presents an opportunity to form quick bonds with people you may or may not know well. Take advantage of it. And if you just don't like sharing information about yourself, then you're out of luck. You might as well close this book now because good conversation requires a degree of sharing.

Lower Your Standards and Start Small

Many of you reading this have high standards for conversation. I know I used to. It's time to lower them. Half of the small talk "skill" isn't anything practical – it's mental. Lower the pressure to perform and impress, and your nerves relax. Successful small talk stems from training your brain to be less picky. It's about being okay with occasionally saying a mistake or something silly. Authentic comments are often the most interesting and fun. Subsequently laughing at your mistakes is all part of the small talk game.

Say what first comes to mind. Small talk is about acting on your feelings and initial thoughts without over-analyzing. Small talk is about delighting in the small moments and small things in life.

 Quick Practice: Do what improv comedians do and try the **"Yes, and..."** technique. Next time you're chatting, try to continue the conversation by adding "and" to the end of your (or their) comments. This technique essentially forces your brain to continue in a more uninhibited way, *even if you feel like you have nothing left to say.* Try it now with the topic of "cats." Start talking about cats, and right when you feel like stopping, say "and..." and force yourself to continue your monologue, no matter how silly you feel.

If you have trouble coming up with something to say, you're likely putting up too many mental road blocks – expressions can't escape past all the "that's too stupid" or "that won't work" or "that's not clever enough" inner doubts. Do you find that your conversations with your best friend are better than with other people? It may be the result of the mental roadblocks you take down when you're talking with your friend.

Make a game out of talking about very ordinary things. Over the next few days, aim to achieve the most simplistic conversations possible.

Quick Practice: Pretend I just called you on the phone. In the next few minutes, tell me the boring details of what you have been doing over the past two hours – but act enthusiastic about it. Talk about the ham sandwich you made for lunch. Talk about filling your car up for gas. And as I've mentioned multiple times – half the battle is *how* you talk, not what you actually say. If you seem enthusiastic about how good the ham sandwich was, others will stay engaged! If you manage to tell an interesting story about the ham sandwich, *and sound enthusiastic about it* – even better!

Rhino Butts and the Art of Being Polite

My friend and I were at a work function a few years ago, and I'll never forget a woman who went on and on about her trip to the local zoo. Granted, I always appreciate when someone else carries the weight of the conversation. I usually try to go along with whatever they are discussing, but this case was a little different.

The highlight of her experience was how she was warned not to go near the Rhino's butt. Why? Because it frequently sprays urine with as much power as a fire hose. I found that tidbit entertaining, but she kept going for a while about her zoo tour and I noticed myself mentally checking out. My friend, however, continued the small talk and asked her question after question about her zoo experience. My friend made a friend that day. Afterwards, I felt a little guilty for not contributing to the exchange, and I admit, I acted selfishly.

I realized that even though small talk sometimes feels fake – that's okay. It seems fake because it sometimes is. But I'd argue it's a polite form of fake. You can't possibly be interested in everything everyone says. It's polite to just play along in the name of keeping a positive social experience. *I guarantee people have feigned interest in what you had to say* at some point as well.

Sometimes you just have to talk about Rhino butts.

A Closer Look at the Parts of Small Talk

We're going to look at a few real-life small talk specimens under a microscope. The first sample is of the shallowest variety.

Two strangers in line at a grocery store start chatting.

JIM: Looks like it's going to be raining any minute.
BOB: Looks like it. Good thing I'm done shopping for the day.
JIM: Me too. I can't believe how much it's been raining lately.
BOB: I tell you what, it sure is good for my lawn though.
JIM: You can say that again.

Notice how Jim kicked things off with a good *Environment Feeler*. The weather. A classic. Bob disclosed a little personal information. There were a few generic comments. End of story.

The aforementioned example is what gives small talk a bad rap. Many comments are truly clichés or platitudes, like "Sometimes you just gotta roll with it," or "Isn't that something?" However, the generic comments serve a purpose: They are incredibly safe, innocuous and won't offend anyone, but they still help maintain the conversation.

What we don't see from the aforementioned example is what happened *next*. If time allowed, and if both parties were interested, Jim and Bob may have delved deeper into a new topic. Bob revealed a little clue about his personal life: He has a lawn that he cares about. That may seem insignificant at first, but if Jim wanted to, he could inquire further about the lawn (including what kind of mower he uses, if he bothers with lawn fertilizer, if he gardens too, etc.). The lawn topic may lead to all sorts of other – more interesting – topics.

Small talk sometimes acts as a proving ground to determine if both parties would like to continue the relationship. In a similar vein, the small talk before and after the official job interview is often just as important as the interview itself! The hiring manager is tasked with determining if the candidate would be a good fit within the culture and/or team, not just from a skills perspective, but from a social cohesion perspective as well.

The Me Too Technique

Small talk is daunting to some of you because sometimes it's the simplest statement that is hardest to respond to. If someone brings up a point about global politics, it may be easy for you to form a connection. But if you ask someone "How are you?" and they respond glumly with "Oh, it's one of those days," that can be much more challenging! What would you say to that?

Next time you're struggling with small talk, try the *Me Too* technique. It doesn't always work, but keep it in your back pocket. One of the major goals with small talk is to find similarities and form rapport. Next time someone says, "Oh, it's one of those days," you could say, "Yeah, I've definitely had those days." Next time someone says, "I'm getting some lunch soon," you can quickly respond, "Yeah, I'm probably going to look for lunch soon too." Easy, huh?

So what about those times when you don't share the same experience or feelings? You could do the opposite and highlight the contrast between you both. For example, they state, "I'm trying the triple burger," you could respond with how you're the opposite, "Oh, I could never eat that, I'd have heartburn for two weeks!" Or "I wish I had the stomach for that, I usually don't get more than a salad for lunch." Of course, a general rule of thumb is to find and discuss commonalities with people, but occasionally highlighting your uniqueness/differences is important too.

The More Substantive Parts of Small Talk

Let's go a little deeper into the pool and examine a more substantive slice of small talk.

Two co-workers / friends run into each other while getting coffee.

PEGGY: I love your shoes.

SUE: Thanks! They're Carl Johns. Yours are cute too.

PEGGY: I want shoes like yours - my husband thinks spending money on shoes is silly, though.

SUE: Really? That's too bad.

PEGGY: He just doesn't understand. He still owns the same
    shoes he wore in college.

SUE: Wow! I can't believe it.

PEGGY: I know! Can you believe it? I mean, who does that?

SUE: I couldn't go a year with the same pair of shoes! Anyway, I
    need to go look like I'm working.

PEGGY: Yeah, I should go back too. See you at lunch?

SUE: Yeah, see you then.

Peggy kicked off the convo with a good *Them Feeler* regarding Sue's shoes. Sue provided a little information. Peggy followed up with her feelings about the shoes and disclosed a quick personal anecdote. A few more generic comments were exchanged, and then it was over.

I want to remind you of the PAT types (Comments, Knowledge, Opinions, and Autobiographical) from a few chapters earlier. If you recall, everyone has stored a collection of previously assembled thoughts in their conversation storage tanks. These thoughts are close to the surface and are recalled quickly – which is great for small talk situations. It may not appear like it at first glance, but many comments included in my examples, and in your everyday social interactions, are PATs. The more small talk you engage in – the more PATs your brain automatically stores away for the next occasion. Let's see how PATs fit in with small talk:

A conversation occurs between two friends.

JOE: I went golfing with one of my buddies yesterday.

FRAN: That sounds like fun.

JOE: I loved it. Golf courses are always in the prettiest
    areas…near lakes, forests…

FRAN: Oh I know. I'm jealous.

JOE: My buddy and I golf a lot, but we're not competitive - I
    think I love driving the golf cart more than the actual golfing!

FRAN: Which course was it?

JOE: The West Isle Country Club.

FRAN: Oh nice. I've always heard that the North Shore club was good too.

JOE: Yeah, I love it there.

In the previous example, Joe started by mentioning a recent event. Then Fran responded with a simple **PAT Comment**. "That sounds like fun," which is probably used a millions times a day around the world as a response. Fran probably used it at least a thousand times in her life. Joe followed up with a **PAT Opinion**, "Golf courses are always in the prettiest areas...near lakes, forests..." It's general enough that he probably used that opinion many times before when talking about golf. Joe later mentioned an **Autobiographical PAT**, "My buddy and I golf a lot, but we're not competitive – I think I love driving the golf cart more than the actual golfing!" Joe probably used a variation of that line before, too. They both employed **Fact PAT**s when talking about the different golf clubs they know.

As discussed already, PATs are great and all, but no one can remember enough PATs to fill up every conversation. It's critical to feed your brain better instructions for quickly generating good comments in any social situation, PATs or no PATs. This next section covers a mental model you can apply to all of your future social interactions, which will help provide your brain direction as it sorts through all the possible thoughts and memories.

Achieving Conversation Flow with FOOFAAE

After feeler statements kick-start the conversation, how do you maintain the small talk? How do you achieve a conversation flow, or what I affectionately refer to as "The Sweet Spot." When the conversation flows at a lively and engaging pace, you've reached a conversation sweet spot. Feelers are designed to get the ball rolling, but to reach the sweet spot, you'll have to offer a little more.

Say "Hello" to my little friend: *FOOFAAE*.

The FOOFAAE guide was created with the intention of providing you something slightly more specific and useful than anything thus far. When analyzing ECs, I discovered that they typically generate comments from one of the following seven categories, in the form of a statement or question: **Feelings, Observations, Opinions, Facts, Action statements, Autobiographical, or Events.**

Exceptional conversationalists routinely cycle through the FOOFAAE options during every social interaction. It's habitual and second nature to them. You need to reach that point. Poor conversationalists tend to rely on a few of the FOOFAAE categories too heavily, and therefore limit their total options.

You're reading this because you want to improve your ability to drive a conversation. You may be sick of letting other people control the conversation. You may feel like you often don't know what to say or how to contribute to the overall conversation. Starting with FOOFAAE as your guide for initiating and maintaining conversation provides a fantastic mental framework for your brain to follow and eventually habitualize. You'll feel more comfortable in every conversation when FOOFAAE is second nature to you.

Without further ado, let's look at FOOFAAE in action. In the following example, you visit a friend and meet their dog. FOOFAAE provides your brain a framework for an assortment of comment possibilities to cycle through.

FEELING: I absolutely *love* your dog.

OBSERVATION: You have such a well-behaved dog.

OPINION: I think Pugs are the best kind of small dog breed.

FACT: I was reading that Pugs are usually...

ACTION STATEMENT: I want to adopt a dog like that.

AUTOBIOGRAPHICAL: My brother has a Pug too...

EVENT: Did you hear Frank just adopted a dog last month?

FOOFAAE Comments Excel at Driving the Conversation Forward
The FOOFAAE drivers will help you expand your repertoire beyond ordinary feelers and PAT types. They are the seven most useful types of statements/questions ECs utilize. I suggest studying each type. Practice them until you know them like the back of your hand. None of the individual FOOFAAE categories should be foreign to you. **Feeling** comments are simply anything to do with your preferences, feelings, expectations, hopes, desires, etc. **Observations** are typically more objective statements than **Opinions**. **Facts** is information or knowledge. **Action statements** are any comments that involve an action (including a potential or past action). **Autobiographical** comments, like the PAT we discussed already, involves personal details, stories, etc. Unlike the PAT types, however, FOOFAAE separates out **Events** – past, present or future – into its own category.

Try to be mindful of which types you lean too heavily on and which types you tend to neglect. Do you love providing facts but avoid offering feelings? Maybe you focus too much on events and not enough on opinions? ECs balance their conversations with statements from each of the FOOFAAE categories. And ECs often string together a bunch at a time.

FOOFAAE should be one of your main tools for driving the conversation forward. However, not all conversation drivers were created equal. Some encourage a variety of responses and give your partner flexibility in how they respond. Sticking to the facts with statements or questions like "How old is your dog?" is likely to lead to very few types of responses and offers limited flexibility for the other person. Disclosing something about yourself and asking a related question, like, "I'm thinking of getting a dog, is your dog good with kids?" opens up the conversation to a host of possibilities. It also provides the other person plenty of room to guide the conversation in a number of directions.

Similarly to tailored feelers, the secret to achieving the conversation sweet spot, is offering more specific and substantive FOOFAAE comments, tailored to the other person/situation. Don't feel bad if you can't immediately reach a conversation sweet spot with someone unfamiliar to you – without enough knowledge about someone, it's difficult to offer anything too detailed or tailored. Sometimes it simply takes more time and more investigative work before you reach a good flow.

> **Disclaimer:** I don't attempt to draw hard lines between feelers, tailored feelers, and FOOFAAE comments. There's often overlap. Ditto with Observations and Opinions. Observations are typically more objective than opinions, but not always. I only make distinctions among them for purposes of instruction.

Ice Cream and FOOFAAE: A Case Study

One time, I ran into a friend at the local ice cream shop. My two young sons, Kaerigan and Rowan, were with me at the time, so it was natural to pivot the conversation around them. Because he was a good friend, we skipped introductory exchanges and jumped right into the conversation sweet spot. It was understood we only had ten minutes or less to chat, so we kept it light and avoided serious or deep discussions. He is also a good conversationalist, and we were both quick to introduce new topics as soon as one started to fade – this kept the conversation very lively and engaging.

Take a look at how our conversation proceeded. I've taken the liberty of breaking down each topic into small abridged vignettes. Note that all of the following conversations were driven forward by a variety of FOOFAAE comments:

Vignette 1

Event

ME: We're here to celebrate the end of kindergarten today.

Opinion and Action
FRIEND: Oh wow! That's a big deal. Congratulations Kaerigan. *You'll be going to school with the big kids soon huh?*

Vignette 2

Observation and Opinion
ME: I like your jacket - it makes you look pretty suave.

Autobiographical and Feeling
FRIEND: Thanks. Yeah, I figured it was time to shop somewhere other than Salvation Army for my clothes. I figured I can afford it now.

Vignette 3

Event
FRIEND: I heard you finally sold your house, right?

Autobiographical, Fact, and Feeling
ME: Yep, two weeks ago. We actually got $2,000 more than we asked for - I'm so relieved!

Vignette 4

Event and Feeling
FRIEND: We're actually on our way to Traverse City later tonight. I figured it would be fun to get away for a few days.

Autobiographical and Fact
ME: I haven't been... but I heard the wine tasting is awesome there.

Vignette 5

Action and Opinion

FRIEND: Oh, I want what you're having Kaerigan. That looks delicious.

Fact and Opinion

KAERIGAN: It's peppermint fudge brownie. It's really good.

Opinion, Feeling, and Action

ME: He's kind of addicted to that. But I can't blame him! I want it too!

Because there was a preexisting comfort level between us, we could take chances with riskier or more personal comments. We could tailor our observations and opinions to topics the other would be interested in discussing, and we could reference events or experiences that we wouldn't just disclose to a casual acquaintance.

 Quick Tip: Trying to be too precise or accurate with your details can slow down and damage the flow of conversation. Don't worry about telling someone *exactly* when or where something occurred if you're struggling to remember. Just paint a general picture and get to the point. Instead of "When I was a kid, I think when I was nine, or maybe it was when I was ten...," just say "When I was around nine or ten."

Buy Time with Small Talk Fillers

You might be saying, "FOOFAAE is great and all, but I can't think about each option quickly enough to keep the conversation flowing smoothly." And you're not alone, many people prefer to mentally digest something before offering a comment. Unfortunately, too much time spent deliberating equals stilted or disjointed conversation. But I have good news. First, practicing the FOOFAAE options will naturally speed up your ability to utilize them. Secondly, get to know the **Small Talk Fillers**.

No human on the planet is capable of effective lightning speed comments all the time. You may assume that ECs think at exceptional speeds and always have responses ready, but they often rely on buying time before their next comment. Even a few seconds gained is a lot of time for the human brain. Sometimes it's the difference between generating a bland statement and an interesting one. Take a page out of the exceptional conversationalists' handbook and incorporate more small talk fillers into your daily lexicon. They're easy to learn, and no one notices or remembers them; what people do notice is the conversation flowing!

I was at a bar one time where I overheard a guy (let's call him Slick Rick) buy himself time with every single response. The woman he was talking to said comments like, "I wish someone would buy me a drink." And Slick Rick would paraphrase first, "Oh you want someone to buy you a drink, huh? I guess I could be that someone." Later during the conversation, the woman would say, "I work in accounting." Slick Rick would say, "Oh, you work in accounting? How do you like that?" See what I mean? There's a reason he's called Slick Rick!

Let's examine a few useful small talk fillers:

Initial Reaction
That's awesome! I can't believe that.
Are you kidding me?
That sounds like a lot of fun.
I could never do that.
Oh my gosh, that is so creepy.

Rephrase, Paraphrase, or Summarize
I can't believe how fast you bought your house.
Sounds like you're close to stopping their service.

Rephrase, Paraphrase, or Summarize as a Question

You work in accounting, huh?
You bought the house already?
He's really going through with it, huh?

Similarity or Difference

I did the same thing last week!
I think we should too.
My son talks the same way - that is so funny.
I'm not sure I would do that.

Each type of small talk filler plays nicely with other types. Feel free to join different types together to buy even more time. For example:

REACTION: Really? That's so cool.
REPHRASE AS QUESTION: You really pet a rhino on the butt?
SIMILARITY OR DIFFERENCE: I'm not sure I could do that.

Let's get even more generic and shallow shall we? Platitudes and generic stock phrases serve to fill the gaps when more substantive responses are out of reach. Even the simplest comments have a place in small talk – don't overlook them. Some phrases have universal appeal; you can plug and play them into any type of conversation. If you're short on fluffy gap-fillers, here's a few to peruse:

You can say that again!
Yeah, that's the story of my life.
When it rains, it pours.
I can't believe we're doing this right now.

One time I was going upstairs with a few people on my way to the office. A man and woman had a perfectly normal exchange. But if you listen closely, the man actually employed a lot of small talk fillers throughout the conversation. I *italicized* the fillers for you:

WOMAN: You guys go first, I'm sure you'll go faster than me.
MAN: *Oh, I wouldn't bet on that.*

WOMAN: I didn't think it would be this heavy.

MAN: *I'll give you credit there*, that's a lot to carry up the stairs.

WOMAN: This will be my workout for the day.

MAN: *You can say that again.* With this many stairs, you could count it as two workouts!

WOMAN: That's for sure!

Small talk fillers rarely get noticed, but they serve an important function as gap fillers between more substantive statements. If your small talk seems to stall a lot, you may be under-utilizing fillers.

Speaking of utilizing small talk fillers – baseball announcers are the kings of small talk fillers. Why? Because their job is to fill up dead air time for three hours whenever nothing is happening in the game – which, if you watch baseball, is quite often! Rephrasing themselves two or three times is very common. Notice all the rephrasing and small talk fillers in the following example:

Wow, look at that hit...it doesn't get much better than that...I haven't seen a hit like that in a long time...he looks like a young John Smith out there...that's why they call him a true pro...boy I tell ya, if he can keep doing that...he's going to be something special...I just can't say it enough. That's a special kid.

Rephrasing your comment in a different way is a smart strategy for buying a little more time. Additionally, some rephrases end up producing more interesting comments – you may surprise yourself!

If you still require more time – simply asking a question and putting the conversation ball back in their court buys the most time. The best types of questions will be covered in the next chapter.

 Quick Tip: Nervous about an impending social interaction? *Be socially prepared.* If you mentally run through the following checklist, you'll improve your chances of having a good conversation:

✓ A feeler statement to help initiate
✓ A question tailored to the specific person
✓ A few relevant/interesting topics to mention in case the conversation stalls
✓ A *recent* story you can tell in under a minute
✓ Information about a personal event in the *near* future.

The Seven Steps to Successful Small Talk

1. Open, Confident Body Language

Look approachable and friendly. Smile sometimes. Maintain eye contact (but not in a creepy-staring-without-blinking-way).

2. Stay Light and Upbeat

Keep comments on the lighter side. Inject some energy into your expressions. Try to stay fairly positive unless they desire to go negative.

3. Tailor Comments to Their Interests

Discuss intersecting interests, but still try to customize your comments to what the other person would find interesting.

4. Self-Disclose

Share information about yourself; your feelings, preferences, experiences, stories.

5. Observe

Share observations about your surroundings, the other person, culture, etc. Dish out a few compliments.

6. Balance

Small talk requires a balance of quick observations, feelings, and questions. It requires a balance between partners in the form of turn-taking. Finally, it requires a balance between seriousness and playfulness.

7. Listen and Follow Up

Actively listen, and then ask follow-up questions. Match the vibe and energy of the moment. Expand on what they are saying.

The Seven Steps to Successful Small Talk is a good guideline to remember. Steps four, five, six and seven will all be addressed in the coming chapters. The remaining book will continue to add skills and techniques designed to build upon the small talk foundation thus far.

CHAPTER 10: USE IT OR LOSE IT

1. Over the next few days, talk about something incredibly simple and ordinary.
2. During one of those instances where you're discussing something very ordinary – add more enthusiasm than you normally would. Notice what happens.
3. Pick a TAPP topic, and see if you can offer a comment from each of the seven FOOFAAE categories. Try it in live conversation also!

CHAPTER 10: REVIEW

Before this chapter:
- ✓ Pay attention to the movie you're showing people
- ✓ Add energy and variety to your voice
- ✓ The four primary PATs: Comments, Knowledge, Opinions, and Autobiographical stuff
- ✓ The TAPP topics: Things, Activities, People, and Places
- ✓ Take advantage of your flaws
- ✓ Focus on making your words more interesting, descriptive, exaggerated, and colorful
- ✓ Gain confidence by going first
- ✓ Become an Interest Hunter and seek out commonalities
- ✓ Initiate with Feeler statements (You, Environment, and Them) and Problem Feelers

From this chapter:
- ✓ Small talk builds rapport and is the gateway to more meaningful conversations

✓ FOOFAAE: Feelings, Observations, Opinions, Facts, Actions, Autobiographical, and Events
✓ Leverage more Small Talk Fillers to buy time

Key takeaway from this chapter:
Half of small talk isn't a skill – it's mental. Lower your standards and need to impress. Focus on small things. Mastering the FOOFAAE framework will help jump-start and maintain your conversations.

Coming up next:
A crucial skill for initiating and maintaining any kind of conversation is knowing how to ask better questions – that's next.

Preview: *Asking questions is a fundamental skill for asserting yourself and keeping the conversation flowing. Learn how to ask the right questions to initiate, maintain, and control conversations.*

[CHAPTER 11]

EXPAND YOUR RANGE
OF QUESTIONS

conversations a day begin with a single question. ns, in the simplest sense, are nothing more than an ? between asking and sharing information. Initial conversations – and many forms of small talk – are heavily dependent on your ability to ask quick questions and share quick responses. A lot of questions function as feelers, but questions can travel much deeper and obtain much more substantive information than a feeler is designed to do.

Journalists always start and keep a conversation going because they are masters of the question. In addition to their solid grasp of question types, they also show interest in the interviewee. That is a simple but powerful combination. However, if you merely acted like a news journalist, you would probably scare most people away!

In everyday conversation, no one wants to be interrogated! Instead, act like a *conversation* journalist. Learn how to gently probe. Start in the shallow end, then gradually dive deeper. But remember, balance your questions with FOOFAAE statements about yourself when appropriate. Where a news journalist simply seeks information, a conversation journalist seeks *information and commonalities*. One of your primary goals should be to find shared interests, feelings, and events (remember the Venn diagram from the previous Chapter 8: *Adapt the Active Mindset and Initiate with Anyone?*).

Do you have trouble coming up with questions? It's helpful to think about adjectives that relate to the topic. Many people internally create "mind maps" to do just this. If someone is talking about a dog, what adjectives come to mind? How about "fun," "furry," "dirty,"

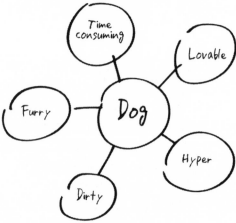

"expensive," "time consuming," "lovable," and "hyper"?

The benefit of surmising these adjectives is that your question can often ask about whether the adjective applies to the current topic. For example, if the adjective is "hyper," your question can ask if the dog *is or isn't* hyper. Pretty simple, huh?

Let's look at the most effective question types. The goal is not to memorize every type, but to familiarize yourself.

The Closed and Open Question Types

Most questions are either **closed** or **open-ended**.

Closed questions look for specific answers and tend to close the conversation (for example, "What time is it?").

Open-ended questions tend to open the conversation up and encourage the speaker to expand on a topic. For example, "How do you feel about the new boss?" Open-ended questions are much better at maintaining conversation. Good open-ended questions are often evocative and elicit feelings, or provocative and ignite thoughtful discussion. Here's a great first date question for you: "What's your favorite thing in the world?"

 Quick Tip: When appropriate, think of an answer for your own questions also. Don't ask "What's your favorite thing in the world?" without considering how you would answer it.

The Interrogative Question Types

Keep in your back pocket the **six interrogative** question types: *Who, What, Where, When, Why,* and *How.* You will rarely be at a loss for words if you can quickly cycle through those question types. For example:

Who else was there?

What happened afterwards?

Where did it come from?

When did he finally show up?

Why did he do that?

How did he even get in?

My three year old son is in the "Why?" phase and can keep a conversation going for five minutes by simply asking "Why?" to every comment. But I don't recommend trying that technique!

The FOOFAAE Question Types

Many questions can be organized under the FOOFAAE (Feelings, Observations, Opinions, Facts, Action Statements, Autobiographical, and Events) model for driving conversations. Of course there are plenty of exceptions and overlap among question types, so please refrain from emailing me examples that don't fit perfectly!

FEELING / OBSERVATION / OPINION Questions

Some of the best questions for initiating conversations and getting the ball rolling fall under the first three FOOFAAE categories. Most of them are low risk and easy for the other person to answer because they don't require deep knowledge of any given topic and aren't overly personal. This is key: hard-to-answer questions don't belong in fledgling conversations.

Look for Agreement/Confirmation.

Isn't this food good?

Do you find it cold in here too?

Looks like you're doing some serious gardening over here, huh?

Ask their Feelings/Attitudes/Preferences.

How did you like it?

Really? What did your wife think?

Compare or Contrast to something else.

Doesn't it feel like you're at a bachelor party right now?

Isn't this better than _____?

FACT Questions

When you don't have all the facts, or just want to obtain more facts, ask for information. Place yourself in the role of the student and learn more about a topic from the expert. Everyone is an expert at something – you just have to find out what. Do they just work at a clothing store in a mall? Then they're still an expert at working retail in malls. Try to learn something you didn't know about that occupation or topic.

Ask for more information.
Is it true what they say about _____?
You repair those? How do you avoid being _____?

Additionally, you could ask for help. (Remember the problem feeler from Chapter 8: *Adapt the Active Mindset and Initiate with Anyone?*). Nearly everyone enjoys helping a little.

Ask for help.
Do you know when the second presentation is starting?
Do you know if they're open on Sundays?
Who should I pick for my team this week?

ACTION STATEMENT Questions

These questions involve *doing* something.

Do you want to get out of here?
Should we get something to eat?
Have you ever tried _____?

AUTOBIOGRAPHICAL Questions

Some questions help you obtain more personal information. There are many levels of self-disclosure. The depth of your questions should depend on the comfort level and familiarity between you and the other person. Some of the best and safest questions to ask initially involve finding out how they are attached or connected to the event:

How are you involved with the _____?
Are you a friend/employee/consultant/related to Jim?
How did you end up at _____?

Once the conversation ball rolls along and the comfort level increases, it's usually safe to dive a little deeper:

Are you from the area?
What do you do?
Do you have any kids? Pets?

EVENT Questions

Ask them about an experience or event. Just think: every Monday you can ask about someone's weekend. And every Friday you can ask if they have anything fun planned for the weekend!

Have you been able to do ____ yet?
You're going to _____ this weekend? That's cool - have you ever
   been there before?
How did the _____ go last month?

 Quick Tip: Don't forget to bounce their question back at them if it makes sense. For example, after answering their question about how you entered your current line of work, simply ask them the same question back!

The Insightful Questions

Many comedians draw from this technique. If you notice something unusual, or ironic, it can be fun to speculate on how it came to be, who thought of it, what they were thinking, the plausibility of it, etc.

Why do they even make shoes for babies? Are there actually
   babies who can run around?
How does the bald, fat guy end up with the prettiest girl on the
   show? That's not even realistic.

Who gets the jobs of painting those ceilings? I'm glad it's not me!

Why do they make baby clothes with so many snaps? Are they trying to torture us?

Is someone actually paying her to do that? Who would pay money for something like that?

Did you hear about that guy from MSU who robbed the bank? How does someone go from college to criminal in the same year? What happened to them along the way? Did they just wake up one day and say, 'I don't think I'll go to microbiology class today, I think I'll go rob a bank instead!?'

Questions don't always need to be answered to start good conversation. Rhetorical questions, like many of the previous examples, are perfectly capable of initiating discussion without requiring direct answers.

Stay in touch with your sense of wonderment. Curious people ask the best questions – that is, if they decide to share their questions! Many people withhold questions if they don't serve a purpose or lead to direct answers. But wondering something aloud sometimes sparks great and interesting conversation.

One time a woman was talking about growing up in the country and dealing with wild animals. The person listening didn't ask the woman a direction question, but instead wondered aloud, "I always wondered how raccoons can steal all my food, but I never actually see one, ever." The woman didn't offer a specific answer, but she provided a guess and kept the conversation going with additional comments about animal shenanigans. Another time I heard two people talking about the eating behaviors of their kids. One person said, "I always wondered, if I let me son eat anything he wanted, would he just eat candy and ice cream all day until he passed out from the sugar crash? Or would he actually attempt to eat something healthy?' This elicited more interesting comments.

The Time Question

Similarly to the Time Feeler, when you can't think of what to ask, you can always think of something related to *time*. Good conversation topics revolve around how people *willingly* spend their time. When you find out what people choose to spend their time doing or thinking about, then you have probably discovered what interests them.

Who are the people they spend time with? What are the things they spend their time using/consuming/thinking about? What have they spent their time doing in the past, and what are they planning to do with their time in the future? What about you - how do you choose to spend your time? You may notice that many of the time related questions naturally overlap with TAPP topics.

In addition, everyone has a timeline. Talk about the past, present or future of their timeline.

> Any weekend plans?
> It sounds like you try to _____ a lot?
> What are you going to school for?
> Do you go to _____ a lot?
> What made you go into that field?
> Are you going to the _____ afterwards?

And of course, in the interest of keeping the conversation balanced, don't forget to reference how you spend your time also!

Don't Forget to Bring Some Question Assistants

Asking questions puts you in the temporary driver's seat of the conversation. And when you ask a question, you may think you're done. But that's not always the case. Exceptional conversationalists anticipate possible pauses or roadblocks in the conversation. The other person may need a few moments to process the question, or may not know how to answer at all.

ECs always keep a comment or second question available in their back pocket, just in case. Don't get me wrong, ECs don't plan out elaborate conversation diagrams. Sometimes just having a general sense of what your next comment or question could be is sufficient.

When you ask a good open question, like, "What did you think of the speaker today?" you may sense the other person won't have an immediate answer. Instead of stopping at the question, staring at them, and waiting through a period of awkward silence, you could add your own thoughts to keep the conversation flowing and the spotlight off of the other person. "I thought he was pretty interesting," or "I thought he was brilliant – I wish I had that much experience with _____." Obviously you don't want to cut someone off, but it's also important to serve as a good conversation partner by helping the other person either think of something to say, or buying time until they can contribute.

Your question assistant can literally be what triggers the other person to think of their next good comment. The aforementioned question about the speaker was very open-ended. By adding your own thoughts, for example, "I thought he was great – I love how he mentioned the effects of climate change," you not only clarify your own position, but you provide specific fodder for them to connect to. Instead of answering directly about the speaker, they could latch on to your comment about climate change.

Think about someone you enjoy conversing with. What do they do when you struggle to connect to something in the conversation? They may utilize space filler techniques like question assistants to fill in conversation gaps, buy you time to think, and otherwise help maintain a fluid conversation.

For example, you saw a good television show recently and ask your friends, "Did you see that XYZ show yet?" And *regardless of how they respond*, you can usually still articulate a version of your second question/comment:

1) **If they watched the show:** Wasn't it good? My favorite part was the chase scene around the volcano; that was so cool.

2) ***If they didn't watch the show:*** It's really good, I think you'd like it. There's this awesome chase scene around a volcano. It was pretty cool.

One time I noticed my new neighbors digging giant holes in their yard. I assumed they were preparing to build a fence, but I wasn't 100% sure. I wandered over and threw out an easy softball question to open up a dialogue, "Hey, are you guys building a fence?" Or since I could probably assume it was a fence, I could have left it open-ended, "Hey, how's the fence-building going?"

Although open-ended questions generate more conversation options, they don't trump closed-ended questions in every situation. Sometimes a simple closed question works better because it doesn't force the other person to exert much effort while they search for a response. New conversations usually flow better if they remain simple and easy to respond to. But if you ask closed questions, be prepared for short answers.

I could predict, in a general sense, how the conversation script was going to play out initially (Remember scripts from Chapter 3: *Increase Your Conversational Awareness*). My neighbors were going to say something predictable to the extent of "Yeah, we're coming along slowly but surely," or "Well, we're trying to anyway, it's taking a little longer than we thought." It's not like my neighbors were going to start talking about something random like the pros and cons of medical marijuana. (Okay, my neighbor might, but probably not your neighbor!) Before the words even left my mouth, I was already thinking about possible follow-up questions or comments. I could respond with "Great, let me know if you need a hand – I'm pretty good with a hammer." Or "I was thinking about building a fence too – did you use any outside help to dig your posts?"

This technique works well for one of the most feared of all social situations – breaking into a new group of people. You may start with a confirmation question like "Are you guys talking about buying houses?" And a receptive group would respond affirmatively, and elaborate or fill you in on what they have been discussing. Make sure you rack your brain for a follow-up nugget to help ensure the transition is more natural and not stilted and awkward. But the group may say nothing more than "Yeah."

Remember the FOOFAAE (Feelings, Observations, Opinions, Facts, Action Statements, Autobiographical, and Events) options to help you follow up with a comment after your initial feeler question is sent out. For example, if you run into a "Yeah," you could follow up with the *autobiographical* option, "That's cool, I've been thinking about moving into the _____ area for a while now."

Some question assistants simply provide your *reason for asking*. If someone mentions how they are attending a local college, you could ask: "Are the professors difficult there?" You could then slip in some self-disclosure by following up with your reason for asking. "I'm starting a new job and I don't feel like working all weekend on homework!"

Your question assistant (*italicized*) could provide your intentions. "Do you want to try the new Cajun restaurant? *I'm really hoping you say 'Yes!'*"

After enough practice and application, this concept of preparing backup comments and questions will become second nature and you won't even realize you're doing it!

The Secondary Superlative Questions

You don't need to exert too much mental energy thinking of a good backup question if you remember the *superlative questions*. Superlatives offer great follow-up options after you received some information from your conversation partner. For example, after they answer your first question, ask about the *biggest, worst, best, least, most,* aspects of the topic:

What was the hardest part about it?
What is the best place you recommend moving to?
What's the craziest thing you saw there?
What's the most amount of money you made doing that?
What's your favorite part of the entire thing?

Look Around More

Let the environment help you. Something standing out in a familiar environment should trigger a host of questions. Say someone brought in a box of Peppermint Patties to your work for everyone to share. You could go about your work, or take advantage of the new object in the environment. "Who is the angel who brought those to us today? I want to thank them!" Or "I love those – have you ever tried putting them in coffee?" Or "I'm not sure I can control myself, do you think we can take more than one?"

A while ago one of my wife's friend's stopped by to drive my wife somewhere. While my wife was getting ready, her friend and I found ourselves standing in awkward silence in the kitchen. I didn't know her friend well, so I quickly looked around for something safe in the environment to comment on. My kids were in the family room watching a show on Netflix, so I first asked, "My kids love Netflix, do you guys have Netflix too?" She said she did, and that got the ball rolling. The door was open for me to add some more interesting comments related to Netflix. "We love it. I still remember the time before Netflix, when we were stuck watching whatever came on PBS at 6am...Usually it was cheesy infomercials!" She laughed and added, "Or Yoga! Which is funny you mention that because when I was a kid I actually preferred the reality-based shows. I never liked cartoons. I still remember watching General Hospital with my mom every week!"

Questions in Observation Clothing

You don't always need a question mark at the end of your statement in order to elicit more information either. Noticing someone drinking a giant beer mug and asking, "Why are you drinking all that beer?" may come off awkwardly. But observing nonchalantly "That's a lot of beer," gives the person an option of offering an explanation, or not.

Seeing a few guys walk by with V-neck T-shirts could prompt the observation, "Those guys look silly in V-neck T-shirts," or a question,

"What is with all the men wearing V-neck shirts these days?" The resulting discussion is often the same.

 Quick Tip: Want to know how to appear more confident when asking someone out on a date? Simply express your request as a statement first, rather than only a question. For example, James Bond wouldn't say, "Would you like to go to dinner sometime?" James Bond would say, "I want to take you out to dinner. What are you doing this Saturday?" Confident people assume the other person would want to go out with them. Questions naturally put you in a subordinate position and sometimes imply insecurity.

Don't Trap Anyone with Your Questions

Sometimes questions turn your conversation into a job interview or an interrogation. Some questions feel forced, and coincidently force others to answer. Your questions should be easily answered by your conversation partner or you could cause frustration and awkwardness. If I inquired about your favorite rugby team, you may not have the slightest idea. Poorly aimed questions can trap your conversation partner in an uncomfortable position.

Couching your question with another statement or question assistant can be an effective way to give your conversation partner another way out in case they feel trapped or unsure how to answer. Simply asking, "Have you owned any Fords before?" doesn't offer any clear options besides responding with "Yes" or "No." However, saying "I'm thinking about buying a car, have you owned any Fords before?" provides more context to what answer you may be looking for. The other person could offer a related comment in case they can't speak to owning a Ford. "I bought a _____ last month, and I had a great experience with the XYZ dealer, you might want to try them."

When you listen to friends talk, you'll notice that *statements* dominate the conversation, as opposed to back and forth question and answer sessions. This is how people talk when they aren't consciously *trying* to make conversation.

Remember, don't force the conversation if it's not meant to be. Look for warning signs. Is the other person truly participating with more than simple comments? Are they too distracted? Are they becoming upset? Are they asking questions also? Don't hesitate to pull the plug on a poor conversation if your partner doesn't seem inclined to contribute. There are plenty of reasons someone may not be interested in chatting with you and many of them have nothing to do with you.

CHAPTER 11: USE IT OR LOSE IT

1. Pick three questions types you typically don't incorporate into your everyday conversations. Over the next few days, try to ask a question from each type.

2. Proactively think about a follow-up question or comment to add after your initial question.

CHAPTER 11: REVIEW

Before this chapter:

✓ Pay attention to the movie you're showing people
✓ Add energy and variety to your voice
✓ The four primary PATs: Comments, Knowledge, Opinions, and Autobiographical stuff
✓ The TAPP topics: Things, Activities, People, and Places
✓ Focus on making your words more interesting, descriptive, exaggerated, and colorful
✓ Gain confidence by going first
✓ Become an Interest Hunter and seek out commonalities
✓ Initiate with Feeler statements (You, Environment, and Them) and Problem Feelers
✓ Initiate with comments related to Time: the past, present, and future
✓ FOOFAAE: Feelings, Observations, Opinions, Facts, Actions, Autobiographical, and Events

From this chapter:
- ✓ Look to FOOFAAE for help thinking of good questions
- ✓ Be proactive and consider a second question or comment
- ✓ Don't trap anyone or ask difficult questions

Key takeaway from this chapter:

The Time Question is one of the most useful to remember. Asking about how someone spends their time is likely to maintain the conversation. Also, remember that the secondary question or comment is sometimes just as important as the initial question.

Coming up next:

So far we've focused heavily on initiating conversations, but sharing interesting thoughts about yourself, and your surroundings, is the meat and potatoes of maintaining great conversation. The Share habit is next.

HABIT FOUR

SHARE

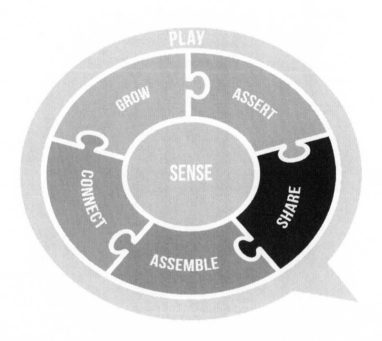

Preview: *The quality of your conversations rely on your ability to describe your environment, yourself, other people, and abstract concepts. This chapter focuses on better methods for describing yourself and painting a self-portrait others would enjoy. The more people know you, the more comfortable they'll feel, and the more easily they can form connections to you in the conversation.*

[CHAPTER 12]

PAINT YOUR PORTRAIT WITH EFFECTIVE SELF-DISCLOSING

Successful small talk – and conversation in general – relies heavily on your ability to self-disclose. It's the fourth step in the Seven Steps to Successful Small Talk, and necessary to achieve conversation balance.

Your conversation storage tank may be the size of Fort Knox and contain millions of interesting thoughts – but it's useless unless you open it up to the public. Think of yourself as a café owner in the busy town of Conversationville. There's a lot of competition, so if you want to attract customers, you'll need to leave some free samples of your thoughts out front. If a customer enjoys the free sample, they may come in and ask for more. If you're a savvy business owner, you'll offer free samples *customized* to meet the needs of each customer.

Some poor conversationalists struggle with talking too much and offering too many details, but for this chapter I'm operating under the assumption that you don't offer enough. Disclosing quick personal information is one of the easiest and most effective ways to keep the conversation humming along.

Serve Your Customers Small Chunks

Serving your thoughts in small chunks is a smart first step to offering exceptional expressions. Notice the two different self-descriptions below:

> BOB: Anyone want something chocolate for dessert?
>
> LONG-WINDED LARRY: I really don't like chocolate dessert that much. If it were up to me, I'd rather have some fruit, especially anything in the melon category, because they just taste better and I usually just choose watermelon or something. Or grapes are good too.
>
> SUCCINCT SALLY: I'm not really into chocolate desserts - I'm more of a watermelon kind of girl.

Long-winded Larry isn't necessarily ineffective – but he probably could have left out a few details. Exceptional conversation isn't about talking as much as you can. The succinct statement is often more interesting and packs more punch than if you drag something out. Good, succinct statements, can of course be chained together to form groups of effective statements. (If you have a great story to tell, and your conversation partner is giving you the green light, then chat away!)

Look at some additional short disclosure statements below:

> I'm one of those people who loves a good horror flick.
> I'm not a big fan of football.
> Sometimes I just see things in black and white.

All of the above have something in common – they're meaningful, yet succinct. Add a little non-verbal enthusiasm, and these statements are even more effective. As you learned with feeler statements, they don't have to be complex to be effective. In fact, many of the statements in this chapter could be consider feeler statements and initiate conversations – I purposely make no distinction.

Exceptional conversationalists are exceptional at speaking in chunks. Try to articulate your feelings and preferences in digestible bite-sized pieces, or tidbits. If you're ever fortunate enough to be asked to appear on television or radio, one piece of advice someone will surely offer you is to speak in "sound bites." A sound bite is just like it sounds: a quick thought listeners can metaphorically sink their teeth into. Politicians, corporate executives, and managers have been honing and collecting sound bites for most of their careers. Sound bites allow people to quickly and persuasively convey an opinion.

Keep in mind, speaking succinctly doesn't mean speaking briefly. A long story can be told succinctly. When you can, trim the fat off the meat of your message by removing any extraneous details that wouldn't be interesting to the listener. On the flipside, if you're having a playful conversation (and no one's crunched for time), random tangents and thoughts can be fun and add a lot of a value.

The One-Two Punch

Notice below that many sound bites start with self-disclosure, and then continue with a *supporting statement*. These one-two combos are very effective and a favorite of ECs. A supporting comment could include an example or explanation that supports the initial declaration or observation. Check these goodies out:

> I love seafood - especially a good salmon.
> I like carpentry. I actually used to volunteer for Habitat for Humanity.
> Last time I was up there, I got this sandwich called the 'The Godfather' - it was fantastic.
> I'm not a big fan of football. I could probably think of 20 other things I'd rather do with my time.
> I love this kind of weather - it's perfect for camping.
> I only drank half my coffee - which you know is very uncharacteristic of me and my coffee habits.
> I've read that book. I know, I'm a nerd like that.

What Kind of Coffee Drinker Are You?

Did you answer? Or did you just keep reading?

 Quick Practice: Considering the number of times you'll encounter coffee in your life, this is a great self-disclosure exercise. In exactly two statements, describe what kind of coffee drinker you are. Essentially, tell me your tastes, and tell me why. Then continue reading below for some great examples.

Look at some actual coffee revelations I've heard; notice the two-part succinct structure?

> I'm a purist - if there's color other than black I won't drink it.
> I've got a sweet tooth so I love all the sugary flavors - the more it resembles a milkshake, the better.
> I'm a premium roast guy. I don't do the cheap stuff.

> I like simple coffee - if it has more calories than my dinner, it's too much.
>
> I'm kind of a Frappuccino addict. It's been years since I actually drank plain coffee.
>
> I'll drink anything - I'm not picky.

Like feeler and setup statements, sound bites like these can also help you set up topics. Before you wax poetic about the philosophical underpinnings of a political dichotomy, try a sound bite phrase first to test the waters. This does two things: First, if your partner isn't interested, you'll find out quickly by their reaction and you'll know to move on. Second, if you have a tendency to ramble, it can keep the conversation balanced, so your conversation partner can add their own input.

The Golden Ratio of Conversation (ISPC)

Many classic fields like art and architecture have discovered golden ratios – perfect proportions that are always aesthetically pleasing and balanced.

Golden ratios also exist within conversational expressions. ECs often structure their statements in the following order:

1. **Initial comment** (usually an observation or opinion)

2. **Support the initial comment** (usually with an example, explanation, or story)

3. **Post comment** (comment about something you just said)

4. **Connection** (connect back to your partner or another topic)

The ISPC framework certainly isn't a cure-all for conversation, but it's a great foundational standard to keep in mind as you practice enhancing your conversations.

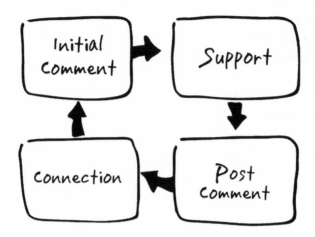

Let's borrow from one of the coffee examples. "I'm kind of a Frappuccino addict. It's been years since I actually drank plain coffee." It contains the first two elements of the golden ratio:

Initial comment (observation/opinion/self-disclosure)
I'm kind of a Frappuccino addict.

Support (with examples, explanations, or stories)
It's been years since I actually drank plain coffee.

You could add the third element by adding color commentary *about* something in the previous comments. For example, "I'm such a coffee snob aren't I?" Let's look at some examples of the golden ratio in action.

Example 1:
Initial comment
I love red wine.
Support
I'll drink anything - even the $2 cheap stuff.
Post comment
Maybe I'm just un-civilized.
Connection
What kind do you drink?

Example 2:
Initial comment
I hate naps.
Support
It takes me forever; I'm not like people who fall asleep in minutes.
Post comment
I'm really just jealous of those people - it's so unfair.
Connection
What's your trick - how do you fall asleep so quickly?

Example 3:
Initial comment
I love that place, it's my favorite fancy high-class restaurant.
Support
Except you have to order one of those sirloins - or they'll look at you weird, like you're barbaric or something.
Post comment
On second thought, maybe we shouldn't go there!
Connection
We could just go grab some overly greasy burgers and fries.

Paint More of Your Self-Portrait

Have you ever noticed how some people are easier to shop for than others? Why is that? What would someone think of purchasing for your birthday? People with strong personalities who reveal information about themselves are easy to shop for. Revealing tidbits of information about yourself over time is how you paint a colorful picture of your character. Shy people, who keep their thoughts and personalities hidden, are more difficult to shop for. That's why they end up receiving sweaters, candles, and bath products every year for Christmas. Sound familiar?

The first time someone meets you, they only see a blurry image of you. Your goal is clarity – help them see you better. The more context someone has, the more they'll get out of every piece of information you offer. The more someone knows about you, the more comfortable they are speaking with you. Others can more confidently reference or introduce certain topics because they can surmise how you would feel about those topics. Not sharing information is actually a very selfish act. That's right – if you don't share a lot of information, I'm calling you *selfish*. Help put people at ease and get rid of your cloak of mystery and the invisible barriers that exist between you and others. Conversation will flow more easily when your conversation partner knows more about you.

A girl I knew in college pulled me aside one evening and voiced a very insightful concern. She asked why I never really talked about myself. She was disappointed that she had hung out with me on numerous occasions throughout the years in our mutual group of friends, yet hardly knew anything about me. And I wondered why I had trouble connecting with people! I am proof it's never too late to make a change.

There have been studies indicating that the sheer act of disclosing causes others to like you more – even if they have no interest in the content of your message. Disclosing – at appropriate levels – can build and strengthen relationships. (Too much too soon and you could scare someone away!)

You may have some unique perspectives on world politics or Miley Cyrus. You may have a hilarious story about the time you fell off a tractor or bombed an interview. Unfortunately, too many people make the mistake of waiting for the perfect time to disclose information. Many people make the mistake of assuming that if the other person never asks, then they must not be interested. This is a huge mistake. Unless you're on a date, most people won't barrage you with questions about yourself. Disclosing is an active process.

A large part of what you collect in your conversation storage tank should be interesting little vignettes about yourself (Remember Autobiographical PATs?). Make a conscious effort to bring up short stories from your life and you'll build more highways to them for quicker access later. If the conversation topic turns to *gardening*, I could offer this anecdote:

Last year I spent a lot of money on some quality plants and vegetables for once. I figured I'd try to grow a legit garden, you know? All that work resulted in like two tomatoes and one gonzo-looking zucchini by the end of the summer. I'm just not cut out to be a gardener I guess. I'm really good at growing weeds though!

Personal statements don't have to be witty or creative in order to be effective. Similar to the section on taking advantage of your flaws (Chapter 6: *Keep Growing*), admitting what you *don't know* or *can't do* magically opens conversation doors because it puts people at ease. And if someone else knows anything about it they'll be more inclined to offer comments. You don't need to be a brainiac to engage in small talk. Take advantage of your lack of experience, skills, or knowledge in certain areas. If you only feel comfortable talking about what you're good at or interesting things you've done, you'll be short-changing your conversation options! Remember, ECs always take advantage of their flaws and turn them into conversational strengths.

For example, at a kid's party, you may find out that the beautiful cake was made at *Froger's*, the local grocery store. You could make a simple comment, "Really? That's cool," but that's boring. Express a humble personal statement. "Really? That's impressive; *I wish I could bake* a cake like that. *I can't even* get pancakes to turn out right!" Or "Really? That's impressive; *I never knew Froger's* made cakes like that. I'm going to have to go there more often."

Here is another example:

JACK: Wow, that's an awesome tattoo.

JILL: Thanks, my husband George actually drew it.

JACK: Really? I wish I could draw like that - I could probably draw a 3D cube but that's about it. My skills don't get much beyond cubes - and half the time I even mess up the 3D part!

These types of statements are also great to toss around in order to paint your self-portrait with a little shade of humility. Look a few more examples:

I never knew/experienced _____.
I didn't expect/think I'd find _____.
I never knew there were _____.
I was expecting a _____, not _____.
I didn't think I'd have this much fun at _____.

Sneak in Personal Information

Many PCs hate talking about themselves. But it's not necessary to shine a spotlight on yourself in order to self-disclose. Exceptional conversationalists are savvy at sneaking some personal information into the context of other phrases. Notice the *italicized* parts where the personal tidbit is inserted:

That's such a great sweater - *I love turquoise* - I don't see enough clothes with turquoise.
Really? *I'm not a car guy*, but that doesn't sound right to me.
I can't believe he didn't like the XYZ movie. *I like pretty much anything by John Smith*. Maybe he should watch it again.
I didn't even notice it - *and you know I'm picky about hair* - if I didn't notice it, then I don't think anyone else did.

How You Feel is the Real Deal

Expressing feelings and preferences are the easiest statements to muster when you need something quickly or just need to take up space. They also help open a window to your personality. And I'm not talking about the lovey-dovey, gooey-ooey mushy feelings. Feelings and preferences are easy because they don't require extensive knowledge about anything! Take advantage of their simplicity. Most of the examples I cover are also feeler statements – they excel at jump-starting conversations or keeping them going. They may not always offer much substance or flavor – but that's okay. Let's have some fun and look at a sample conversation consisting of just feeling and preference phrases.

Andy is meeting Jen's parents for the first time. Andy and Jen happen to love talking about feelings. In fact, they'd fit right in on the popular reality show The Bachelorette on ABC. Notice how their conversation is maintained with little more than feeling and preference statements:

ANDY: I'm excited I could finally make it here.

JEN: I'm so glad you could come.

ANDY: I'm looking forward to _____.

JEN: Yeah, I love this place.

ANDY: I really like the _____. I'm really comfortable here - this is my kind of place.

JEN: That makes me feel good then - I'm glad I chose it.

ANDY: I'm excited, I think it's gonna be fun.

JEN: I know, *I can't wait.*

ANDY: I like coming to new places like this.

JEN: So are you nervous about meeting my parents?

ANDY: Yes...and no... I'm excited and nervous, but in a good way.

JEN: I know how you feel - I was so nervous to meet your family.

ANDY: It will be good though. I feel good about it.

JEN: I'm glad you feel that way. That makes me feel better.

That was a simple conversation; however, there are some very important elements within it. The phrases may not be very substantive, but they are necessary building-blocks that help push conversations along. They are easy to add and pretty low-risk. They let others know where you stand. They also make fantastic small talk filler statements if you're at a loss for words.

Expressing your feelings, desires, preferences, hopes, and expectations go a long way towards painting your self-portrait. Check out a variety of examples below, and note that you could probably use these in a thousand different contexts. (Some may appear boring in print – but remember half the battle is about *how* you say them, not the actual words themselves.)

I wasn't expecting to see _____!

I hope they don't come over here.

I was worried we wouldn't _____.

I didn't realize they had _____! That's hilarious.

I love that they gave us free _____ for just showing up.

This is my favorite part, especially when they _____.

I won't touch that. I don't like _____ (slimy/miniature/spicy) things.

I have a weakness for _____ sales! It's probably my favorite place to shop.

I'm strangely enjoying this. Even though I probably shouldn't be.

I don't think anyone loves comfort _____ (food/fish/chocolate) more than me/you.

Notice that some of the aforementioned examples highlight what you didn't know or didn't expect. In the following examples, notice the effectiveness of the minimalist comments versus the substantive opinions.

YOU: Did you like the show?

GILL: I did.

YOU: Great. I did too.

The conversation might end there. But if you simply added your feelings about something, it could be rejuvenated. Let's try again.

YOU: Did you like the show?

GILL: I did.

YOU: Great, I did too. I was hoping you would. I was worried you wouldn't like the dancing parts.

GILL: Oh yeah, the dancers were the best part - especially that guy that kept tripping over the frog statue!

Don't Forget Your Friends and Family Ammo (AKA Your *Fammo*)

Your ability to contribute to a conversation immediately improves by 15% (give or take a little) if you include information about friends, family, and people you know. Your self-portrait also includes anything personal to you – your family, friends, pets, etc. Let others into your world a little bit. Take advantage of the interesting people in your life and borrow from their experiences or thoughts on topics.

> That's so funny - one of my buddies used to do the same thing.
>   Except he _____.
> My friend had a dog like that, and it would even _____.
> I've always done it that way, and for my entire life, my mom
>   always told me to _____.
> My husband would be shocked if he knew what I was doing right
>   now, he'd probably be like ` _____.'

Fammo is especially helpful if you don't have any direct experiences to share, but still wish to make a connection somehow. Someone asked me if I run, and instead of only offering, "No, I don't anymore," I said, "I don't run anymore, but my good friend runs all the time. He actually just finished an ultra-marathon. I have no idea how he has time for that!"

Examine the following conversation *with* and *without* a reference to a friend.

With a friend reference:
JACK: Nice tattoo.
JILL: Thanks, do you have any?
JACK: No, I don't.
JILL: My friend got a sword on her arm… She likes it because she's edgy now. She's always wanted to be edgy. But she's *so not edgy* - I don't care how many tattoos she gets!

Without a friend reference:
JACK: Nice tattoo.
JILL: Thanks, do you have any?
JACK: No, I don't.
JILL: Oh, okay.

The following fammo examples all contain some elements of the first three parts of the ISPC structure (**Initial comment, Support,** and **Post comment**):

> That sounds like my friend Steve - he always wears socks with
> sandals! He's such a dork. But he's a lovable dork.
> My wife is always telling me to eat better, but how am I supposed
> to pass up a double decker cheese sandwich? No way!
> Joe would absolutely love that. He is obsessed with anything
> fish-related. I don't get it.
> It's funny, my mom couldn't tell you one thing about my job. I tell
> her I got a raise and she's just like, 'That's great honey,
> keep up the good work.' It's actually more sad than funny.

Quick Tip: Be careful of "over-sharing" or "steam-rolling." Having a successful conversation should trump any desire to contribute more information. Be careful of sharing too much information too quickly with someone you just met. If the other person is in a groove telling a story, don't try to wedge in your own story just for the sake of sharing something.

CHAPTER 12: USE IT OR LOSE IT

1. Pick five TAPP topics (Chapter 5: *Fill Up Your Conversation Storage Tank*) and think of a self-disclosure comment for each topic that helps paint your self-portrait.

2. Convert the previous five comments into interesting sound bites utilizing the one-two punch technique, if you didn't already.

CHAPTER 12: REVIEW

Before this chapter:

- ✓ The four primary PATs: Comments, Knowledge, Opinions, and Autobiographical stuff
- ✓ The TAPP topics: Things, Activities, People, and Places
- ✓ Become an Interest Hunter and seek out commonalities

✓ Initiate with Feeler statements (You, Environment, and Them) and Problem Feelers

✓ Initiate with comments/questions related to Time

✓ FOOFAAE: Feelings, Observations, Opinions, Facts, Actions, Autobiographical, and Events

✓ Be proactive and consider a second question or comment

From this chapter:

✓ The One-Two Punch is a great formula for sound bites

✓ The Golden Ratio of conversation (Initial comment, Support, Post comment, Connection) is a great way to structure many comments

✓ Aim for clarity and paint a better self-portrait of yourself

✓ Your self-portrait also consists of your friends and family

Key takeaway from this chapter:

Starting with how you feel is a very easy and natural way to maintain the conversation. Adding clarity to your self-portrait is critical to helping others make more connections and feel more comfortable with you in conversation.

Coming up next:

This chapter covered how to share better internal observations and information. In the next chapter, we'll dive deeper into how to share better external observations and opinions.

Preview: *Offering observations and opinions about everything in your environment, including the people, are cornerstones of any conversation. Small talk is especially dependent on solid comments about your surroundings. This chapter will upgrade your ability to share external observations and opinions.*

[CHAPTER 13]

SHARE MORE EFFECTIVE OBSERVATIONS AND OPINIONS

Have you ever witnessed relatives meeting a newborn baby for the first time? The rapid fire succession of observations is amazing:

> Oh he's so sweet!
> Look at his chubby little cheeks!
> He's got such pudgy arms.
> He's got Daddy's big brown eyes.
> Look at that dark hair - she is definitely Jenny's baby.

You've been commenting about your surroundings since you could say your first words. Observations and opinions about everything in your environment, including the people, are cornerstones of any conversation – and especially small talk. It's critical to learn a variety of methods and techniques for improving your external observations and opinions.

Opinions and observations breathe life into conversations. Observations and opinions have the potential to be much more interesting than feelers, yet still originate from one of the three primary categories: yourself, the environment, and your conversation partner. The previous chapter covered observations and information about yourself. This chapter covers the rest – primarily your surroundings and other people. By surroundings – I also mean something much broader than comments about immediate surroundings, like "Hey, that plant is huge." For example, "That house is in bad shape, but the neighborhood is really nice. I bet someone could make a nice investment flipping it." Or more abstract surroundings – maybe someone on the radio mentions something the president did. You could offer an opinion, "He keeps trying to strike a deal with the _____. There's no way that would work – he should try to make an arrangement with the _____."

Go Beyond Objective

Observations and opinions take many forms, from simple and objective, "That's a revealing statue," to a little more subjective, "That's a very R-rated statue," to very subjective and opinionated, "That's a very R-rated statue – someone needs to get him some pants!" While there is certainly overlap between the terms observation and opinion, for the most part, observations are more objective, and opinions are more subjective.

Many PCs fail to go beyond simple objective observations like, "She's wearing a lot of mascara." There are many options for converting simple observations into interesting opinions. Can you think of a few ways to convert "She's wearing a lot of mascara" into a stronger opinion? Start by making your observation more subjective and less objective, then add some exaggeration and colorful language.

> She needs to take a break from the mascara!
> She may want to take some makeup lessons from someone other than an eight-year-old.
> That's a ton of makeup… I wonder if she even owns a mirror.
> She needs to lay off the clown makeup.

Of course, the statement "She's wearing a lot of mascara" can come off as strong or mild depending on *how* you say it. (You can also come off mean or playful, depending on how you say it and who the person is – celebrity or stranger?) I have worked in many customer service roles, and I learned quickly that if I was dealing with an angry customer, and I *didn't* want an emotional reaction, I needed to talk more like a computer – in neutral, objective statements – preferably in third person. For example, "Some people might say that she has more makeup on than average."

Opinions typically offer something more substantive for the other person to mentally chew on; an opinion can be connected to, agreed with, disagreed with, or added to. An opinion can paint something in a new light, can show a new perspective, or add an interesting angle.

Opinions can prove you understand a topic. For example, someone was talking about the challenges of raising their first child. Adding "I always say parenting is like making pancakes. That first one is usually burnt, but then you get better at it the more you make!" immediately demonstrates that you understand the situation to some degree.

What Conversation Soup are You Serving?

My wife is a master at creating something out of nothing in the kitchen. Just when I think there's nothing good to eat, there she is, like a magician, adding *this* to *that*. I eventually discovered the secret often lies in the combination of spices.

Think of conversations as serving soup. Are you merely serving soup to keep someone nourished? Or are you serving soup that tastes good – that not only nourishes, but provides a pleasant experience? By stating something literal and serious like, "I'm hungry," or "When do you want to go to the store?" you're merely keeping the conversation alive. You might as well serve them a bowl of Ramen noodles without the chicken flavor seasoning. Conversation is more than just a means to achieve an objective. If you want them to *enjoy* the soup, you'll have to add some ingredients that make soup (and conversation) interesting.

Remember, go beyond what a robot would say. Exceptional conversation is about everything else you sprinkle on top of the message – all the fun "human" stuff that adds the unique zesty flavor. Descriptive words, energy, feelings, self-disclosure, stories, interesting observations, and opinions will keep your conversations thriving. Sadly, PCs often possess the "just enough" mentality and serve their conversation partners

just enough nourishment to get by. They too often forget to realize eating is just as much about the enjoyment of the experience as it is about nourishment.

Let's look at the difference between a cyborg and an exceptional conversationalist. The topic of having a garage sale comes up and both the cyborg and the EC offer their thoughts:

CYBORG: A sign on the road will increase traffic.

EC: You have to have a good sign on the road if you want to increase traffic. You can't be like those people who let their toddler scribble something on the back of an old pizza box!

Conversation itself is more than just a way to learn or share information – it's a medium for expressing ideas, feelings, and thoughts in interesting and figurative ways. Exceptional conversationalists revel in the conversation itself, rather than aiming solely at accomplishing an objective. They enjoy playing with the conversation.

Channel Your Inner Actor

I am not an excitable person by nature. That doesn't mean I don't possess just as many emotions as the next guy. If you don't naturally express emotion or feeling, you may consider acting a little until you get used to expressing yourself more colorfully. Yes, I'm saying to act. At least a little. If not for yourself, then for the sake of making the conversation experience more interesting for the other person.

The Hollywood movie industry is successful for a reason. People prefer a little drama and hyperbole. Maybe your friend tells you they just returned from trying the menu at a new ice cream shop and it was delicious. If they are excited about it, try to *reflect and share* their energy. Don't bring down the mood with a somber "Cool." Share in their joy or excitement with something like, "Really? I'm jealous! I wanted to try that place...what flavor did you get?" Celebrating or showing excitement over "trivial" things can be fun for all. Enjoy life's little pleasures. At the time of this writing, a woman shot to fame from her YouTube video showing how excited and happy she was over her new Chewbacca mask. She was even invited on to talk-shows because her exuberance was so entertaining!

One time I had to take my car in to have new tires put on. While waiting, I overheard a mechanic nearby exclaim in genuine astonishment, "*I have half a Butterfinger left! Awesome!* I completely forgot I left it there." All the other mechanics around him laughed. In print, his statements are nothing special. But the *way* he said it and the excitement he felt in that moment is what mattered. No one laughed because he told a witty joke, or some entertaining story – all it took was acting excited about finding a half-eaten candy bar.

PCs often fall short when it comes to expressing a lot of human characteristics. Did your friend get a raise? Show you're thrilled and happy for them! Is this the first time seeing them in a few weeks? Act excited to see them! Did someone bring up some shocking event on the news? Did you see something out of the ordinary? *React!* Are you nervous about an upcoming presentation? Are you excited about a new movie coming out? Don't just say it, *show it!*

Many poor conversationalists are very analytical and tend to sit and process information on an intellectual level before reacting. Taking time to think through everything is a terrific strategy for those times when you need to buy stock or run a business, but you risk sucking the life out of conversations.

Sprinkle Flavorful Opinions on Everything

"To avoid criticism: say nothing, do nothing, be nothing."

– Aristotle

Don't succumb to a passive mindset – be proactive and freely offer your opinions and observations. Exaggerate. Dramatize. Consider what a chat bot would say – and then say more. Most people won't ask your opinion. Don't wait for the other person to ask. Initiate the conversation with your feelings and preferences. Are you going to a concert Friday night? *Let people know how much you're looking forward to it.* Just saw the concert? Initiate a conversation by telling about your experience. Did it disappoint? Was it better than expected? Was it similar to something else? Share your experiences and stories. If you just saw a movie; what was your favorite scene? Was it better than the book? Why do you love going to movies?

Don't wait to be asked. Have something positive, playful, or complimentary to say about the other person? Say it!

> That is really creative. How do you come up with that stuff?
> You're always thinking of the neatest ways to do _____.
> You're a life saver.

Does the chocolate cake at the restaurant look good? Or does it look like a five year old baked it? Then say so! Express how you feel about it. If you order the cake, go beyond saying "This chocolate cake looks good." Use an exaggeration to make the point more interesting. "A day that includes chocolate is a good day." Take it even further by saying, "I think I may have an addiction – someone may have to stop me before I order three more slices." Fun is contagious! Catching your playfulness, perhaps the other person replies, "Maybe you should find a rehab center specializing in cocoa addiction." To which you could respond "Well, admitting you're an addict is the first step toward recovery, right?"

Adding opinions and support to a bland, factual statements, can instantly make them more multi-dimensional. Check out this example:

> OBSERVATION: They're selling Laffy Taffy over there.
> ADD OPINION + SUPPORT: And they have strawberry! That's the best flavor - I could eat a whole bag right now.

Apply the Right Amount of Seasoning

Exaggerated opinions are more interesting, but of course, they aren't always appropriate. You won't always know the temperature or vibe of the conversation until you test it with a feeler statement. Generic opinions help you figure out which direction to steer the conversation when you're unsure. They help you to broach subjects and introduce topics without too much risk. For example, "I'm not sure the Lions would be happy with how they played last night," or "Maybe we should eat at Roscoe's, it might have good food," or "I think there are probably corrupt politicians in every party." Softened opinions aren't always as fun or interesting, but they help you avoid risky conversations. Feel free to add modifying and qualifying words to reduce the strength and limit the meaning of your opinion (e.g. "probably, maybe, usually, I think, and I feel"). Just don't rely on them too much!

Safe opinions will never make a big impact. Nor will they be very entertaining on their own. However, they still count as a contribution to the conversation. Some safe opinions can moonlight as strong opinions. For instance, your manager states "I think we should do what's best for the company." On the surface that statement may appear strong, but it's actually a purely safe opinion. Who is going to argue that we shouldn't do what is best for the company? That kind of statement is more common than you think – especially in the business world. Your boss states, "There's been a lot of change since Bob left." Not sure how to respond, you offer a seemingly strong (but actually safe) opinion, "I definitely think some change is necessary." The word "definitely" adds strength to the statement, but keeping the word "some" offers flexibility in case you need to adjust your opinion a little later.

Trivial = Safe
Strong opinions are best paired with trivial topics. Offering the following strong opinion about a coworker isn't a laughing matter:

> I think Bob's new haircut is horrible - it looks like a small rodent got trapped on his head!

But add a light hearted subject and the opinion becomes playful:

I think Justin Bieber's new haircut is horrible - it looks like a small rodent got trapped on his head!

A strong definitive opinion about trivial topics can spark light-hearted and playful conversation. You typically don't need to "test the waters," so to speak, with trivial topics. Because small talk and casual conversation typically center on non-serious topics, these types of opinions are pervasive in exceptional conversation. Even negative opinions – though normally frowned upon – are perfectly acceptable when aimed at trivial topics. Check out the following three exceptional opinions:

1. I'm obsessed with M&M brownies, there's nothing better on this planet.
2. Is there anything better than a double cheese burger from Five Guys Burgers and Fries? If there is, I haven't found it.
3. It doesn't come with cruise control? That's a deal breaker, I don't want that piece of junk!

Let's strip the above opinions of their exaggerations, superlatives, and playfulness and see what happens, shall we? Now they represent opinions a PC may offer:

1. I like M&M brownies a lot.
2. I like the double cheeseburger at Five Guys Burgers and Fries.
3. It doesn't come with cruise control? That's not good.

Let's compare another PC vs EC example. Someone is telling the story about how their husband bought generic cotton swabs and they're not happy about it. Notice how the EC version was stronger and more descriptive because it exaggerated the traits of the generic Q-tip.

PC: Yeah, buying generic brand Q-tips don't usually work as well
EC: Yeah, I never go generic on Q-tips - there's only one Q-tip. The others are just wannabes. Generic brands are just little sticks that can poke your ear drums out.

Superlatives, Hyperbole, and Definitive Statements are the BEST EVER!

Humans are fascinated with the biggest, best, worst, etc. The Guinness Book of World Records is popular for a reason. Incorporate stronger, more dramatic statements: superlatives, hyperboles, definitive, categorical, and absolute statements. These statements are simply more interesting than wishy-washy, passive statements many PCs trod out. As introduced in Chapter 7: *Expand Your Word Choices*, exaggerating your words, and incorporating superlatives, makes them more descriptive.

Let's look at a few more examples:

> I love it there - they have the best fitting rooms.
> Is there anything more delicious/amazing/gross than grilled steak cheese sandwich from a street vendor? Iif there is I haven't found it yet.
> They have _____ here? This place wins. This place is already the best _____ diner/theatre ever.
> That is the worst character on TV. Everything he does is illogical.

No one was arrested for exaggerating their feelings occasionally with statements like "I would die happy if I overdosed on this ice cream right now." Try to push it a little further than what you would usually say. Let's assume you're a man, and you just screamed like a five-year-old girl after a spider fell on your arm. How could you exaggerate your actions?

> That may have been the wimpiest moment of my life.
> Did I just say that? That's probably the wimpiest thing I've ever said.
> That was probably the least manly thing I've ever done.

Compare the following two examples:

> BORING: I like to read XYZ, it seems pretty trustworthy.
> INTERESTING: I always read XYZ, it's the only magazine I fully trust.

Definitive generalizations are common in small talk. Examine the following exchanges including a PC and an EC response. The EC employs a definitive generalization.

At salad bar.
FRIEND: What's that brown stuff? You should try it.
PC: I don't know, I'm not sure what it is.
EC: Nope. *I don't eat anything* that resembles brown slime.

Picking up child from camp.
COUNSELOR: I'm sorry. Timmy got a few big scratches on his legs.
PC: That's okay. I'm sure he's fine.
EC: That's okay. If you don't get scratched at camp, then it's not a real camp in my book!

Exaggerate What Sticks Out

One summer night at my old house it was very hot and humid. I was lying in bed sweating because our bungalow lacked adequate air circulation. Meanwhile, my wife pulled the comforter over her. Obviously I found her behavior unusual. I simply pointed it out with an exaggerated opinion: "I think you're the *only one in the world* who uses comforters in the summer."

Exceptional observations focus on anything that sticks out. A little embellishment is encouraged! Exceptional conversationalists examine their surroundings based on a "normal" baseline, so to speak, and actively look for discrepancies. When you discover something abnormal, point it out, but also play with it – exaggerate its abnormal traits. Talk about how the abnormal feature affects something else. Question why it exists.

Here are a few examples:

The most disturbing part is the _____ on his face.
I think the weirdest part in all of that is the_____. Why would someone _____?
They actually have a _____! I've never seen one of those.

Sometimes nothing will stick out, but that doesn't mean there isn't an opportunity to exaggerate a trait, situation, or action. For example, your coworker kindly requests, "Can you make a copy of this for me?" And normally you may reply, "Sure." But if you were feeling playful, you could pretend their request was unusually difficult, and therefore exaggerate your reaction. "You're so demanding! I don't get paid enough for this job."

Stick a Label on It

As discussed in Chapter 7: *Expand Your Word Choices*, labels and generalizations are highly effective for adding life to your descriptions and keeping your comments succinct, yet playful. They also happen to function as useful devices for exaggerating how something sticks out from the norm. As a reminder, these are best used with friends who know that you're exaggerating. Time for examples again:

> He's the Babe Ruth of our team. He can win us the game single-handedly.
> Nobody can waste time like you and I; it's a miracle we can get anything done.
> I love sport coats. Everything looks cooler in a sport coat... Sending a fax. Throwing out garbage. It doesn't matter.
> The games are a complete rip off and I never win, but I love playing anyway.
> How come everything looks cute on you, but look at me. I look ridiculous.

Notice how many of the aforementioned comments combine labels and generalizations with supporting comments. When a label or generalization is offered, supporting it with an example or explanation is usually effective. In the following examples, Jill loves to label and generalize:

> JACK: No, I'm way too cowardly for sky diving. I'm not into adventure sports of any kind.

JILL: I wouldn't peg you as cowardly; you look like you would jump off all kinds of things!

JACK: Montreal was completely annoying; they knew French and English, but deliberately refused to speak English to us.
JILL: I think something about speaking French turns people into jerks.

The Sarcastic and Indirect Statement Technique

Many opinions and observations are obvious in nature. Boring people tend to state observations as literally as possible. When presented with any situation, you typically have three choices:

1. Overstate, and exaggerate the facts of the situation.
2. State the facts exactly as they are.
3. Understate, and downplay the facts of the situation.

If you need to say something obvious, it can be twice as interesting if you simply understate or overstate it. Robots love literal and direct statements, but humans? Not so much. Humans prefer more playful language. We like to guess a little; we often enjoy a little intrigue or layer of sarcasm. Let's look at a few examples of these indirect statements (coincidently all involving dogs):

Your friend's dog jumps on you and smothers you with giant slobbery kisses.

FACTUAL STATEMENT: Your dog really likes me.
UNDERSTATEMENT: I have a feeling your dog likes me.
UNDERSTATEMENT 2: Do you think your dog likes me?
UNDERSTATEMENT 3: I don't think your dog likes me very much.
OVERSTATEMENT: I think your dog wants to marry me!

You're discussing your tiny toy poodle.

FACTUAL STATEMENT: He won't scare many people away.
UNDERSTATEMENT: I don't think he would even scare away
the mice!
OVERSTATEMENT: No one will break into my house with such an
intimidating *beast* guarding the place.

Your comments will be more interesting when you choose to understate or overstate, even slightly. You see a guy with hair spiked about a foot high? "I'm not sure his hair is high enough." Now the door is open for more playful support. "...maybe we should see if he needs more hair gel so he can get it a few inches taller."

I would be remiss if I did not take a moment to mention the value of sarcasm in general. Most people already incorporate an amount of sarcasm into their daily conversations, but nonetheless, it's important to remember how effective sarcasm is for creating interesting comments (but only in small doses). On top of being interesting, they're one of the easiest types of comments to formulate.

Is the weather miserable? Instead of stating something literal, sarcastically state the opposite: "Beautiful day we're having, huh?" Maybe the air conditioner breaks at your office and the building quickly becomes unbearably hot and humid. When talking about the situation, you could say something trite, "Isn't it hot in here?" Or you could try some sarcasm, "Are you enjoying our tropical paradise?"

Maybe someone comments on the fact that you're eating cookies for breakfast. Instead of something literal and factual, "Yeah, it's not very healthy," you could respond, "Hey, it's my breakfast of champions." Maybe they aren't excited about something, you could state, "Wow, you sound thrilled."

One time I was giving a new co-worker a tour and introducing them to everyone. I stopped by Mike's desk and said, "This is Mike, he handles the knowledge database. He's very helpful if you need anything." And Mike could have just agreed, but in this case he lightened up the exchange by sarcastically denying everything, "Actually, I'm not helpful at all. I'm actually very selfish and like to keep to myself." We all laughed.

Is it obvious you aren't prepared for the meeting or some other special occasion? You might as well try to lighten up the situation with some sarcasm. "I'm obviously really prepared..."

I was at the movies and we just finished watching a preview of a very depressing, sad drama. The guy next to me said to his date, "Well, that sure looks like a light-hearted comedy," and his date found his comment hilarious. I'm not sure it was hilarious, but it was still more entertaining than stating the obvious!

The Comparison Technique

A friend was telling me about a brand of razors I should purchase. He claimed the shaving experience was so smooth and effortless, it was like a hot knife cutting through butter. I went out and purchased them that day and discovered what he said was true. And that was ten years ago, but I still think of that analogy occasionally when I use those razors. Comparisons and analogies are powerful technique utilized by the greatest orators, comedians, politicians, salesmen, and conversationalists throughout all of time. Compare more things. Just do it.

Larry and Peggy are on vacation. They've been married 20 years and epitomize average conversationalists. Read the following average interactions:

PEGGY: Get your feet away from me!
LARRY: Why? They smell good.
PEGGY: No they don't, they smell bad.

LARRY: You like gingerbread coffee too?
PEGGY: Yeah, I do. It's good.

LARRY: The hotel breakfast looks cheap.

PEGGY: You're right, it doesn't look very good.

 Quick Practice: See if you can help add some flavor to their conversations by adding a comparison somewhere in one of the aforementioned examples. Could you think of anything? Were you planning on just skipping ahead to see what I came up with?

Adding an analogy dramatically transforms each interaction into a more entertaining experience. Take a look:

PEGGY: Get your feet away from me!

LARRY: Why? They smell *like freshly picked lilacs.*

PEGGY: Yeah right, if lilacs were left rotting in a vase for five months!

LARRY: You like gingerbread coffee too?

PEGGY: Yeah, I do. *It's like a little piece of Christmas in a cup.*

LARRY: The hotel breakfast looks cheap.

PEGGY: You're right, *it looks more like a breakfast garage sale.* The coffee machine *looks like it's been sitting in someone's attic until this morning.*

As discussed in Chapter 12: *Paint Your Portrait with Effective Self-Disclosing,* speaking in digestible chunks is very effective – and comparisons pack a lot of meaning in succinct statements. Comparing one thing to another is also a more creative way to express your thoughts and take your descriptions, observations, and opinions to new heights. I've seen the silliest and simplest comparisons achieve success. Analogies and metaphors are key components of figurative language. And figurative language is usually more entertaining and enjoyable than literal language. Comparisons and analogies also help clarify your point, making it more effective. Here are some more to whet your fancy:

He was so happy! He acted like he just won a million dollars.
That looks like a 1970's shag carpet.
We're all getting sick, except John, he's like an ox.
It's becoming like *The Wild West* around here!
What do you think this is? *Woodstock?*
He's like the guy who only calls when he needs something.

The statement "I feel like _____ right now" has limitless potential. You could fill in the blank with "a boy scout," "a loser," "I just got scammed," "a babysitter," or "waiter," etc. Keep in mind, as with many examples found in this book, some of these only work when said with a smile or when it's obvious you're being facetious.

The Silly Human Technique

Develop an eye for noticing subtleties in human behavior and appearance. Talk about the idiosyncrasies of the human condition. Question why people act the way they do. Point out your own experiences and quirks. Remember, it can't hurt to gesture or reenact the behavior or mannerisms. Many of the following examples take advantage of comparisons and analogies.

He's the kind of person who loves the spotlight. If there is a
chance to be on camera, he'll be there!
He gets that evil-villain wrinkle in his forehead - I don't know how
he can make his face do that!
Liam can't go a day without _____ (Coke/Donuts/checking his
hair/etc.)
[Fidgets hands] Sorry, my hands just do that sometimes on their
own! It probably means I should cut back on the sugar.
No one can resist him when he gets that puppy dog eye look.
I don't know...You know how your mind cycles through options but
nothing comes out?
That looks like your _____ (flirting/hungry/angry/bored) face.
That's the worst when a guy comes up to you and says '_____.' I
never know how to respond appropriately.

The Secret Life Technique

Making up observations about someone's hidden agenda or secret thoughts can be great fun. Have fun with it – make up some fun secret motivations for others, yourself, or inanimate objects (anything really!).

Saying "You're secretly a _____ (Metallica/Jimmy Buffet) fan aren't you? I knew it!" can be fun if their music tastes are much different than the band you claim they admire.

Remember the baby example from beginning of the chapter? I included many observations one could make about the baby. Those were mostly pertaining to the baby's appearance. Let's look at opinions that go beyond just appearance, and speculate as to what they baby wants, hopes, etc. For example, you're taking a lot of photos of the new baby when he starts becoming upset:

> Maybe he just doesn't like that angle. Try the other side.
> I think he's worried it'll go viral and really embarrass him.
> He's just camera shy.
> He's like, *'get that thing away from me!'*
> Maybe you should talk to his agent first.
> Maybe he thinks you're just paparazzi...I don't blame him.

Let's look at some other examples of fun secret intentions:

> A co-worker shows up to the work luncheon and heads for the dessert table.
>
> YOU: You're just here for the free dessert aren't you?
>
> *Or you could mention your own secret intention.*
>
> YOU: I'm really only here for the free turkey wraps.

> YOU: They canceled my favorite show. XYZ is no longer on.
> FRIEND: They did? That sucks!
> YOU: Yes! Can you believe it? It's only my shows that get canceled. I don't know what the ABC execs have against me.

Play along if someone makes up fun intentions for you.

FRIEND: I saw you wink at me. Was that intentional?

YOU: *You caught me.* I thought I was being subtle. Just my right eye was flirting with you. My left eye is the shy one.

Due to the crass, immature, R-rated nature of some of my examples, I could not include specific details. However, I preserved the structure of some of them below. I'll leave the rest up to your imagination!

Why is he just standing there? He probably wants to _____.

She looks like she's about to _____ all over the place.

He looks like he's about to _____ any second.

What is that guy thinking? Does he think we're going to just _____?

The Impact Technique

Everyone is interested in hearing how they affected something or someone else – especially in a fun or light way. If you see an opportunity to highlight their impact, point it out. Coincidentally, these examples all involve *doing* something (remember action statements from FOOFAAE?).

Your friend is talking about baking a cake.

YOU: You're making me hungry now. I have a strong urge to go find chocolate…it doesn't matter what kind, any kind.

Your friend is showing off her new shoes.

YOU: You're making me jealous. I think I'm going to go stop at the mall after work.

Your friend shows off her new dress.

YOU: You're going to be fighting off guys left and right tonight at the bar!

The Fix the World Technique

Point out how you would fix or improve something. What laws would you change? What would you do differently? Don't overlook the silly and trivial.

It's winter, and you and your friend are walking to the store and pass a dirty looking snowman. You both offer opinions:

YOU: He looks a little disheveled.

FRIEND: That's the saddest looking snowman I've ever seen.

So far, so good, but commenting on how to fix the situation could ignite even more interesting conversation.

YOU: He could use some makeup or something.

FRIEND: He could probably use a bath. He's kind of dirty.

YOU: But then his face would melt off, he can't do that.

FRIEND: But how's he supposed to pick up snow girls looking all messed up like that?

YOU: I think he's consumed too much eggnog...he's a little fat around the mid-section.

FRIEND: Yeah, he definitely needs to cut back on the 'nog. Maybe just stick to carrots.

YOU: No, he can't do that. Then he'd be eating his own nose. We don't want cannibal snowmen around here.

FRIEND: You're right, what was I thinking?

Let's look at additional examples about fixing a situation:

FRIEND: Is he supposed to be Italian?

YOU: His accent is horrible! Who hired that guy? *They need to hire someone to be in charge of accents* - like an accent coordinator.

FRIEND: My kids waste so much food.

YOU: Mine are the same way. I think the amount of food they leave on the floor *could solve world hunger.* If only I had a little machine that could suck it up and freeze dry it - I'd be a hero.

Observations as Responses

Keep in mind, many observations function as good responses as well. When someone directs a comment in your direction, you don't need to answer directly with a personal statement. Try aiming the conversation back towards them instead.

MATT: You should do it! You'd be great at it.

YOU: That's funny. Matt, you're hilarious.

MATT: Don't worry, I was just looking out for you.

YOU: Oh thanks. *You're like my guardian angel.*

MATT: Don't you know that global warming is just a big hoax?

YOU: You didn't take any science classes in high school did you?

Aiming an observation back at them also serves as a good response when receiving a compliment.

EILEEN: You did great on that project Bob.

BOB: Oh thanks, you're too kind. You were a big help too, thanks for all the input.

For the record, another common way ECs handle flattering words is by taking the ultra-humble approach. After acknowledging the compliment, they often playfully attribute credit elsewhere instead of themselves.

RANDAL: I thought you were excellent in that video. You carried yourself really well.

PATRICIA: Oh thanks. It was all CGI, it wasn't really me.

CHAPTER 13: USE IT OR LOSE IT

Imagine you're looking for your next home. You're on a tour of a few house options and you find a house you really like – until you step into the backyard and observe the neighbor's backyard across from you. The following is what you see:

There's an old army Jeep, three sheds, some other army surplus items, and a bunch of metal scraps strewn throughout the unkempt yard. Good observers zero-in on what stands out from the norm – in this case, a lot! You could offer a secret intention, "Maybe he's preparing for the zombie apocalypse," or sarcasm, "Do you think he's a military guy?" or a comparison, "His yard looks like the war might still be going on." You should be able to offer a number of good observations and opinions about the "atypical" neighbor.

Can you make any of the following types of observations?

1. Secret Intentions/Actions
2. Sarcasm
3. Generalizations/Labels
4. Comparisons

CHAPTER 13: REVIEW

Before this chapter:
- ✓ The four primary PATs: Comments, Knowledge, Opinions, and Autobiographical stuff
- ✓ The TAPP topics: Things, Activities, People, and Places
- ✓ Initiate with Feeler statements (You, Environment, and Them) and Problem Feelers
- ✓ Initiate with comments/questions related to Time
- ✓ FOOFAAE: Feelings, Observations, Opinions, Facts, Actions, Autobiographical, and Events
- ✓ Be proactive and consider a second question or comment
- ✓ The Golden Ratio (ISPC): Initial comment, Support, Post comment, and Connection
- ✓ Aim for clarity and paint a better self-portrait of yourself
- ✓ Your self-portrait also consists of your friends and family

From this chapter:
- ✓ Sprinkle on more flavorful opinions
- ✓ Exaggerate what sticks out
- ✓ Sarcasm and under/overstatements are easy and fun
- ✓ Compare more things

Key takeaway from this chapter:
Aim for stronger opinions over mild objective comments – especially when the topics are more trivial in nature.

Coming up next:
Thus far, you've hopefully learned a lot about initiating conversation, small talk, and maintaining conversation by sharing information about yourself and what you observe. The Assemble habit is next, and dives deeper into what makes comments interesting so you may upgrade your own comments.

HABIT FIVE

ASSEMBLE

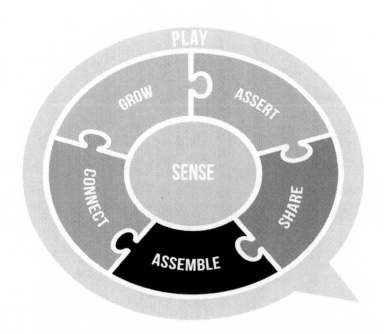

Preview: *It's time to examine exactly how to assemble your thoughts into effective and interesting expressions. You'll also upgrade your ability to support other statements, and thereby improve your overall conversation effectiveness.*

[CHAPTER 14]

LEARN HOW TO EFFECTIVELY SUPPORT YOUR COMMENTS

What do Batman, Sherlock Holmes, and peanut butter sandwiches all have in common? They are all effective on their own, but with support (e.g. Robin, Dr. Watson, and grape jelly) they are much better! And sometimes, the supporting comments are the best part.

Up until this point we've only lightly covered supporting statements and post comments. This chapter takes a wider and deeper look at those two critical components of the golden ratio of conversation (ISPC).

So what's a supporting statement? Supporting statements often take the form of examples, explanations, additional information, or stories. In many cases, they are simply a rephrase of the original opinion.

Let's re-visit an example from Chapter 7: *Expand Your Word Choices*, and add some supporting comments. Observe the following three ways to describe a good-looking person:

> He was very good-looking.
> He was definitely a runway model.
> He was like *Brad Pitt-level* good looking.

You could support each statement with the same hypothetical example emphasizing the man's attractiveness. Check it out:

> He was good-looking. *I would pay him money just to stand around near me!*
> He was definitely a runway model. *I would pay him money just to stand around near me!*
> He was like *Brad Pitt-level* good looking. *I would pay him money just to stand around near me!*

Supporting your statements adds substance to your points. Support can also validate your claims, and prove to the other person you really are who you say, and really do have those opinions. In the following example, Maureen and Geoff form instant rapport by sharing supporting examples.

> MAUREEN: I'll admit, I'm kind of a grammar snob.
> GEOFF: I am too!

Maureen adds validity to her claim by offering an example of what she knows about grammar:

MAUREEN: Are you an *Oxford comma* person?
GEOFF: Absolutely!

Geoff adds information supporting his claim:

GEOFF: Have you ever read the book *Eats, Shoots & Leaves*?
MAUREEN: Oh yeah! It's one of my favorite books!

Let's break down a few other methods of utilizing supporting statements:

FRIEND: I love NPR.
YOU: I do too, it's my favorite station to listen to.
Don't stop there, support your opinion with an example.
SUPPORT: I must have at least three NPR T-shirts. And five NPR buttons on my backpack.

FRIEND: How is the move going?
YOU: We finally got the last of the boxes moved in. It's so hard to find anything!
Add a supporting example that highlights the difficulty.
SUPPORT: Every morning before work it's like being in a giant scavenger hunt just to find my socks!

FRIEND: We were at the mall today and Maggie was choking on a French fry. It was so scary!
You could respond with an opinion.
YOU: Oh my gosh, that's a nightmare to me.
Then you could offer an example in the form of a quick personal anecdote that supports your opinion.
SUPPORT: That's why I never babysat as a teen - I was so scared that the kids would choke and die on me and it would be my fault!

Keep the Comparisons Going!

The importance of comparisons and analogies were introduced already. But in this chapter we'll look at how comparisons and supporting comments work well together. For example, saying, "It's so wet and dreary out," is fine. But adding an analogy takes the statement to a new level: "It's so wet and dreary out – *I feel like I woke up in Seattle and can't escape.*"

The next set of examples start with an **observation/opinion**, followed by an **analogy/comparison** (*italicized*) supporting the initial statement:

This place is so quiet - *I feel like I just walked into a library.*
I'm so sophisticated. *I'm like James Bond over here.*
Look at all the guns. *They have enough for a small military.*
Is it supposed to be this cold in here? *I feel like I just walked into Antarctica.*
You can't just go half-way, *you're either swimming in the ocean or sitting on a beach chair.*
He actually cried. That's so unlike him. *It was like seeing a unicorn - I don't think I'll ever see that again!*
Your TV is enormous. *I feel like I'm at the movie theatre.*
That's crazy, *that's like something out of Narnia.*

Let's reverse it. Let's start with the **analogy/comparison** and finish with a supporting **observation/opinion** (*italicized*):

You're like a starving wolf. *I've never seen anyone eat so quickly!*
Those events take over your weekends like termites. *Before you know it, your entire weekend is gone.*
That looks more like cat puke than an omelet - *I'm not eating it.*
I feel like I'm stuck in a bad romance novel... *and I'm the girl who ends up alone with only her cats to comfort her.*
These are great seats - it's like prime real estate over here. *I feel like we just bought Park Place and Boardwalk.*

In Chapter 12: *Paint Your Portrait with Effective Self-Disclosing*, we covered how exceptional conversationalists excel at speaking in bite-sized chunks. Pairing an effective opinion or comparison with a supporting statement is a terrific technique for creating more digestible and interesting conversation.

Work Together with Your Conversation Partner

Conversation is a team sport. Help them. Develop the analogy together. Check out the examples below:

> JOE: I think you just scratched me when you gave me that hug.
> LIBBY: I did? Sorry!
> *Joe could end there, or he could make a fun comparison.*
> JOE: Yeah, it felt like I was hugging a panther.
> *Libby can now play along with the animal theme.*
> JOE: Yeah, you better watch out - I was actually marking my territory.

> You enter the room wearing aviator sunglasses and spiked hair.
> YOU: You thought I was Adam Levine for a minute didn't you?
> *Your wife continues playing along with the analogy.*
> WIFE: Oh yeah. I was about to run over and rip your shirt off and throw you on the couch, *and then I realized it was just you.*

Observations/Opinions Taste Better with Support

Fast food employees are often trained to ask "Would you like to make it a combo?" And let's face it, a burger plus fries and a drink just go so well together. As with food, there are naturally good pairings of statements in conversation too. Don't always just serve the burger when you can serve the fries and drink also! The following combos will help you chunk your statements better. Make it a habit to become more aware of them and take advantage of their awesome powers.

Observation + Personal

This is one of my favorite combos (and a favorite of many ECs also). Pair the observation with your own personal point of view or experience. It's a great technique for extending the length of your statement, while instantly providing a good contrast between external and personal comments.

In the following examples, the personal comment is *italicized*:

> That jacket's a good look on you. *I need to get something like that, mine is stuck in the 90s.*
> I can't believe you do that. *It would make me crazy!*
> Driving in snow is fun. *My friends think I'm weird.*
> You've got such thick hair. *I'll probably lose mine by the time I'm 40!*
> You look shocked. *Did I do something to scare you?*
> It's funny seeing you in shorts. *I'm used to you in suits.*
> You haven't gained a single pound since college. *I've gained five pounds just in my neck. I have neck cellulite!*

Recently I ran into a friend at an outside restaurant on a nice summer night. He was looking sharp and had his shirt open a bit so his abundance of chest hair was on full display. I decided to play around.

> ME: Wow, you have such luxurious chest hair. *I'm jealous - I'm suddenly really insecure about my own.* Can I have some of yours?
> FRIEND: Sure, I have plenty to spare!
> ME: Or maybe I can buy some? Do they sell chest toupees?

Observation + Action

Express an action after the observation. In the following examples, the action statement is *italicized*.

> This is so good, *you have to try it.*
> I smell BBQ...is that BBQ? *I have to find out.*

Okay, time to get ice cream. *This is going to happen. Finally, the ice cream is almost here.*

Did you see how steep that is? *There's no way I'm doing that.*

Check out those kayakers. *We should do that! That would be so much fun!*

I don't think I've watched even five minutes of that show - *and I don't plan to either!*

Observation + Exaggerated Example

Exaggeration has come up again and again as a primary theme of many techniques in this book. And it's back again to remind you that rather than just supporting your comment with a regular example, try an exaggerated example just for fun. The supporting examples are *italicized*:

Wow can those glasses get any thicker? *I could see to Egypt with those things.*

They're really skimping on their frozen pasta dinners. They used to have all kinds of stuff in the bag - *now it's basically a bag of pasta with two pieces of shrimp and a chunk of red pepper!*

She played the creepiest soundtrack for my massage. *I mean, she may as well have been playing the Friday the 13th movie soundtrack.*

I like him, he's probably my favorite TV actor. I'm not obsessed though - *you won't find any full size posters of him in my bedroom!*

Stories Sprout from Support

Stories are important parts of exceptional conversation. Stories are the mental candy most people crave, as demonstrated by the billions spent on books, TV, movies, etc. We have already emphasized building roads to stories in order to improve your thinking speed, but if you struggle to introduce stories in the first place, the ISPC (Initial comment, Support, Post comment, Connect) is your solution. Unfortunately, mentioning the word "storytelling" often sends shivers down the spines of most people.

Let's make one thing clear – successful stories can be short and sweet. Stories do not (and probably should not) need to sound like a page out of Homer's epic tale *The Odyssey* and launch into details of Odysseus's ten year struggle to return from the Trojan war. Simple stories about the dullest topics can be more interesting if spoken in a certain way. For example, here's a simple story about seeing a bug:

> I was taking the trash out yesterday, and looked up and saw the biggest black beetle I've ever seen on the hallway ceiling. I just screamed and ran! I didn't know if it was going to jump on me or what. Luckily it wasn't there by the time I got back.

Instead of trying to "force" a story into the conversation, focus on elaborating and expanding your supporting statements. This method opens the doors to potential stories and provides fertile ground for a story to grow, without all the pressure that accompanies formal "Let me tell you a story..." storytelling. When you make a point to add support, sometimes a story organically takes shape, and sometimes it doesn't. Either outcome is fine!

 Quick Tip: Good stories typically follow a basic structure: a retelling of an unexpected event/action, your reaction to the event/action, what occurred after the event/action, and a conclusion.

Let's look at a few examples of expanding the support within the ISPC framework:

> COMMENT: I'm not sure I'd go there. I have mixed feelings about that place.
> SUPPORT: When I was there last month, the server actually gave me someone else's order.

Expand your support by answering additional questions: How did you react? What happened next?

EXPANDED SUPPORT: I couldn't believe it. I ended up telling his manager - I think I got him in trouble.

POST COMMENT: I feel bad now though. He was probably just new to the job.

CONNECT: The food was still good - hopefully you'll have a better experience!

COMMENT: When we adopted my lab, she and the cat didn't get a long at all.

SUPPORT: Actually they hated each other, they were basically mortal enemies.

How did you react? What happened next?

EXPANDED SUPPORT: I was actually more worried about my dog getting attacked by my cat. We had to put the cat in the dog's crate for over two weeks!

POST COMMENT: It's funny because they're best friends now.

CONNECT: How do your pets get along?

The aforementioned comments were short, but effective, stories. The more often you offer supporting examples and details, the more likely stories will start rolling off your tongue – sometimes before you realize it!

Ice the Cake with Post Comments

A cake without icing still tastes good – but icing takes the cake to a new level of deliciousness. This section finally dives into what constitutes a **Post comment**. They've been introduced already as the "P" in the ISPC, but I intentionally left them out of focus until now. The post comment takes many forms, but in general, they are remarks about what was just said or done, often in the form of a conclusion, summary, or hypothetical statement. They can be as simple as "Well that was embarrassing." This is a good spot to jump to a few examples:

COMMENT: I just a bought a tuna sandwich from a gas station.

POST COMMENT: I know, I like to live dangerously.

COMMENT: I wasted my entire game playing video games.
POST COMMENT: And it was awesome - I have no regrets!

COMMENT: I found the coolest thing ever - scented candles
   that smell like bacon and pancakes.
POST COMMENT: It's the perfect invention - we should just
   stop trying to invent anything else.

Post comments add a final thought or feeling to a decision you made, sometimes in the form of a realization. Inserting a little sarcasm or understatement works well as a post comment too. For example, "So yeah, hitting a hornets' nest during a soccer game probably wasn't the best idea I've ever had..." Check out a few examples of the most common types below:

CONCLUSION: It was probably the lamest date ever.
CONCLUSION: I'll never be doing that again.
CONCLUSION: So stay away from XYZ, is the moral of the
   story.
SUMMARY: So basically, I'm a jerk... is what it comes down to.
REALIZATION: I have no idea how I ate the entire thing, but now
   I'm paying for it.
REALIZATION: I probably shouldn't call people at 3am anymore.
REALIZATION: I was probably a little too greedy!
HYPOTHETICAL CONCLUSION: He's probably never talking to
   me again.
HYPOTHETICAL CONCLUSION: If she ever sees it I'm screwed!
HYPOTHETICAL CONCLUSION: I almost fainted right there on
   the floor!

Providing a reason, or questioning the reason for why something occurred, also make solid post comments.

QUESTION: Why would someone do that?

REASON: Because that's just how I roll.

REASON: I don't know, maybe I'm just a glutton for punishment.

Post comments are especially tasty if spoken with a little extra energy and enthusiasm.

As discussed a few times already, there is a critical moment right after you finish speaking. In that moment, there is a window where your partner may or not be ready to respond, and may or may not know how to respond. In this moment you risk a potential awkward interruption in the conversation. Post comments are often utilized to fill in the gaps if you notice that what you're talking about may not elicit any good responses, or was possibly misunderstood. Post comments can help shape the other person's response. Help the conversation flow by ensuring your conversation partner stays involved.

Am I just being paranoid, or is that not weird?

Do you see what I mean? He's crazy right?

Did that make sense?

Who does that? Who brings an entire salmon to someone's house?

Or, maybe what you said was inappropriate? The post comment can clarify any possible misunderstanding, and also steer the topic away from a potentially embarrassing moment. For example, at a meeting you could express a strong opinion about a new product. "It's not even good at doing X or Z. You would think for the cost it would help the project more." And realizing that you may have opened a door to a heated confrontation, you could offer a post comment clarifying your position before anyone responds. "...*I'm not saying I don't like it*, because I still think overall it's a good product, but I just have some concerns."

Observations + Support + Post Comments

Earlier in this chapter, we looked at the effectiveness of pairing an observation with a supporting comment. Let's borrow some of the comparison examples listed earlier in this chapter, and add post comments in the form of conclusions, summaries, explanations, hypothetical conclusions, or realizations. Try to think of any additional post comments while you're reading my examples.

Example 1. At a gun shop.

OBSERVATION
Look at all the guns.

SUPPORT
They have enough for a small military.

POSSIBLE POST COMMENTS
Now we know where every gun in the state comes from.
They could probably take over Canada if they wanted to.
If I was a criminal this is the last place I'd try to rob.
When the zombies attack, we're coming here first.

Example 2. Walking into a store.

OBSERVATION
Is it supposed to be this cold in here?

SUPPORT
I feel like I just walked into Antarctica.

POSSIBLE POST COMMENTS
I knew I should have brought my winter jacket.
Mental note, next time bring a sweater.

Were you able to think of any more possible post comments for the aforementioned examples or any other previous examples in this chapter? It's good to get into the habit of offering post comments.

Putting it All Together with the ISPC Formula

We've covered the first three parts of the ISPC formula. The fourth part, *Connection*, will be covered in more depth later. Take a look at how they all work together in a few real-life examples below.

Example 1: A friend makes a sandwich for you.

COMMENT

Oh it's got cilantro? That stuff is awesome.

SUPPORT

I lived in Mexico for a while and they put it on everything.

POST COMMENT

I learned you either love eating cilantro or you die from starvation!

CONNECTION

Have you ever been to Mexico?

Example 2: A new mother is describing her situation.

COMMENT

Now that we have a baby, it's no fun visiting friends anymore.

SUPPORT

You can't even have a conversation without a loud `WHA WHA WHA` every five minutes.

POST COMMENT

Our child completely killed our social life.

CONNECTION

You guys could still reach us on Facebook, but that's about it!

Keep in mind; the *Connection* isn't always needed if something else triggers a connection first. Additionally, all the elements of the ISPC formula don't necessarily need to be said together. You may not say your post comment until after the other person responded to your support comment, or maybe you offer a post comment to *their* support comment, etc.

CHAPTER 14: USE IT OR LOSE IT

1. Go back and add a supporting statement to one of the examples in this chapter.
2. Go back and add a post comment to one of the support examples in this chapter.

CHAPTER 14: REVIEW

Before this chapter:

✓ The four primary PATs: Comments, Knowledge, Opinions, and Autobiographical stuff
✓ The TAPP topics: Things, Activities, People, and Places
✓ Initiate with Feeler statements (You, Environment, and Them) and Problem Feelers
✓ FOOFAAE: Feelings, Observations, Opinions, Facts, Actions, Autobiographical, and Events
✓ Be proactive and consider a second question or comment
✓ The Golden Ratio (ISPC): Initial comment, Support, Post comment, and Connection
✓ Aim for clarity and paint a better self-portrait of yourself
✓ Your self-portrait also consists of your friends and family
✓ Sarcasm and under/overstatements are easy and fun

From this chapter:

✓ Support your comparisons or offer a comparison as the support
✓ Observations pair well with personal statements, actions, or exaggerated examples
✓ Post comments are usually summaries, realizations, conclusions, or hypothetical conclusions

Key takeaway from this chapter:
Support and post comments come in many forms – it's important to know how to wield them effectively and incorporate them often.

Coming up next:
Next we'll dive even deeper into how to structure your observations, opinions, support, and post comments so they're more interesting.

Preview: *The way you structure and frame your comments can make all the difference. We examine how exceptional conversationalists assemble a variety of statements in a more interesting, engaging, and likeable way.*

[CHAPTER 15]

BUILD MORE INTERESTING AND ENGAGING COMMENTS

Angles Make Your Comments More Interesting

We've covered many types of statements up until this point. No matter what type of comment you're making, the *angle* is often the difference between boring and interesting. And I'm not talking about acute vs. obtuse either. The angle is the spin or twist you give a comment or topic. It's the secret sauce – the inherent intrigue or narrative built into the expression. Angles are the "hooks" that lure people in.

The majority of conversation is based around exchanging information. Person A: "Did you eat lunch?" Person B: "Yes, I did." Poor conversationalists lean heavily on factual, literal comments too often and forget the fun, figurative human stuff. As you share information, start looking for interesting narratives to pull out of it.

Journalists are exceptional at converting dry information into interesting stories. They know how to hook you and gain your attention. There's good reason newspapers don't simply list a bunch of scores under the sports section – readers want to read an interesting narrative about a player or drama occurring within a sports organization. Look at the three ways to talk about the same fact.

1. Justin ran for 120 total yards against the Lions.
2. Justin shredded the Lion's defense and ran for a whopping 120 yards.
3. Playing with a broken collarbone, Justin still managed to shred the Lion's defense. He ran for a whopping 120 yards against a stout defense that was ranked highly in stopping the run. Justin may even win rookie of the year honors if he keeps running like that.

Notice how the addition of descriptive words in the second example make the fact more interesting and impressive. The original fact offered no context or emotion. The third example included additional information and multiple storylines – the fact that he was running with a serious injury against a highly rated defense made his run even more impressive. And speculation that he may win a highly coveted award is also an interesting element that helped paint a picture of Justin. Maybe

Justin's grandmother recently passed away, or maybe his wife just gave birth to his first child and he dedicated the game to her. Human interest stories contain the word "interest" for a reason.

Put on your journalist hat and start thinking of ways to convert your own factual information into more interesting comments. You don't need the creativity of an actual journalist to spin your information into something more interesting. Let's break down another simple everyday example. First, the factual statement:

I drank a soda today.

The factual statement contained no narrative or intrigue. Framing the statement even a little differently dramatically improves it. Let's add an angle:

I normally don't drink soda, but I am today.

Now the listener is left wondering, "Hmmm...why don't they normally drink soda? And what is so special about today?" Both are questions a conversationalist is encouraged to ask – simply because the statement was framed with an angle. Let's add more information to the angle:

I told my husband I would be healthy and give up soda for a year, but I can't do it any longer. It's too hard!

Much more interesting! There's family drama. There's temptation. There's a mini narrative that could be expanded on or inquired about.

Let's break down another example:

LIAM: What are you doing this weekend?
CAITLIN: Well, my boyfriend is coming over to my house.

There's nothing wrong with the factual response, however, it's missing some pieces. Caitlin forgot to mention a basic angle – this is the *first time* her boyfriend is meeting her son. Now that's much more interesting. Adding one of the following angles would increase interest in the conversation even more:

ANGLE 1: And I'm really nervous! I hope my son doesn't do anything crazy!

ANGLE 2: And I'm torn about what we're going to do - I mean, my son hates sports and my boyfriend is the biggest sports fanatic and wants to watch the game.

Angles also help your partner select the appropriate follow-up questions or responses. A bland statement like "I bought a computer" probably won't jump-start much conversation. If your partner is interested, they may ask standard questions (e.g. "Oh yeah, what kind?" "That's cool," or "Do you like it?"). And the conversation remains stuck purely in information-sharing mode. But adding an angle can initiate a myriad of rich tangents, and is much more likely to trigger responses from your conversation partner.

Imagine you're on a date. Your brain starts cycling through possible topics. You remember TAPP (Things, Activities, People, and Places) and think about something involving *technology*:

I just upgraded my phone.

Most people have experience buying a phone. What angles could make it more interesting? What mini-plot or narrative could you add? Consider the following:

1. *You need help:* I just upgraded to new phone and I can't figure out how to use it. My old phone was so much easier!

2. *You were surprised by something:* I just upgraded to my new phone. I found out it can do _____, how cool is that?

REMEMBER: Adding an angle to a factual statement is the equivalent of converting a *documentary* into a *drama*. How you frame the information makes all the difference.

To achieve an interesting angle, you may need to exaggerate a little. Check out the following two ways I could have responded to my boss after she tells of her adventures watching her neighbor's dog while they were out of town.

> BOSS: And I don't think I could do it again. The couch was literally ruined and I could tell they weren't happy with me. That dog was crazy!
>
> O.K. ANGLE: That reminds me, I still need to figure out what to do with my dog this Thanksgiving.
>
> EXAGGERATED ANGLE: I'm such a bad dog parent… *I always forget about her until the day before a holiday.* I'm always like, "Oh shoot, where's Lila going to stay!?"

So which angle did I actually communicate? Both! And no, I don't "always" forget about Lila, but the exaggeration formed a much more interesting admission (and angle).

There are hundreds of angles – some work better than others. Framing your angle with superlatives helps add interest. Maybe you're the worst at _____? Or the event you recently attended had the best _____ ever. Open your mind to experimenting with different angles to see what works.

Many angles are interesting because there is a **contrast** between the statements. A contrast of expectations, observations, actions, etc. For example:

> I was hoping for <u>one thing</u>, but I ended up with <u>something else</u>.
> I thought it was going to be <u>good/bad</u>, but it turned out <u>bad/good.</u>
> I didn't like <u>XYZ</u>, but now I do.

We'll dive into the power of contrasts next.

Contrasts Also Make Your Statements More Interesting

"Yes… *I mean No!*"

That one little statement has generated many laughs in the history of human conversation. You may not believe me now, so try it and find out for yourself. Quickly change your "no" response to a "yes" – or vice versa – and watch the smile form on the other person's face.

Why?

People love contrasts! Humans are genetically programmed to notice anything conflicting or opposing. Contrasting statements inherently create interesting angles. Leverage this psychological principle to your advantage when talking. Point out contrasts in your surroundings, or construct your own verbal juxtapositions. Start with a factual statement, and then offer some contrasting support. Exceptional conversationalists attempt contrasts frequently. The best and most humorous stories almost always contain some contrast.

You don't need to be a genius to come up with more contrasts – it's just a matter of structuring your statements a certain way and adding a contrasting comment. Let's look at some simple self-disclosure statements *without* and *with* contrasts.

> WITHOUT CONTRAST: I used to have a lot of goals too.
> WITH CONTRAST: I used to have a lot of goals too... *and then I decided to have kids!*

> WITHOUT CONTRAST: I really loved it!
> WITH CONTRAST: *I didn't think it would be any good,* but I actually really loved it!

> WITHOUT CONTRAST: I told you I'd come...
> WITH CONTRAST: I told you I'd come... *you didn't believe me did you?*

 Quick Practice: Now it's your turn. Try to finish the following contrasts. This practice will start training your brain to structure more statements as interesting contrasts. Remember, these statements could talk about someone or something else rather than yourself. Feel free to alter them as you work your way through.

I hope it's _____, because last time they _____.
I was/wasn't expecting _____, but _____ occurred.
I wasn't sure about _____, but I think I'm going to _____.
I was thinking one thing, but new information changed my mind.
I didn't think I would like _____, but it turned out to be _____.
It used to be good, but now it's _____.
I normally do _____, and never noticed _____ until today.
It was really hard, but paid off in the end.
I never do _____, but this time I am/did.
I might have to _____, which would _____.
I was supposed to _____, but then _____ changed.
This is good/bad, so much better/worse than _____.
Everything is bad/good now, I hope _____ gets/doesn't get better/worse.
Normally I/it wouldn't/doesn't_____, but in this case _____.
I was thinking/going to _____, but instead I _____.
That's like _____, but without the _____.

A previous chapter highlighted the power of comparisons, but explaining what something *isn't* like is a fantastic technique as well. Not only can saying what something isn't like extend the conversation, but it helps add balance and substance to an opinion or observation.

Radio personalities frequently compare – but also contrast – ideas in order to fill air time with interesting topics and discussions.

BORING VERSION: I think he's an excellent quarterback.
RADIO HOST VERSION: I think he's an excellent quarterback - now I'm not saying he's Joe Montana. He doesn't have the same arm strength - but he's still really good.

See how easy that was? The length of the phrase is doubled or tripled by mentioning who someone was not like. Not to mention, the statement is more multi-dimensional. If you listen for contrasts on the radio, you'll hear them all the time. Here's another:

> BORING VERSION: He's a good defensive player.
>
> RADIO HOST VERSION: He's a good defensive player, *and he isn't dirty. Most defensive players play a little dirty and bend the rules, but not him,* he follows the rules to a T.

BAM! Instant contrast.

In the following example, my coworker was telling me about her son August and managed to bust out two quick contrasts/angles.

> CONTRAST 1: He's good... But he just got over another sickness.
>
> CONTRAST 2: I used to be really freaked out about anyone getting too close to him. One time my husband wanted to take him to the mall and I was like, 'Nooo! He's not going anywhere!'... But now that he's three we don't care anymore! He can go wherever he wants!

Let's look at another contrast. This time, each contrast is formed by *contrasting against the comment before it.* Someone asks how it's like being a new father/mother:

> SELF-DISCLOSE: It's been great.
>
> CONTRAST 1: ...but it's exhausting. I feel like I'm part-zombie right now.
>
> CONTRAST 2: ...but I wouldn't trade it for anything. In a weird way it's enjoyable to be woken up by this little creature all night.
>
> CONTRAST 3: ...but if it was anyone else, I'd strangle them!

Pick a Fight with the Straw Man

There is always opportunity to create contrasts, even if not initially apparent. Contrasts are possible everywhere, in every situation. Let's look at an example where at first glance it doesn't seem possible to create a contrast.

JAKE: Did you like middle school?
EVE: I loved it.
JAKE: That's good.

Eve needs help. Eve needs a straw man. Setting up something to contrast against is sometimes referred to as *The Straw Man* strategy. It's a common debate technique. In the previous example, Eve lacked anything to contrast against – because she loved middle school! So instead of relying on just her own experience, she can introduce a straw man to contrast against: *people who hated middle school.*

EVE: Well, it's funny, *a lot of people hated middle school,* because of cliques and puberty and stuff. But I loved it, every minute of it. I guess I was weird like that.

Eve was able to create a much more interesting statement by stating a contrast. Have you ever been at a loss for words to describe something? You could say *what it was not like.* "It definitely wasn't one of those warm fuzzy type situations."

FRIEND: What were you like in high school?
YOU: I don't know - pretty normal I guess.

Instead of stopping there, consider straw man possibilities.

OPTION 1: Well, I definitely wasn't the king of the school or anything. I was more like the Jester.
OPTION 2: Well, I definitely wasn't the weakest kid in school - but I was close!

If discussing wine, you could disclose the following statement and stop:

I love white wine.

Or, you could continue by contrasting your statement against what you *don't* like or who you're *not* like.

And I'm not one of those people who has to drink $70 bottles either - I'll drink anything under ten bucks!

Contrasts enhance your descriptions and add color to your self-portrait too. Check out these examples:

A friend was recently describing a food truck encounter.

FRIEND: I had some great tacos from a food truck.

ADDED CONTRAST: *And it wasn't even a fancy one,* it was one of those 'I've been here for 20 years and I've got weeds growing in my engine' food trucks.

A friend described a recent accident.

FRIEND: I turned around and the glass dropped right out of my hands!

ADDED CONTRAST: *And this wasn't the kind of glass that breaks into a few pieces.* It was the kind that breaks into a thousand tiny shards!

It helps to look for what isn't quite "normal" and find the oddities in another's (or your own) actions, behaviors, conversation, etc. If you understand what is normal, then you can look for what *isn't* normal and simply point out the contrast. Over time your brain will automatically look out for contrasts.

Contrasts Highlight Your Individuality

A general rule of thumb when forming new relationships is to seek commonalities. However, after establishing a common bond with someone, don't feel discouraged about pointing out where your experiences or thoughts differ from theirs. Part of your self-portrait should highlight your uniqueness. Express your individuality within your circle of friends.

Your friend tells a story about the time he wolfed down a barely cooked piece of meat. You could respond, "I could never do that. That would make me cringe. If I see blood in my food I instantly lose my appetite!"

Exaggerating the contrast between experiences is a classic technique of late night talk show hosts to maintain an interesting conversation. Talk show hosts converse with so many types of people and personalities, they inevitably run into challenging conversation situations. They may share nothing in common with the interviewee, yet still need to respond with an interesting comment.

For example, if a talk show host is interviewing someone who just completed a 100-mile ultra-marathon, they may draw a contrast to their own lack of experience:

> Oh yeah? That's great - I can't even run up the stairs without getting worn out.
>
> Oh yeah? That's great - I also like to run. I ran up two flights of stairs instead of taking the elevator this morning.

Also remember the FAMMO technique: borrow information and experiences from your family and friends. Rather than stopping after saying, "I'll drink any kind of coffee," you could continue with a good FAMMO contrast, "but my boyfriend only drinks coffee from Dunkin Donuts – I don't know why, but he's crazy about that place."

Contrasts Also Improve Supporting Comments

Contrasts offer great opportunities to enhance your supporting statements. The previous chapter covered supporting statements in-depth, and primarily suggested supporting statements function as a method to provide additional information, explanations, or examples. But your supporting statements can also take the form of contrasts.

Contrasts are fantastic devices for enhancing observations about your surroundings and drawing out interesting angles. Your statement may start with an innocent observation, "I like this place," but transform into something much more interesting when you add some contrast and expand on it. "Unlike the XYZ coffee shop. Have you been to that place? It's a zoo in there! I couldn't even hear myself think."

Saying "She handled it so well," doesn't offer any contrast. But what if you said "She handled it so well. *I would have been a nervous wreck!*" Much more interesting!

Let's break down an example:

SELF-DISCLOSURE: Yeah, we decided on the birthing center in Granville. It was very nice - they took a very holistic, gentle approach. I really felt at home there.

Nothing incredibly interesting yet. Notice the following statement offers contrast to the first group of statements and makes the entire contribution more interesting.

ADD CONTRAST: ...Unlike the hospital in Rochester. It felt like a baby factory there - you come in, take some drugs, and pump out babies. The doctors were rude. *It was horrible!*

Anything can be contrasted. Someone's current behavior with their past behavior. Your past thoughts to your present thoughts. Let's look at a variety of contrast examples involving self-disclosure statements and observations. Most of the examples contrast your own thoughts/actions/experiences with someone else's (or your own) thought/action/experience.

COMMENT: You went easy on me in there.
ADD CONTRAST: I thought you were going to crucify me about being late!

COMMENT: I started working out of my house.
ADD CONTRAST: Until I realized that working out of your house will make you go crazy and start talking to the dog all the time!

COMMENT: You're cleaning?

ADD CONTRAST: I've never seen you clean before. All of a sudden you're on your hands and knees and pushing that vacuum like a pro!

COMMENT: Dog boarding places freak me out. Even the ones with open play areas. I feel weird about those places.

ADD CONTRAST: But I'm probably just being overly paranoid. My dog would probably be like, 'I'd rather go there than hang out with you all day!'

COMMENT: How do you find time to bake all those cookies?

ADD CONTRAST: I barely find time to get home and make a TV Dinner!

COMMENT: I'm usually not creeped out by anything.

ADD CONTRAST: But that one...he's a little creepy.

COMMENT: He's such a great father to the kids.

ADD CONTRAST: Which is funny because when he was younger, he swore he'd never have kids!

COMMENT: I have simple tastes. I'm happy with steak and potatoes.

ADD CONTRAST: Keep that foie gras and sushi crap away from me!

Keep in mind, your response to someone else's comment can serve as the contrast! Check out the following example:

CO-WORKER: That is so sweet - it says 'we wish Jim the best of luck and appreciate the 22 years of service.'

YOU: That's cool - a lot companies would just send out an email saying that he's no longer with the company - if even that.

Small Talk is More Interesting with Contrasts

Small talk tastes best when it's sprinkled with contrasts. A terrific example of multiple contrasts during small talk:

> JACK: What do you do?
>
> JILL: I'm in the fashion industry. Which is funny, because as a kid I wanted to become an orthodontist.
>
> JACK: Most kids just want play with Barbies at that age - but you were probably like, 'Hey, I think we should straighten Barbie's teeth.'

Check out the following two friends discussing their coffee habits. They each offer contrasts.

> MARGARET: Yeah, I was bad. I was a cup o' Joe addict. Not anymore though, I'm much better now. I've reduced my drinking to about half.
>
> HENRY: That's cool. I don't drink coffee at all anymore. Well, except for those pumpkin lattés during the holidays. I love those things.

 Quick Practice: Contrasts can be very subtle as they're not always framed as cleanly as my examples. Let's look at a fairly meaty example below. See how many contrasts you can spot! I'll review all of the contrasts afterwards.

Jack brought his children to church. After the service, there is a coffee-hour for socializing. While Jack holds his baby, a woman, Jill, comes over to introduce herself.

> JILL: Hi, I wanted to come over and see the baby - my name is Jill.
>
> JACK: Hi, I'm Jack, this is Jack Jr., over there is Jackson.
>
> JILL: I was so glad to see some more children at the service. It's been a while since we had this many sounds of children in the background.

JACK: Yeah, and I was worried we'd be asked to leave!

JILL: No way, they are so well-behaved.

JACK: Thanks. Yeah *this time* they were well-behaved - I never know how they're going to be - we sure got lucky.

JILL: How old is Jack Jr.? Seven months?

JACK: No, actually he just turned one. I know. He's small for his age. My other son is the opposite, he was actually a huge baby. When he was ten months, he looked like he was two years old.

Jill is holding a bagel and a donut in her hand. Suddenly, the baby reaches for the donut.

JILL: Looks like he wants a chocolate donut! I like how he doesn't even care for the bagels - he's already got a sweet tooth!

JACK: Yeah, I should go get him some food - if I don't, he may not be so pleasant anymore! It was nice to meet you Jill.

JILL: You too, Jack. Have a good day.

I counted at least six contrasts, did you? Let's recap the contrasts:

1. Jill offers a contrast when she said she was glad to see more children – and contrasts with the fact they don't usually have many children.

2. Jack adds an exaggerated fear – he thought they'd be asked to leave, in which Jill contrasts with a statement to the contrary.

3. Jack counters with another contrast about how this one particular time they were good, but it's the exception.

4. Jill asks the baby's age and learns that the baby is much older than what Jill thought. That's a contrast of expectations.

5. Then Jack offers a contrast about the difference between his two children.

6. Jack mentions that he should get his son some food – or else he'll turn into something unpleasant. He indicates a contrast between the current, pleasant behavior, and possible unpleasant future behavior.

The Definitive and Exception (AKA "Contradiction") Technique

I love animals...well not llamas. Llamas are lame, but all the other animals are cool.

I hate animals...they're all dirty. Well not llamas. Llamas are cool...all other animals suck.

Definitive statements and **exception** statements are one of my favorite combinations of phrases for creating quick and interesting statements. An easy way to create a contrast is by starting with a definitive statement. The reason? There's an exception to every rule. And the two statements together create an automatic contrast. Examine the introductory examples for this section. They both start with a definitive statement, and follow up with an exception.

For example, you ask the car wash attendant, "Can I wash my truck at your car wash?" This particular car wash attendant loves using definitive statements and exceptions. He responds, "You can wash anything here... *as long as it doesn't bite.*"

I always get a smile out of people after they ask me what I like to eat because I start with a definitive like, "Oh, I'll eat anything..." But then I follow up with an exception, "...except mushrooms. I don't go near fungus!"

The other day someone got a laugh by stating this definitive and exception combo:

I feel like I stayed up partying all night - *except I didn't party at all.* I was just being tortured by my four-month-old son, who woke up every hour.

Our brains notice conflicts because they capture our attention when we were expecting something predictable. In the following example, someone asks you how the amusement park was.

YOU: It was really fun.

Boring, right? Now notice what happens when you add an exception (*italicized*):

EXCEPTION: ...*although I spilled soda all over my pants,* but other than that, it was a blast.

Let's examine a few more examples. Exceptions are great for bringing attention to one interesting detail.

YOU: I love you man - *even if you smell like vinegar.*

FRIEND: You had their green tea? Did you like it?
YOU: I did, *it looked like sewage water,* but it still tasted good!

FRIEND: There's no way I'd vote for John Smith.
YOU: *I never would either, but he's got great hair,* you can't deny that.

Some exceptions function as a means to clarify or quantify your previous statement.

EXCEPTION 1: He's sexy...he reminds me of my ex...*except with better abs.*
EXCEPTION 2: He's sexy...he reminds me of my ex...*except without the beer belly.*

Exceptions also include what something *is* or *isn't*, what something *could* or *couldn't do*, etc. For example, "He could do anything – *well he couldn't tie his own tie* – but he could do anything else!"

Exceptions help clarify what you mean and what you don't mean. "I love llamas – *I don't want to own a llama farm or anything* – but I love looking at them and petting them once in a while." Or "I love people watching – *not in a creepy psycho way though.*"

Sometimes, just stating a pseudo-definitive statement will elicit an exception or contrast phrase from someone else.

The Playful Disagreement Technique

A disagreement, at its core, is a contrast of opinions. Unfortunately, confrontations, arguments, and disagreements can be a source of fear and frustration for poor conversationalists. Obviously, it's important to find commonalities and shared interests, but it's equally important to maintain your individuality. If your sole mission is to please and agree with the other person, you'll end up appearing like a parrot instead of a person. You can't please everybody – and if you try, you'll fail. Besides, light-hearted disagreements add fun and engaging contrasts within a conversation. Anyway, let's look at some examples, shall we?

YOU: What are you doing?

SPOUSE: I'm doing my yoga. This is called the '*downward facing dog.*'

YOU: It looks more like the '*distressed dog*' to me!

FRIEND: If Mark was a super hero, he'd probably be a smaller version of the Incredible Hulk. He even kind of has his skin tone.

YOU: No way! He's totally more like the Wolverine. He's too hairy to be the Hulk!

CO-WORKER: Winston Cunningham is going to be a great quarterback in the NFL.

YOU: Don't tell me you're a Cunningham fan - we may not be able to be friends any longer!

CHAPTER 15: USE IT OR LOSE IT

1. Go back to the TAPP topics (Chapter 5: *Fill Up Your Conversation Storage Tank*). Pick two topics, and challenge yourself to add an angle or contrast.

2. Express a Definitive and Exception combo in one of your next conversations.

CHAPTER 15: REVIEW

Before this chapter:

- ✓ The four primary PATs: Comments, Knowledge, Opinions, and Autobiographical stuff
- ✓ The TAPP topics: Things, Activities, People, and Places
- ✓ Initiate with Feeler statements (You, Environment, and Them) and Problem Feelers
- ✓ FOOFAAE: Feelings, Observations, Opinions, Facts, Actions, Autobiographical, and Events
- ✓ Be proactive and consider a second question or comment
- ✓ The Golden Ratio (ISPC): Initial comment, Support, Post comment, and Connection
- ✓ Aim for clarity and paint a better self-portrait of yourself
- ✓ Observations pair well with personal statements, actions, or examples
- ✓ Post comments are usually summaries, realizations, conclusions, or hypothetical conclusions

From this chapter:

- ✓ Angles and contrasts are crucial for sounding more interesting
- ✓ The Definitive and Exception technique is an easy way to form contrasts

Key takeaway from this chapter:

Angles and contrasts are the number one method for sounding more interesting and keeping people engaged in what you're saying. Devote a lot of time to practicing contrasts!

Coming up next:

You've learned how to strengthen your observations, opinions, support, and post comments with angles and contrasts. The Connect habit is next. It explores the fourth part of the golden ratio – adding a connecting statement to the other person or something else. But the Connect habit also goes much further into the secrets of keeping the conversation flowing smoothly.

HABIT SIX

CONNECT

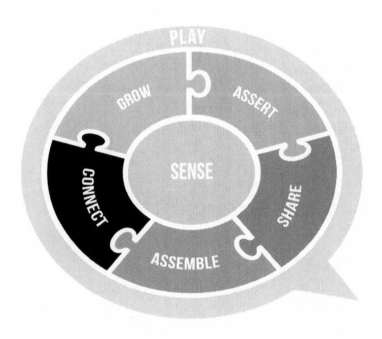

Preview: *You will have the power to maintain conversations longer if you know how to offer connectable opinions and topics. Connecting is all about keeping the conversation flowing in interesting and effective ways.*

[CHAPTER 16]

OFFER CONNECTABLE OPINIONS AND TOPICS

What do all the previous examples of exceptional comments in this book have in common? They are more "connectable" than the average comment. The more connectable your comments, the more the conversation will flow. This chapter dives into the nuts and bolts of ensuring your comments are as connectable as possible. Coincidently, the next chapter examines how *you* can be a more connectable conversation partner.

Maintain Better Conversation with Connectable Opinions

A major obstacle for even the best conversationalists is maintaining an interesting conversation for an extended period of time without too many long pauses or awkward silences. Not all FOOFAAE comments are made equal. It's important to offer FOOFAAE comments that inherently elicit and evoke more substantive discussion if you want to contribute to maintaining a longer, more interesting conversation.

The first question you have to ask yourself is what kind of conversation drivers are you relying on? Have you ever played golf? Golf clubs come in all shapes and sizes. Some are designed for hitting great distances, and some for precise short ranges. "Woods" are designed to propel the ball the farthest, up to about 350 ft. "Irons" and "Wedges" for mid-range, and finally "Putters" for specific and precise short distances.

Comments that maintain conversation could be classified in a similar way. Many comments/questions will only hit the conversation ball a few feet, while some will drive the conversation great distances.

If you only use putters, your conversations will start and stop quite a bit. Asking "What time is it?' or "How old is your dog?" are putter-type statements. Many feeler statements could be classified as putters – they are simply designed for starting or filling in conversation, not eliciting or evoking substantive conversation. If you rely on putters for your entire golf game, your conversation may feel forced or disjointed, and you may never achieve a conversation flow.

You've already learned many techniques discussed earlier to help you reach the conversation sweet spot: disclosing interesting information, connecting to engaging stories, asking better questions, offering interesting observations, support, and framing your opinions with angles or contrasts. If your opinion elicits additional comments, connections, or otherwise keeps the conversation train chugging along, then it's called a **connectable opinion.**

Can you think of something food-related right now to start a conversation with a friend? The other day I overheard someone mentioning an issue they have with cooking:

> I have so many cookbooks, and I always say I'm going to make these amazing recipes, but I never do. I really should start trying to cook more!

It was a great conversation driver. Why? Because it involved a *popular* and *relatable* topic – food – and it was framed with an intriguing *angle* – she has always wanted to _____, but never does _____. Her conversation partners could form a number of different connections, because most adults can relate to the struggles with cooking. (If her angle was how talented of a chef she was, it may not be as relatable!) For example:

> I'm the same way! I'm so optimistic, but then who has time for all of that? I mean with...
> I was the same way, but I started making a cooking journal and setting a goal for myself of ….
> See, I'm not even that ambitious, I just try to make something edible that won't poison my kids and I'm happy...

So remember, connectable opinions involve popular topics, relatable topics, and are framed with interesting angles.

On a side note, check out the aforementioned responses to the cooking opinion. They're each interesting in their own way, share additional information, and help move the conversation forward.

Connectable Opinions are Strong but Gentle

Pick an angle and offer a strong opinion, but not in an argumentative "I'll fight anyone who disagrees with me" kind of way. One time a group of my friends and I ordered takeout Chinese. One of my friends offered a great opinion that lead to a number of fun comments:

> I think Chinese food and pizza are the hardest foods to *ruin*. I mean, have you ever had *bad* pizza? Even badly cooked pizza is still edible. It's basically impossible to mess up.

The opinion was strong, but about a light-hearted topic. It naturally opened the conversation up to additional comments about types of food that are hard to mess up, food that is easy to mess up, cooking, ordering takeout vs cooking, and a lot more. All because of one super connectable opinion. (Feel free to store this PAT opinion in your conversation storage tank and offer it yourself next time you're eating Chinese food or pizza with friends!)

Have you ever listened to a group of sports fans talk sports? Sports conversations can continue ad infinitum because the topics are ripe for taking strong positions on trivial topics; everyone involved understands the opinions are open to debate. Let's look at three baseball fanatics: Dave, Jay, and Mark. They've been friends forever and love discussing baseball. Their conversations last for hours. Let's look at a short snippet:

> DAVE: Did you hear that Rodriguez just signed for 122 million dollars?

Each person offers an opinion:

> MARK: I'm happy for him, but that's crazy. That's way too much for a relief pitcher, don't you think?
> JAY: Yeah, but it's the going rate. It's about average. It's not a shock to see that deal.
> DAVE: I think he should have been paid more - relief pitchers are undervalued as it is. At least that's my opinion.

Look at each opinion from a high level. Mark views the contract amount as **too much,** Jay thinks it's **about right**, and Dave thinks it's **too little**. Like *Goldilocks and The Three Bears* – the soup can be too hot, too cold, or just right. Of course, after each opinion is made, the guys could offer support for their respective views.

Connectable, interesting opinions take a solid position. They are either *for or against*, they see either *the good or the bad*, etc. However, make it clear you're open to discussion. Post comments may be needed in case your opinion came off too harshly (e.g. "That probably sounded worse than I meant it," or "But that's just my opinion, I'm probably in the minority.").

Let's examine an example involving the topic of restaurant servers.

> FRIEND: Our server looks really stressed out - we should leave him a good tip.
> BORING OPINION: Yeah, you're right. That would be a good idea.

Let's try again, but with a more connectable opinion.

> CONNECTABLE OPINION: You're right, we should. I think everyone should work at a restaurant at least once in their life - it builds character, don't you think?
> FRIEND: Absolutely! I wasn't ever a server, but I worked behind the desk at a hotel during college - now that kept me humble. I had to deal with so many arrogant jerks!

Support the opinion with additional information.

> SUPPORT: Oh yeah, and when I was a server, I used to have to
> _____. It was crazy.

Check out at an example that centers on a very connectable topic – pets.

> FRIEND: My dog threw up on the rug again.
> BORING OPINION: That's not good.

So far the conversation lacks a connectable opinion. Let's try again.

FRIEND: My dog threw up on the rug again.
CONNECTABLE OPINION: That's not good. See, that's why I
have a cat - I think they are much lower maintenance.

That's a connectable opinion. The friend now has something to agree or disagree with, and explain why. Just in case the friend doesn't offer any comment immediately, you could add some support and beef up your connectable opinion:

SUPPORT: I can leave for a week and come back and my cats
are fine. I don't come back to ripped-up couches.
FRIEND: Yeah, that's true, but I think dogs are much better at
_____, even though...

Connectable Opinions Offer Many Connection Possibilities

In the aforementioned example about pets and servers, a little support was added to the connectable opinion to provide even more conversation fodder and give the conversation partner more time to think about how to respond.

I recently heard Jack, Jill, and Jake talking about buying a car. Unfortunately, Jack's opinion was good, but lacked much substance. Notice what occurs when Jill offers a *connectable* opinion. We'll look at Jack's opinion first:

JACK: I don't think you should buy a new car.

His opinion isn't bad by any means, but it may not help carry the conversation far. It doesn't provide much food for thought. Take a look at Jill's opinion:

JILL: I don't think you should buy a new car either! I was at the
dealer recently...and this guy says I should buy a new Hyundai,
but I was like, no, I only want a used car. I personally think

you should only buy used. I don't want to pay $10,000 more for something brand new. It's not worth it.

Notice how Jill's opinion offered much more substance because she supported her opinion with additional information and thoughts around the idea. She told a quick story about her experience at the dealership. She clarified her first opinion by saying two years is perfect, and then explained why.

Does her contribution follow a familiar pattern? She stuck to the golden ratio of conversation! She offered a strong opinion, then interesting support, then an interesting post comment. She could have even tried to connect to something or someone else if she sensed the conversation was going to stall.

Her entire opinion plus supporting comments were very *connectable.* She helped her conversation partners, Jack and Jake, think of a number of options for continuing the conversation. She may have helped trigger a response about their own experience at a dealership, their own thoughts on the best time to purchase a car, whether they should buy new or used, the brand Hyundai, etc.

The best conversation drivers open and expand the conversation, are light in nature, yet substantive. They provoke thought and feelings, without intimidating. They create fertile ground for others to plant comments and form a variety of connections.

Maintain Better Conversation with Connectable Topics

Speaking of pets, restaurants, food, and sports... they are timeless topics most people can relate to. Exceptional conversationalists cram their storage tanks with thoughts and experiences on hundreds of popular topics.

> **REMEMBER:** The best opinions not only stick to relatable and common topics that most people *can* contribute to, but also focus on "hot topics" that your conversation partners *want* to contribute to.

Tune in to how your friends feel about topics. I have friends who love discussing sports, video games, and movies, but not much else. Other friends become energized when discussing politics or global issues. Keep a mental note of the hot topics for each person you know.

One time my friends and I were talking at lunch. One guy was talking about how his fridge was bare and there was nothing to eat at his house. It was a pretty standard conversation lacking any hot topics. I stated a pretty average opinion, "You should go buy a bunch of Hot Pockets."

Bingo! Connectable topic introduced. But wait, that doesn't look like a very connectable opinion does it? I didn't realize it at the time, but the simple comment hit on a very hot topic that everyone *could* contribute to and *wanted* to contribute to.

Apparently every person involved with the conversation had experiences, opinions, and knowledge of Hot Pockets. Here are some actual comments that grew from introducing the Hot Pocket topic:

I love Hot Pockets. They have these new kinds I think called Pretzel Pockets - they are so good. I could eat them every day.

I think you can buy *breakfast pockets* too - you could seriously eat Hot Pockets for every meal!

You eat Hot Pockets? I never thought you were a bachelor-type guy.

Have you ever heard of Jim Gaffigan? He has the funniest skit about Hot Pockets not cooking all the way. I can't remember it exactly, but he said something like _____.

That's so true. Why can't mine ever be hot all the way through? Maybe they should be called *Hot and Cold Pockets* or *Hot-on-the-outside-Pockets.*

Maybe I just need to learn how to use my microwave correctly.

I want to buy a freezer for my basement just for Hot Pockets, like 500 of them.

You'll never go hungry again - and when the apocalypse comes, you'll be ready!

But if there's a power outage, you'll have 500 *Moldy Pockets!*

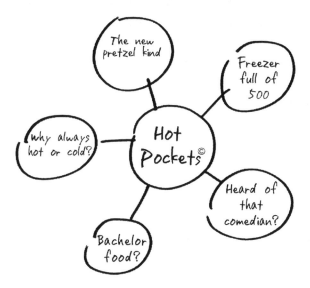

The conversation became fun, lively, and exceptional; I had Hot Pockets to thank for the experience. In fact, many of the opinions that sprouted from my simple opinion were themselves connectable. But how do you know what topics are likely to spawn more conversation and what topics are likely to stop the conversation in its tracks? Keep reading.

Increase Your Ability to Contribute with TAPP Sub-Topics

The TAPP topics were strategically selected because of their likelihood of appearing in conversation and their innate connectability. Go back to the TAPP topics (Chapter 5: *Fill Up Your Conversation Storage Tank*) and really flesh out your thoughts on each topic (research additional supporting material if you become stuck). Expanding your knowledge around topics is key to being able to contribute more connectable information and opinions. If you want to expand your knowledge around a topic, read more opinion-pieces. Think more deeply about every topic you come across. What personal anecdotes could you add?

Additionally, try to apply different techniques to each topic. Can you form a safe and/or strong opinion with a good angle? What about a good analogy? What support could you offer? Try a superlative; think of the best, worst, cheapest, most expensive, etc. In addition, there are plenty of connectable sub-topics within each TAPP. For example, Hot Pockets is a good sub-topic under the topic of food. I included a handy list of TAPP Sub-Topics to help you expand your knowledge.

If you're feeling ambitious, peruse the list of TAPP Sub-Topics below and make an effort to form a comment related to each one. This is a great mental association exercise. Pretend each one just came up in conversation – could you contribute immediately?

Keep in mind, you don't need a tattoo to talk about the topic of tattoos. Do you have any friends with an interesting tattoo? What are your feelings towards tattoos in general? What tattoo would you get?

TAPP Sub-Topics

Tattoos, Gambling, 80s or 90s bands, fashion trends, 3D printing, urban legends, worst teachers, worst ex boy/girlfriends, best vacation, interesting hobbies, places you'll never visit again, near run-ins with the law, where to get the best taco/burger/steak, scariest moment, how long Facebook will last, new apps, what apps need to be invented, best or worst restaurant chains, how many pets is too many, the future of phones, plastic surgery, strange addictions, cruises, veganism, fad diets, irrational fears, strange habits of your family members, alternative energy, future of electric cars, transportation, secret societies, how long the latest pop star will last, new science ideas, cures for hangovers, ghosts, best drinks, virtual reality, first computer, TV vs movies vs books, specific TV shows, bad or good TV channels, future of cable, a TV show that should be made, pet breeds, strange animal facts, interesting Halloween costumes, crazy international leaders, crazy celebrities.

Interesting angles can also be pre-thought out before the topic is ever introduced into the wild. Many conversation drivers can be Previously Assembled Thoughts (PATs) discussed in Chapter 5: *Fill Up Your Conversation Storage Tank*. By mentally processing interesting aspects of topics before the conversation ever starts, you move those thoughts to the outer layers of your brain, ready for quick retrieval during a fast-paced conversation. It's important to build those highways to interesting tidbits of information by thinking about them more often.

When an opinion offers a unique twist or observation about a topic, it's often called *insight*. I throw around the term "insight" loosely; for conversational purposes, it doesn't need to be profound or philosophical. It's more about looking at a topic – or something in the environment – in a new way and forming connections that may not be obvious. Insightful thoughts add another, deeper layer to all conversations (and impress other insightful people!).

Let's take the topic of Sports; more specifically, the Olympics. You could state simply "Usain Bolt is so fast" or "I like watching the swimming event," but of course you can do even better. What's an overlooked aspect? Think beyond talking about the ceremony and the winners. How about: "It would suck to be the *fourth place guy*. I'd be like 'screw you, Dad, for making me run 15 miles a day my whole life! I didn't even get a medal to show for it!'"

Insight often depends on unique or uncommon knowledge about a topic. Learning a unique fact about TAPP topics will boost your conversation abilities – because a fact offers opportunities for *comments about the fact*. "Did you hear they have to pay taxes on their medal? It already costs thousands to train every year!" And then you could add a personal hypothetical statement. "Right! If I won, I'd be like '*No thanks – please keep it. I can't afford it!*'"

"I Read a Study That Said..."

The world is full of smart and interesting people. A great deal of research concerning every topic under the sun has already been conducted.

Luckily for the rest of us, some of the smartest and most interesting people make their insights available for free (or less than $20.00 if they are selling a book!). It's no secret some of the best insight is simply borrowed from someone else. Go forth and copy!

A long time ago, I watched a social psychologist present his ideas on why someone ultimately votes Democrat or Republican and how it can be traced to the way they were raised. He claimed Republicans tend to be raised with more emphasis on fear and respect for authority. On the other hand, Democrats were raised to question authority and think more creatively. These ideas, vague as they may be, still make for provocative conversation fodder. (Do you agree with his assessment? Hmmmm?) To appear insightful, I simply reference the content of the study and possibly take a position. Ninety-nine percent of the population will never ask for the specific source of your information. (Notice how I never told you who the social psychologist was?) But ninety-nine percent of the population can relate to a study about Democrats and Republicans – just be careful who you bring it up with!

Your goal from now on should be to offer more connectable opinions and introduce more connectable topics.

CHAPTER 16: USE IT OR LOSE IT

1. Devote time to converting what you see, read, hear, experience, and think about, into connectable opinions.
2. Rummage through the TAPP Sub-Topics if you haven't already, and think of opinions and supporting material for as many as you can.
3. Think of five of your own TAPP Sub-Topics.

CHAPTER 16: REVIEW

Before this chapter:

✓ The four primary PATs: Comments, Knowledge, Opinions, and Autobiographical stuff

- ✓ The TAPP topics: Things, Activities, People, and Places
- ✓ Become an Interest Hunter and seek out commonalities
- ✓ Initiate with Feeler statements (You, Environment, and Them) and Problem Feelers
- ✓ FOOFAAE: Feelings, Observations, Opinions, Facts, Actions, Autobiographical, and Events
- ✓ Be proactive and consider a second question or comment
- ✓ The Golden Ratio (ISPC): Initial comment, Support, Post comment, and Connection
- ✓ Post comments are usually summaries, realizations, conclusions, or hypothetical conclusions
- ✓ Angles and contrasts are crucial for sounding more interesting

From this chapter:

- ✓ Connectable opinions are strong, but gentle
- ✓ Connectable opinions are relatable and encourage multiple ways to respond
- ✓ Study the TAPP Sub-Topics for more popular topic ideas

Key takeaway from this chapter:

Focus on opinions and topics that your listeners *can* and *want* to contribute to.

Coming up next:

Next we'll look at techniques for being a connectable conversation partner.

Preview: *Mastering the art of making connections is imperative to maintaining exceptional conversation. This chapter focuses on connecting to others and becoming a more connectable conversationalist.*

[CHAPTER 17]

BE CONNECTABLE AND MAINTAIN THE CONVERSATION

Conversation, at its core, boils down to a series of connections; from one topic to the next; from riding horses to eating ice cream; from describing a movie to feelings towards the president. Mastering the art of making connections, connecting to others, and helping others connect is imperative to exceptional conversation. The previous chapter covered how to be proactive and introduce connectable opinions and topics into the conversation. But it's just as vital to be able to connect to someone else's comments or topics.

This chapter focuses on critical techniques for speeding up your response time, avoiding awkward silences, and keeping the conversation fluid and dynamic. Essentially: being an exceptional conversation partner.

It's important to prime your brain to look for more connections than you do currently. How quickly can you answer the following questions?

> What time is it?
> Where are you from?
> How long has it been since you last ate breakfast?

Not too difficult, huh? Unfortunately conversation isn't that easy! Conversation can be intimidating because a response is often expected in only a few seconds, but with endless possibilities, a good response is hard to deliver. When you need a quality comment in a hurry, look no further than feeler categories. Not only do they excel at initiating conversation, but they double as lightning fast responses.

Remember, feeler statements come in three primary categories:

1. You
2. Environment
3. Them

A friend tells you a story about how **they accidently fell asleep on a bench while visiting a famous monument.**

How would you respond? The options are limitless, aren't they? Your brain can quickly become overwhelmed if it searches for every possible response option in the recesses of your memory. Focusing your brain to look through feeler categories is the first step to speeding up the time it takes to generate an interesting response. Check out a few possible feeler responses to your friend's aforementioned story:

You: Relate it back to yourself. Did you like it or not? Have you done something similar? Do you know it or not? Do you want to do it or not?

I would be mortified if I did that.
I've done my share of embarrassing things like that too.
I don't think I've ever done anything that embarrassing before.

Environment: Comment or question how it relates to the surroundings or people in the immediate environment. Does the action or statement impact anything?

Did anyone notice?
Were there a lot of crowds?
I can't believe no one woke you up!

Them: Comment or question their actions or something they said. Point out something interesting or unusual. Gather more information.

You fell asleep for three hours? You must have been exhausted!
How long were you asleep for?
That sounds dangerous, I'm glad you didn't get robbed!

Connect More Effectively with FOOFAAE

Feeler statements are suitable for many needs, but three categories may not be specific enough for helping you generate responses. In Chapter 10: *Start Small with Small Talk*, we reviewed how each FOOFAAE category functions as a great option for initiating conversation. Like feelers, FOOFAAE options offer another advantage: they double as a great way to respond also.

Let's revisit example FOOFAAE statements and questions designed to initiate:

FEELING: I absolutely love your dog.

OBSERVATION: You have such a well-behaved dog.

OPINION: I think Pugs are the best kind of small dog breed.

FACT: I was reading that dogs are partially colorblind.

ACTION STATEMENT: I want to adopt a dog like that.

AUTOBIOGRAPHICAL: My brother has a Pug too…

EVENT: Did you hear Frank just adopted a dog last month?

For the sake of making a point, it's possible to respond to each previous FOOFAAE statement using the *same* FOOFAAE category. If someone starts with a Feeling comment, you could respond with a Feeling comment. Take a look at the responses to each of the aforementioned *FOOFAAE* statements:

FEELING: I love him too, I wouldn't trade him for anything.

OBSERVATION: Yeah, surprisingly, he's acting pretty good now.

OPINION: I do too, but I'd probably say Shih Tzu's are a close second.

FACT: Someone told me they could only see in blue or yellows, do you know if that's true?

ACTION STATEMENT: You should! You could go down to the shelter this weekend, I think they're having a big adoption event.

AUTOBIOGRAPHICAL: That's funny, I used to have a dog like that who always _____ too.

EVENT: Did he? I wonder if he adopted from the big adoption event the shelter had last month.

Of course, you could respond to any FOOFAAE category with any other FOOFAAE category.

Quick Practice: Now it's time for you to practice. Your friend discloses to you, **"I'm thinking of traveling to Madagascar."** Try to respond to your friend with a comment from each FOOFAAE category: *Feeling, Observation, Opinion, Fact, Action, Autobiographical, and Event.*

When you're done, look at the following examples (Don't look ahead!). Of course, some comments could fall under multiple categories – don't get hung up on that.

FEELINGS
I would love to go to Madagascar - I don't know anything about it.
I don't think I'd ever want to go that far away.
Are you nervous about going?

OBSERVATION/OPINION
That's very adventurous of you.
You're starting to sound like the next Indiana Jones or something.
You're always going on trips. You have such an interesting life.
You would love it there.

FACTS
I heard they like to wrestle cows there. I think it's some sport they play. We have baseball and they have cow wrestling.
Do you know much about that country?
I bet it's really hot there. I hope you like the heat.

ACTION STATEMENT
You should go. If I had the money I would go right now!
I want to go with you! Could you pack me in your suitcase?

AUTOBIOGRAPHICAL
That's awesome. I've seen the movie Madagascar with my kids,
   but that's the closest I've come.
What made you decide to pick Madagascar?
I didn't even know Madagascar was a real country until last year!
   Geography was never a strength of mine.

EVENT
If you do go, you'll have to buy a _____ for a souvenir.
That's awesome. Remember when Andy went to Egypt? He said it
   was the time of his life.

If you still can't think of anything within the FOOFAAE categories, there a few more options for keeping the conversation flowing. First, remember the small talk fillers for buying time. You can always summarize or paraphrase what they said.

PARAPHRASE
You want to go to Madagascar huh?
Wow. You're thinking of traveling to Africa?

Second, if you can't think of anything, and asking a follow-up question isn't preferable, maybe it's time to change the topic.

CHANGE TOPIC COMPLETELY
That's cool but I'd be a little nervous. Did you hear about what's
   happening in Kenya right now?
I could never do that. I'm perfectly happy traveling in this
   country. I'm actually thinking of going to Yellowstone, have
   you been?

Pivoting too far away from their topic is not ideal unless you feel strongly about not continuing with their topic.

Develop Your Keyword Radar

Keywords (or Key Phrases) aid your ability to respond faster, with more specific comments. Keywords or phrases act as a trigger that aims your brain towards a target. If your brain has to only search for responses related to a keyword, the search becomes ten times easier. Before we dive too deeply into keywords, check out some examples of keywords in action:

DAVE: How's it going? Living the *dream*?

YOU: Yeah, I don't know about *dream*. If it was a dream, I don't think I'd be writing a research paper right now - I'd probably be boating on a lake.

HENRY: That's the *swanky* bar all the rich people go to.

YOU: Yeah, you're right. I can smell the *swank* from here - and it's kind of sour, like rotten milk.

ART: Your salad looks good - it looks very *Mediterranean*.

YOU: I love olives and feta - I guess I'm just a *Mediterranean* kind of guy.

BRANDON: You can't hear the vocal *fry* in her voice?

MALCOLM: No, I guess I lack a good *fry* filter!

ISAAC: You look *lost*.

YOU: The only thing *lost* is my mind.

YOU: How was your weekend?

WILLIAM: *Busy.*

YOU: *Good* busy or *bad* busy?

PAT: Your dog is so *weird*.

YOU: He's not *weird*, he's *introspective*.

Keywords often stand out from the rest of the comment in some manner. Some people deliberately choose uncommon words, or place extra emphasis on certain words, or a combination of both. The "key" is to know when you hear them. Do you struggle to respond quickly? You may be getting hung up on cycling through many possible response options without a clear sense of direction or target to aim at. Your brain quickly becomes overloaded if it isn't focused on something specific.

Let's practice some keyword recognition. A colleague approaches you with a concern:

Hey, can I steal you for a minute? I need help with something.

Did you notice any keywords in that statement? Does any word stick out now? The person asking purposely chose the word "steal," instead of something more standard and ordinary like "see" or "talk." You can have fun with that word, and maybe pretend to take it literally.

Sure, you don't need to steal me though... I'll come willingly.

(Admittedly, some examples appear cheesy in print, and definitely require playful conversationalists to work well!)

Here's an example of the small talk that occurs when people first meet at a gathering. I've italicized the keywords each person connects to. Tom and Hank are friends and just ran into each other at Hank's party:

TOM: There he is, the *head of the house.*
HANK: *Head of the garage* is more like it. The only head of the house is standing over there. (Points to his wife)
TOM: Ha! It's good to see you.
HANK: Tom, I'm glad you could *make it.*
TOM: *Make it?* I wouldn't miss it! Plus, *I bet* there's better drinks than the crap I have at home.
HANK: That's probably a safe *bet,* and only one way to find out.

Examine the example below to see how a few keywords make the difference between bland and engaging conversation. The first example lacks anything in particular that would trigger an interesting response:

ERIN: Last week he was sick.

KATE: He was?

ERIN: Yeah, he was out for a few days.

KATE: But he's better now, right?

ERIN: Yeah.

KATE: That's good.

Saying the word "sick" is pretty ordinary, and is less likely to trigger any additional connections. When it's replaced by something more interesting/meaningful, check out what happens:

ERIN: Last week he looked like he might have *scarlet fever*.

KATE: He did? I haven't heard of anyone getting that. It sounds so Victorian.

ERIN: I know, doesn't it?

KATE: Wasn't that what the little boy had in the Velveteen Rabbit?

ERIN: Exactly! I didn't think anyone got scarlet fever these days!

KATE: But he's better now, right?

See how well that worked? The words "scarlet fever" trigger many more possible connections than the word "sick." And even if he didn't have scarlet fever, it could have been referenced anyway. "He wasn't feeling good...we were just glad it wasn't *scarlet fever* or something!" Or, "At least he didn't have *scarlet fever* or something..."

Listening for keywords will aid your ability to respond, but try to return the favor. Purposely add keywords to your comments so others have an easier time responding. Some words are just going to spark more discussion and reactions than others. You don't always know what people are going to bite on and connect to. However, as you start noticing keywords, you'll discover trends and patterns for the people you socialize with. Throwing out keywords is kind of like going fishing. Half the battle is knowing your audience, but the same word could be interesting to one group and boring to another. For example, some people may have a lot to say about "scarlet fever" and for others, it may pass right over their heads.

In Chapter 7: *Expand Your Word Choices*, I covered the importance of experimenting with words – by experimenting, you'll come across many more keywords. Saying something looks good isn't as fun or interesting as saying it looks *Mediterranean*. As soon as the word Mediterranean is introduced, it offers other connection possibilities.

Remember contrasts from Chapter 15: *Build More Interesting and Engaging Comments*? Try offering a statement about what you're *not like*, or what you *don't like*, what you *don't need*, what you *don't care* about, etc. It also buys you more time and is surprisingly good for adding keywords. Let's examine an exchange where you can't think if a good response:

FRIEND: Before you come over, I've gotta clean up the place.
YOU: Don't worry, that's fine.

Now check it out after adding a comment about what you're not like or don't care about.

YOU: Don't worry, that's fine. I'm *not Martha Stewart* - I couldn't care less if you left out a plate of *macaroni* or something.

Now your friend has more options for connecting to your statement. Your friend could respond to the *Martha Stewart* keyword or the *macaroni* keyword.

FRIEND: Good, because I think Martha Stewart would faint as soon as she walked in my apartment door!

Or:

FRIEND: Funny you mention that, because stale macaroni is my favorite delicacy.

Whether you're initiating or responding with connectable opinions, topics, or keywords, the goal is the same: create conversations rich with options for all parties involved.

Let Free Information Be Your Guide to Better Responses

Look for *free information* to guide you. *Free? What? Where?* Free information is the clue to what topics may resonate with someone. People give away free information all the time. It's your job to look for it and take advantage of it. Free information is simply the information the other person brings up during the conversation that provides a glimpse of what they may be interested in talking more about (*or what they aren't interested in talking more about*). When you recognize this free information, try to connect with it.

In the following example, Justin proves he isn't skilled at picking up free information:

> JUSTIN: Hi Randal. How was your weekend?
>
> RANDAL: Good, we had a great time. I wasn't able to do much dancing, but that's fine.
>
> JUSTIN: Well, I'm glad you had a good time.
>
> RANDAL: Yeah, we did.

If Justin had read this book, his conversation may have proceeded more like the following:

> JUSTIN: Hi Randal. How was your weekend?
>
> RANDAL: Good, we had a great time. I wasn't able to do much dancing, but that's fine.
>
> JUSTIN: You weren't able to dance? Why not?
>
> RANDAL: Well, actually, what happened was...

The second time around, Justin picked up on the free information Randal offered and steered the conversation to the topic of why Randal couldn't dance. People won't always advertise with flashing signs what they desire to discuss. Stay alert for free information and hot button topics. People tend to add a little extra energy behind certain comments if they are more interested or invested in that topic.

The other day I was at a park with my four-year-old son. We were sitting on the grass when suddenly a large yellow lab came sprinting up to us. A woman, walking briskly after him, shouted to us, "Sorry!" As she got closer, she continued, "He likes to chase squirrels!"

She offered free information.

I simply acknowledged her statement with something straightforward, "Yeah, I can see that!" But the better approach would be to inquire further or offer free information in return. Try to connect to mutually shared interests and information. Find commonalities. Listen for the keywords. I should have responded with one of the following:

> OPTION 1: Hey, I have a Pug who does the same thing!
>
> OPTION 2: If I had to chase a dog like that I wouldn't need a fitness club!
>
> OPTION 3: That's okay - my son likes to chase squirrels too!

The sharing of information goes a long way toward creating and building rapport. All of these phrase options help establish a social connection – a relationship based on shared information, interests, and experiences.

Are You A Good Conversation Partner?

As a child, I remember asking my youngest brother to play tennis with me. After a few games of beating him soundly, I realized the experience was no longer enjoyable. We didn't play tennis again. It wasn't his fault, he just couldn't hit the ball back to me consistently enough to keep the game engaging. (*Update: Now that we're in our thirties, he would like everyone to know that he can kick my butt in any racket-related sport.)

It's important to always ask yourself if you're being a good partner. Saying "Yeah, I know" or "That's cool" or "I bet" is the equivalent of swatting the ball out of bounds. It essentially tells the other person you're willing to play the game, as long as they do most of the work and keep hitting the ball. If your conversation partner wants to keep talking, then by all means let them. In that case, nodding your head or acknowledging what they are saying is acceptable; but eventually they will want you to participate also. Look at the following exchange:

MEREDITH: I love your dog.
WILLY: Thanks.

Many conversations die an early death in exactly this manner every day, especially if one of the conversation partners refuses to disclose much information or expand on a thought or topic. *Don't make it difficult for others to converse with you.* Make conversation as effortless as possible. Help others draw good connections. Offer free information on relevant topics and give them options.

In the latter exchange, all Willy had to do was offer one little free nugget of information and it could have sparked an entire conversation. Let's visit a parallel universe and visit the second example again:

MEREDITH: I love your dog.
WILLY: Thanks. *He's getting very old.*
MEREDITH: Yeah? So is my dog - he's already nine years old - I can't believe it. The other day he...

Boom! Did you hear that sound? An interesting conversation was born.

It's bad enough if you fail to pick up on the free information, but even worse if you fail to offer free information. Remember the importance of painting your portrait and offering samples in Chapter 12: *Paint Your Portrait with Effective Self-Disclosing.* Let's look at a simple everyday example of the consequences of keeping the free stuff to yourself.

You're sitting down with your child and a lady notices your child's interesting shirt.

STRANGER: I have to tell you, I really love your son's shirt.
YOU: Oh thank you.

The conversation could end there. But you might continue the conversation by adding a piece of free information.

YOU: I bought it from the XYZ store - they have some great deals.
STRANGER: Oh yeah? The XYZ store over on 15 Mile Road?

YOU: Yep, and they have tons of shirts with the best images and characters - both my boys love their shirts.

STRANGER: Great, I've always wanted to go there. I have two sons as well.

Suddenly it becomes a real conversation, all because you gave them a little free information. Don't be an information hoarder! Give some away for free. In fact, have a fire sale! You will be amazed at the conversations that blossom if you just plant the seeds of free information.

Tailor your free information to your conversation partner's interests. When in doubt, err on the side of agreeing with them and supporting their feelings and thoughts. Recently a friend was telling me about a *new* car they bought. I responded:

That's awesome. I love new cars. Especially that new car smell when you first get in.

Later, another friend approached me with news about their purchase of a *slightly used* car. I responded:

That's great. I think that's the way to go - it doesn't make sense to buy brand new because you lose so much value right away.

Was I being dishonest? No, I have strong opinions on buying cars, and I chose aspects of my opinion that fit well with what each person was telling me.

Receiving compliments are notoriously hard because after you respond with "Thank you," what then? Providing a detail about what they're complimenting is often all that's necessary to keep the conversation flowing. For example, someone compliments your shoes, "I love those high heels, I don't know how you pull it off, but it all works really well on you." Rather than stopping the conversation train at "Thank you," add an additional detail they can latch onto. For example:

I got them on sale at XYZ Shoes, aren't they nice? I fell in love with them as soon as I saw them.

I wasn't sure if they'd be comfortable at work but so far my
feet feel great.

I only bring them out for special occasions, and since it's my
husband's anniversary today...

If you can't think of any new content or information to add, then at least ask a follow-up question so they are inclined to expand on a specific topic.

One of your primary goals should be to create social experiences the other person finds enjoyable. And part of that is making the conversation as effortless as possible. Stick to topics that intersect. Give them options you think they'd be interested in. Give them time to think by filling up space when needed. When you tell a story, lace it with hints about other topics for them to latch onto.

If you don't know the other person well, you may have to look for clues or rely on common/popular topics, until you find a hot topic that sticks. Part of the utility of small talk is its ability to reveal potential connections and specific hot topics.

Don't Be a Connection Blocker

If someone attempts to add information and you deny, or negate it, you may inadvertently slam the door on the conversation. That's right kids, don't do drugs, and don't be *a connection blocker*.

I recently picked up pizza and the guy taking my order was particularly chatty. It was winter, and during the course of paying, he asked, "Is it snowing out there?"

It wasn't snowing. I could have just answered truthfully, "No," and blocked or stifled additional connections. That's all he was asking, right? Wrong. His question was simply his go-to device for starting conversations with customers. He didn't give a crap about the weather! He probably asked the same question to most of his customers that night! I felt like seeing where the conversation with the pizza guy could lead, so I added a simple connection.

ME: No, but knowing this state, we could get a blizzard any minute!

PIZZA GUY: Isn't that right! I'll tell ya one of these days I need to move south. I'm not sure I can handle this weather much longer.

ME: Yeah, I know. I wouldn't even have to move far. I'd be fine with going to _____, I heard they have the best _____ there!

One of the most common questions of all time for initiating a conversation with a friend is: "Have you seen/listened to _____ yet?" If you are asked that question, instead of blocking with "No, I haven't," and ending the conversation there, try to consider the following:

Why haven't you?
What prevented you from watching it?
What have you heard/read about it?
What are you missing out on?
What do you plan to do about it?

If you address even one of those questions, your response would be much more interesting, and would help your partner to connect. The following example responses are alternatives to "No":

No, I haven't - but I really need to. Everyone keeps mentioning it. I'm like 'why is everyone talking about this lady who rides a horse everywhere?' I'm so confused - I need to see it soon.

No, I haven't. Maybe I'll watch it tonight - even if my husband doesn't want to, I'll force him to watch it with me. I'll tell him it's a fair trade for going to a baseball game with him!

Another common scenario involves someone telling you something you already know. "Hey, did you hear about _____?" Or "I was reading that only the female Mosquitos bite people." Many PCs would be inclined to block the conversation at "I know." However, ECs may say "I know," but they would add another detail. ECs may also employ the contrast technique to elaborate on how they didn't know either, until some event occurred. "Yeah, I actually didn't know that until I went to _____, and they mentioned _____. I used to always think _____."

But What If I Can't Connect?

A while ago I visited a Halloween event, and a man dressed as a pirate tried to initiate dialogue with me. He initiated with "I knew a pirate with one leg, named 'Peggy'!" I was speechless. Of course I chuckled, but then what? How do you respond to something so random?

Sometimes you can't, and that's okay. Don't feel bad. If you really need to be bailed out by saying something – anything – then save yourself by talking about how you don't know what to say. "I have no idea how to respond to that." It's the break-in-case-of-emergency option.

Remember, some of the best conversationalists have thousands of previously assembled thoughts (PATs) ready to go for any occasion. But even most ECs aren't prepared for pirate jokes. Luckily, in this case, I witnessed a classic PAT response while watching the very same pirate talk to someone else later. He asked a stranger, "What is a pirate's favorite letter? ....Rrrrrrr." The gentleman had the perfect response ready, "I thought Pirate's preferred the 'C'!" Get it? The gentlemen may have been an exceptional conversationalist (and probably used that corny line before). And now you have a PAT for your next pirate encounter. You're welcome.

How many times have you been to an event where you asked someone what they did for a living and had no idea how to respond? Sometimes you'll know *nothing* about their occupation and could risk dragging the conversation through boring land if you ask too many questions about it. No offense to engineers, but living around Detroit I have witnessed my share of engineers who ended up killing the conversation prematurely with details about their occupation (unless they're talking to other engineers). I eventually discovered a technique that works well: Admit your ignorance right away. Maybe someone brings up their obsession with a type of country music, and you can't even remember the last time you heard a country song. Saying "I honestly have *no* idea who that even is. I'm so clueless when it comes to _____!" is a playful way to indicate that their conversation topic may not fare well. You could also try "I know nothing about _____, do you like it?" or "And I thought my job sounded complex, I have no idea what that is." Next, you can either ask them to try to explain it further, or pivot to something else before any awkwardness sets in, like, "My brother always makes fun of me for not knowing anything about XYZ – but he doesn't know anything about WXY, so we're even."

Before I had children, one time a colleague was telling me a story about how she was overly anxious to take her baby anywhere for fear of getting him sick. I couldn't relate at all to her experience. So I just admitted my lack of experience, and tried to mention something similar. "Yeah, I know it's not even close, but I'm paranoid to take my dog to any boarding place; I can't even imagine how you must feel taking a little human somewhere."

Answer the Invisible Questions

Great conversationalists often avoid awkward silences by answering questions *before* they are asked. This technique is useful when you can't think of what to say next, or you have to carry the load for a struggling conversationalist. Think of questions the other person may be wondering, or soon wonder, but hasn't vocalized or thought of yet.

I once worked for a small company where every few months, a very awkward event took place. Every time someone had a birthday, a group of coworkers would surprise the lucky person at his or her cubicle. As many as ten people would huddle around the coworker, present cupcakes, and offer the standard well-wishes. After the obligatory congratulations were over, the huddled coworkers always stood there in silence, anxiously waiting to hear from the birthday person. But if the lucky coworker couldn't carry the conversation for a few minutes, the nice gesture quickly turned to awkwardness. The people who fared well would anticipate possible questions, and simply answer those questions before being asked.

A typical birthday question is "What are you doing to celebrate?" You can answer that question *before anyone actually asks it*. "Well, I didn't really plan anything for my birthday, maybe I'll go see a movie – I'm so boring. Does anyone have any good ideas?"

If you're at a loss for words, or dealing with a reticent conversationalist, it helps to think about what they could be wondering or curious about. In fact, many people state the invisible question out-loud. "Why did I do that? Well, because I _____."

Sometimes You Have to Carry Their Weight

Exceptional conversationalists excel at creating good conversation with anyone. But how is that possible if the other person isn't contributing much? ECs adjust their style to adapt to their partner. If they see someone struggling, they help them out. Sometimes this even means putting words in the other person's mouth. This happens more than you realize – often when an extrovert and introvert talk (or an EC and PC). During my shy days, I noticed extroverts doing this to me frequently.

An EC might ask, "Do you like going out?" And noticing I'm struggling (or just taking too long), the EC may interject, "I bet you like just hanging out at home on a Saturday night, right?" Which made responding easier for me, "Yeah, exactly."

ECs sometimes carry the load for PCs by guessing or observing the PC's feelings. "You're probably like, 'I just want to get out of here!'" My wife and I have had many conversations with other couples, where often the chatty wife would talk for her more reserved husband. "John loves fishing too, don't you John?" Be careful of cutting people off too quickly though.

> **REMEMBER:** *Extrovert* does not equal *exceptional conversationalist.*
> It's been discovered that the most successful people are actually
> "ambiverts" – people who could tap into both their introverted and
> extroverted personality traits. They are more conversationally
> flexible, more intuitive, and more influential. Sometimes it helps
> to be outgoing and social, and sometimes it's prudent to sit back
> and let the other person do the talking.

The following conversation took place at a hair salon. (I admit it's a
long example, but I promise it has a surprise ending!)

PERSON A: Did you go watch any fireworks?

PERSON B: I used to go to all of them as a teenager.

PERSON A: I was so crazy - I would drive all over town looking
for them. I didn't care if someone hit my car.

PERSON B: I used to drive this big boat car. It was probably as
big as my living room. People would try to threaten me too.
They'd say 'move or I'll hit your car!' and I'd say 'go ahead!'

PERSON A: They don't make them like that anymore. I was just
at a car show in Detroit.

PERSON B: Did you see that new X hybrid? Apparently it's like
the Rolls Royce of hybrid cars. Honestly, I'd rather just buy
a house.

PERSON A: That's a lottery car - you only buy that if you win
the lottery.

PERSON B: But actually if I won the lottery I'd probably buy
something else - maybe a deluxe Winnebago. I'd see the
states. Quit my job. Tell my boss to go shove it where the *sun
don't shine!*

PERSON A: We can dream can't we?

What I forgot to mention is that PERSON A and PERSON B were
actually the *same person*: Linda. She was the hair dresser and was forced
to make all the connections because her conversation partner (the client

– let's call him Pete) only gave her an occasional *nod* or a "Yeah". Pete was a major information hoarder and probably the worst conversationalist I have ever witnessed. Granted, he may not have been in a mood to talk, but he was very rude about it. The hair stylist just connected to herself over and over again in order to keep the conversation going. She could have had this conversation with her goldfish, it didn't really matter who the other person was.

The aforementioned conversation is not that rare. Sometimes it's necessary for you to carry a conversation until you hit upon something the other person can contribute to (or wants to contribute to). Sometimes you may feel like you're forcing the conversation to occur through sheer will-power and brute force. And obviously if you're not receiving any positive signs, maybe it's time to press the abort button and move on to something else.

CHAPTER 17: USE IT OR LOSE IT

It's important to prime your brain to look for more connections than it currently does. We're going to try two free-association activities.

1. See how many connections you can make to each of the single generic words from the list below. Can you generate five statements related to each word? 10? 20? Push yourself to form connections in a few seconds or less.

2. Go back and choose one word to start with, then choose one word to end with. Form a series of connections that lead from the starting word to the ending word. This is good practice for steering conversations.

    "FOOD"

    "FISH"

    "HOME"

    "CAR"

    "SCHOOL"

    "DRINK"

CHAPTER 17: REVIEW

Before this chapter:

- ✓ The four primary PATs: Comments, Knowledge, Opinions, and Autobiographical stuff
- ✓ The TAPP topics: Things, Activities, People, and Places
- ✓ Initiate with Feeler statements (You, Environment, and Them) and Problem Feelers
- ✓ FOOFAAE: Feelings, Observations, Opinions, Facts, Actions, Autobiographical, and Events
- ✓ Be proactive and consider a second question or comment
- ✓ The Golden Ratio (ISPC): Initial comment, Support, Post comment, and Connection
- ✓ Observations pair well with personal statements, actions, or examples
- ✓ Post comments are usually summaries, realizations, conclusions, or hypothetical conclusions
- ✓ Angles and contrasts are crucial for sounding more interesting
- ✓ Connectable opinions are relatable and encourage multiple ways to respond

From this chapter:

- ✓ Connect faster with FOOFAAE as your guide
- ✓ Free Information will help direct your responses in the right direction
- ✓ Listen for keywords
- ✓ Don't be a connection blocker

Key takeaway from this chapter:

It's important to give your partner options, listen for free information, and avoid being a connection blocker.

Coming up next:

Finally, the entire book culminates with being an exceptional listener and growing the conversation as a team.

Preview: *Exceptional listening is so much more than staying quiet and paying attention – it's about forming genuine connections with people. This chapter helps you upgrade your listening skills, develop deeper relationships, and learn how to collaboratively grow the conversation.*

[CHAPTER 18]

LISTEN AND GROW THE CONVERSATION TOGETHER

"Hey You! Are You Listening?"

What does it mean to be a "good listener" anyway? Or better yet, an "exceptional listener"? Exceptional listening isn't easy. It requires effort. Exceptional listening is so much more than simply staying quiet and paying attention. Everyone's listening behavior falls into one of the four levels below:

The Four Listening Levels

The Narcissist Level

They are inattentive, distracted, and impatient. They change the topic prematurely, talk over people, and exhibit poor eye-contact.

The Pet Dog Level

They offer minimal responses and acknowledgement (e.g. "Yeah" or "That's cool."). They stay relatively quiet.

The Nice Guy Level (AKA Effective Listening)

They maintain good eye contact and use substantive phrases to indicate understanding and acknowledgement (e.g. "That must be very hard to deal with."). They paraphrase and reflect facts/feelings of what the talker said (e.g. "Wow, so basically they really don't want to fix the car?"). They ask follow-up questions and show genuine concern and interest. They actively seek similarities and discuss mutual interests.

The Exceptional Listening Level

See The Nice Guy Level. They expand on the talker's thoughts and ideas. They add unique comments and help *grow* the conversation in general.

In the following exchange, Larry attempts to be a good listener based on the self-help books he's been reading.

PEGGY: I don't think I like that show.

LARRY: If I'm understanding you correctly, you're saying that you don't like that show, is that correct?

Let's be real – if you observe real conversations long enough, you realize people rarely respond in the manner Larry just did (except on bad TV shows or stuffy self-help communication books). Many books offer advice based on the perception of what good listening is versus the reality of good listening. Sure, Larry, demonstrated that he heard what Peggy said, but he also demonstrated he'd make a better trial lawyer than a good listener.

Being an effective listener isn't difficult. That's why I'm shocked at how many dreadfully bad listeners I encounter. Communication experts dedicate large sections of their books to listening skills because there's a shortage of good listeners in the world. Effective listening – and especially exceptional listening – requires effort. Your listening skills remain critical to not only maintaining genuine conversations, but to maintaining genuine relationships.

The reality is most people understand the core principles of how to be at least an effective listener. Poor listening habits stem from something beyond a lack of effective techniques: bad listeners often don't care. No book is going to inspire you to care – that part is up to you. Some people are too selfish or lazy to try. (We all know someone like that!) "Caring" also means caring about the other person more than the infinite amount of distractions in daily life. Be in the present moment with the other person. Focus on them, not your cell phone. Fully engage. Don't show off your multi-tasking skills and attempt other activities while listening. Give 100% when you can (but don't psycho-stare either). The other person will notice if you're not fully engaged – but rarely will they voice the concern to your face.

 Quick Tip: Grow your relationships like you would grow vegetables. Good relationships, like bountiful harvests, require effort, energy, and regular watering and care. For these reasons, selfish people often find it difficult to keep long-term relationships.

If you care about improving your listening skills, then the following seven techniques will send your listening skills to the next level.

The Seven Steps of Exceptional Listening
1. Pay Attention to the Entire Message
2. Echo Their Message
3. Encourage Sharing
4. Be the Source of Positivity
5. Grow Their Topic with Them
6. Take Advantage of Hypothetical Statements
7. Maintain Some Balance

Step 1. Pay Attention to the Entire Message

Exceptional listening starts with hearing and receiving the correct message – the *real* message, not just the words on the surface. The real message also exists within the other person's body language and emotions bubbling beneath the surface. It's important to pay attention to their entire body of signals within the situation and conversation context.

Everyone desires to be fully understood. If you feel that you're receiving mixed signals, try to seek clarification. Not much is more frustrating for someone than being misunderstood.

Pay attention to both the situational and emotional wavelength. It's not a bad idea to relate to the facts of the situation you find yourselves in, and then move to the emotional aspects. Dialogue over the facts of the final exam, restaurant, sports team, etc., can kick-start great conversations, but the deeper bonds form over the expression and exchanging of emotion. Exploring the joy, regret, frustration, etc., is the wavelength many poor listeners fail to connect with. Check out the example below:

LARRY: How's it going?

PEGGY: I'm okay. I just missed a deadline and my boss is not going to be happy.

LARRY: That's not good...why did you miss the deadline?

Larry did an admirable job, but he didn't sync with the emotional wavelength very much, instead he focused on a factual detail. Let's give him another shot.

LARRY: How's it going?

PEGGY: I'm okay. I just missed a deadline and my boss is not going to be happy.

LARRY: That's not good...I've done that a few times myself. Do you think he'll understand?

Much better Larry! He quickly connected on the emotional wavelength. Pay attention and try to acknowledge both wavelengths if possible.

Step 2. Echo Their Message

The simplest and easiest tool for both echoing sentiment and demonstrating understanding is the *Rephrase* or *Paraphrase*. The rephrase was mentioned in Chapter 10: *Start Small with Small Talk*, as a fantastic way to buy time, and they come in handy for listening too. They require little thought or effort, but still indicate to the speaker that you understand and you were paying attention at a basic level. Sometimes all that's required is that you say what they said, in a slightly different way. (You can even repeat the exact words, but change the inflection/energy level a little.)

Jason and Joyce love to rephrase each other:

JASON: I like oysters.

JOYCE: Yeah, you *really* like oysters.

JASON: You like oysters too.

JOYCE: Yeah, I love oysters.

Rephrasing helps you quickly form connections and express similarities. It's a quick way to indicate that you're on the same page as your conversational partner and that you're paying attention.

Another option is to *rephrase and confirm* the significance of what they just said.

YOUR MANAGER: I feel like we should buy XYZ.

YOU: Yeah, buying more XYZ is the right thing to do.

These types of rephrases occur a million times a day in the corporate world. They are perfect for letting someone know that you're on the same page, but at the same time, give the impression you have your own opinion on the matter.

Rephrases don't have to be simple, though. Try to add some creativity to your rephrases. Echo the sentiment, but take advantage of more original and colorful words and ideas.

PEGGY: I don't want to just give up on it.

LARRY: Yeah, *you can't push the eject button yet.*

One level beyond rephrasing is *summarizing.* Summarize the main points – wrap everything into a neat little package. Summarizing also has more potential to be entertaining and fun.

Check out some example below:

So you're basically saying your dog is more masculine than me.

So you're basically saying that you want to break up with him, right?

It sounds like you really wish you had a new job.

So he's essentially a hot dog addict, is what I'm thinking.

Summarizing sounds simple enough – but there is a subtle art to it. Many summaries take the form of conclusions. (Think back to post comments from Chapter 14: *Learn How to Effectively Support Your Comments*). One time I was telling a story about how I offered potato chips to my three-year-old son as payment for bringing me things. After finishing the story, one of my friends offered a great conclusion/summary, "So the secret to Rowan's heart is *junk food* – good to know." Check out a few more conclusion/summaries (*italicized*) below:

> MARGARET: My Bloody Mary had too much asparagus and cucumbers.
> WILLIAM: *So basically you drank a salad.*
> MARGARET: Yeah, exactly!

> MARGARET: How was the trip?
> JOE: It was fun, but also kind of stressful with the kids running around everywhere.
> MARGARET: I bet! *You almost need a vacation from your vacation!*
> JOE: Exactly!

Step 3. Encourage Sharing

Help them explore their thoughts. Pull them out. Many people won't naturally spill their can of beans without some effort on your part. Everyone has two main layers of information they share: **public** and **private**. Public information (e.g. details about their trip to the super market, how they feel about the weather, etc.) is easy to pull out and sufficient for small talk. More personal information (e.g. specific details about their family, feelings on important topics, etc.) require a certain level of trust, respect, and safety. They need to feel like you understand them and won't judge. It's also important to prove you're interested, without being overly nosy.

Part of your job as the conversation partner is to notice the hint (or *free information*) and encourage them to extrapolate. Many people appreciate the co-exploration of their thoughts and feelings because they may not have fully fleshed out how they feel about certain things.

Regular Listening vs Therapy Listening

My book focuses on everyday listening situations. There's another type of listening I refer to as "therapy listening": The situation where one person is experiencing a highly traumatic event and is pouring their heart and soul out on the table. In such situations, it's important to proceed with caution and let the other person do most of the talking. Offering too much advice is risky. Being that I'm not a therapist – and my wife is – I'll refrain from writing about how therapy conversations should proceed.

Rephrasing won't always encourage someone to continue elaborating. Leverage the power of observations to point out some part you'd like to explore. Check out some observations that encourage additional comments:

> You look like you want to get out of here.
> That's really nice - it's great that you're helping them.
> You sound like there's more to it.
> That's crazy - I'm glad you made it out okay.

Don't forget to take advantage of techniques already covered in this book, like superlatives, labels, etc.

> How did you know that? You're like an encyclopedia of cheese facts.
> You're the only one I know who would have done that!
> That's the craziest thing I've heard in a while.

Your follow-up questions also serve to validate their feelings. Thoughtful follow-up questions not only signal that you were paying attention, but that you have thought about what they said in more depth than simple rephrasing would indicate. Some are straightforward:

> Hey, I was wondering, did you ever take _____ to the _____ ?
> So what happened next? Did you ever seen him again?

How did _____ ever work out? Did it go OK?
Is that what you want to do?

And some are lighter and more playful:

Do you feel like you're just running around putting out fires all
day?
Were you like, 'Listen dude, I don't want any more!'?

Step 4. Be a Source of Positivity

Shit happens. And for some people, shit happens a lot. Our perspective is important to how we all deal with the pain in our lives. People will sometimes talk to you about something negative, depressing, painful, or disappointing. Exceptional listeners act as more than just a shoulder to cry on, but actively help the other person reframe their thoughts into something more positive. You can help others alter their perspectives and see positive aspects when their visions may be clouded or biased. You can be a beacon of hope or light in their world. Obviously, it's important to acknowledge their pain and what they are going through, however, positivity always trumps negativity when it comes to exceptional conversation. Instead of echoing their sentiment with only "That sucks," try adding "Well, at least..."

You arrive to work.

YOU: Good morning, how are you?
COWORKER: Eh...it's Monday. I've been better. You?
YOU: Hey, at least we're not in Boston right now, they're
getting about two feet of snow right now from the
snowpocalypse.
COWORKER: True! I'm so glad I'm not there. My drive in was a
piece of cake compared to what they're going through.

Your friend complains about how they had to host their obnoxious cousins for Thanksgiving.

FRIEND: It was horrible. I had to cook and clean for everyone – and no one even thanked me.

Rather than solely rephrasing their negative experience, you could add a positive spin.

YOU: That doesn't sound fun. Well at least you didn't have to drive anywhere and battle through the snow drifts right?

Clichés certainly have a place in the listening world. In fact, many people use them as filler when they can't think of a better response or want to offer some advice in a safe manner.

For example, I could respond to your situation with: "Well, as they say, *all's well that ends well* right?" or "There's always *one rotten apple* right?" or "You *win some you lose some*," or "*Everything happens for a reason*, you know?"

Platitudes like those can also offer comfort. In fact, they frame the situation in a way that's well-known and understandable; they acknowledge the fact many other people have experienced a similar situation. The exception to the positivity rule? When you're talking to someone who revels in cynicism – as the saying goes, *misery loves company*. There's actually another exception: Sometimes going negative and disparaging the person or thing that has been hurting you is cathartic. If your friend needs to release some anger – by all means join in the ex-boyfriend/ex-girlfriend bashing.

At a primal level, we all desire to feel important and know our thoughts and feelings matter. You can prove this in interesting ways. Show the other person's impact. Express their positive affect on you or something else.

How did you get so good at _____?

I'm glad you're here. If I had to _____ one more time I'd go crazy!

I wish I could draw like that.

You always know how to fix things like this, I'm sure you'll
eventually figure it out.

Hide a little flattery in your statements. Sincere and subtle flattery will
sometimes yield surprising results – you may even receive some flattery
in return!

YOU: These cookies are delicious!

KATHLEEN: It's my new recipe. I'm glad you like them.

YOU: I don't know how you always make them stay so moist. You
should start a cookie blog or something!

One a side note, the quickest route to negative conversations is
through judging, criticizing, and arguing with each other. Not much will
derail a conversation faster. If you disagree on a serious topic – don't
jump into an argument too quickly. Ask exploratory questions in an
objective way. It can be challenging to reel in the emotion, but it's
important to stay neutral during potentially risky conversations. I've
been in 1,000 arguments in my life, and there were two times where
someone actually said, "Yep. You're right. Your argument convinced me
to change my mind." Those two times don't make up for the 998 people I
annoyed. If you insist on pushing the issue, bring up your points more
objectively. Explore instead. Find out why they think the way they do. If
you must try to convince them, try indirect questions that help them lead
to the conclusion on their own.

Your goal should be to leave people feeling better after talking with
you than how they felt before the conversation started. Someone may
express frustration or embarrassment in a subtle manner, but there may
be more to the story than they're letting on. Regardless, help make them
feel better; put something into perspective/context, offer a compliment,
etc. Check out the following example where Ruth acknowledges Sarah's
concern, and also puts everything into perspective so Sarah doesn't feel
as bad about the situation.

SARAH: The festival was fun, but Jaden wouldn't go on any
rides.

RUTH: Oh, poor guy... were they scary looking? Maybe he just
needed some time to get acclimated.

SARAH: Maybe. He's kind of a scaredy-cat in general though. I
hope he gets over it one day.

RUTH: I bet that happens to a lot of kids though, roller coasters
can be scary. I'm still scared of the X ride at Cedar Point!

Step 5. Grow Their Topic with Them

Reflecting the other person's message in a new way helps them work
through sides of the issue or topic they may not have thought of before.
ECs expand and grow the message beyond the original intent. Your goal
is to grow more than just their thoughts – *grow the topic in general*. When
you offer your unique contributions, stories, and opinions, the
conversation as a whole benefits.

Notice in the following examples how Kenny picks up on underlying
meanings/feelings and offers Steph another way to express how she feels.
Kenny also offers his own feelings on the topic to help keep it balanced
and develop the rapport.

KENNY: What are you doing this weekend?

STEPH: Well, Steve is out of town so I'm just going to sleep in
and relax.

KENNY: I hear you - sometimes you just need a day to unwind
and do nothing at all. I call those my 'lazy-days.'

STEPH: Exactly! I haven't had a 'lazy-day' in a long time.

KENNY: Yeah, I don't think I can remember the last time my kids
let me sleep in.

Expanding the other person's message and topic with new thoughts
not only proves you're digesting and processing their words and
meanings, but offers new connection possibilities and improves the
overall flow of the conversation.

In the following example, notice how Cat expands on Mark's initial
statements. Mark doesn't ask a question or ask for feedback on anything,

but Cat takes the initiative to offer new connections and share thoughts (all the while keeping it focused on Mark's topic).

> MARK: I think I'll try the sandwich with bacon. *I love bacon.*
>
> CAT: *Yeah so do I.* You can put bacon on anything and it would taste good...salads...omelets...I can never get enough.
>
> MARK: I know! It seems like bacon is all the rage this year - everyone's talking about it.
>
> CAT: Yeah, I feel like every cooking show is using it this year. Every time I go get fast food I see a sign for a new bacon burger. Have you tried the Baconator yet?

In a sense, once someone plants a seed, the exceptional listener helps it grow larger than it would grow on its own. Exceptional listeners aim to be the "gardeners" of messages and don't worry too much about the quantity of contributions they are making, but instead focus on the quality of the conversation itself.

Examine the following conversation between two friends. *The names are intentionally left out because it doesn't really matter who contributed what.*

> I hate split peas.
>
> Me too! When I was a kid I announced that all peas were my mortal enemy.
>
> I think most kids did probably did.
>
> True, probably because they're so mushy.
>
> Most vegetables are usually served mushy, that's probably why kids don't usually like vegetables in general.
>
> Broccoli especially.
>
> That's an entirely different level of hatred.
>
> But carrots, I've always loved carrots.
>
> I just had the best carrot side dish at Peart's Steakhouse.

Each person contributed to the growth of the conversation, and that's what matters in the end.

What if you simply agree and can't think of anything else to say? Try to follow the ISPC guidelines if you can. Did the other person stop after offering an opinion? If yes, *maybe you can provide the support?*

Check out another interaction where Melissa not only expands the general theme/topic of the conversation, but adds support to Libby's initial statement.

> LIBBY: Now that my son is four he's growing so fast.
>
> MELISSA: Yeah, I'm surprised you can even find time to buy all the new clothes for him.
>
> LIBBY: Yeah, I'm not sure how I get it done. Isn't it crazy how they grow like weeds at that age?
>
> MELISSA: Aiden is six and he finally started slowing down - thank goodness, because I was tired of shopping every month!

Every opinion has two primary responses – agreement or disagreement. If simply agreeing is too boring, the straw man strategy from Chapter 15: *Build More Interesting and Engaging Comments*, should prove helpful. Watch Bridget put it into action below:

> MEGAN: We're thinking of getting a dog soon.
>
> BRIDGET: Oh yeah? What kind?
>
> MEGAN: I'm not sure, probably a lab. I love labs. They get along with anyone.

In this case, Bridget wants to agree, but instead of sticking with a boring "I love labs too," and stopping there, she connects to Megan's last few words about how they get along with anyone.

> BRIDGET: Yeah, I don't get people who have dogs that want to fight or bite everything. What's the point of having a dog if you can't take him anywhere?

Notice how Bridget employs the straw man technique beautifully by setting up a straw man (people who intentionally buy mean dogs) and offering an opinion on them. It serves as an interesting contrast to

Megan's opinion, while still agreeing with her and growing the topic. Bravo Bridget!

Step 6. Take Advantage of Hypothetical Statements

The hypothetical statement is a perfect option for growing a sentiment in an interesting and playful way. Talk about what *could, should, or would* happen. On the flipside, mention what didn't happen. Let's break down an example below:

> A colleague expresses their frustrations to you about a situation at work.
>
> COLLEAGUE: I don't know if I handled it correctly.
> YOU: I think you did a good job.
>
> *So far, so good, but it could be much better with a hypothetical statement.*
>
> YOU: At least you didn't storm into his office and say something offensive like, 'And another thing! I think your new hair-cut sucks!'

The aforementioned hypothetical proves that you understand what they were thinking and feeling – but in a more dynamic way. It also helps them express their feelings in a new, playful way. Here's an example with the hypothetical italicized.

> You're at the movies with a date.
>
> DATE: I just wanted a small cup of water but they made me pay for the normal size fountain drink!
> YOU: Really? What's the deal with that? Like they can't afford to give you a cup just for water. It's not like *you're going to jump over the counter and steal some Sprite while they're not looking!*

Injecting yourself into their story is another technique for offering hypothetical statements. Think about those times where someone just finished telling a story, or describing a particular situation, and you can't think of how to respond. Inject yourself into the situation or story. If you experienced the events in the story, how would you respond? How would you act? How would you be affected? Examine how Catherine injects herself into Mark's situation:

> MARK: And then the water started flooding my basement and I started seeing sparks...it was not good.
>
> CATHERINE: That scares the hell out of me. If I saw sparks and water, I'd be like 'Honey, we need to get out of here! *Now!*'

Step 7. Maintain Some Balance

Remember your primary goal for most conversations: Create a pleasant social experience for everyone involved. Don't spend time worrying about your "grade" as a listener.

The role of an exceptional listener comes with many responsibilities. One of those jobs includes maintaining the balance among contributors. Just because someone else is talking ad nauseam doesn't mean they desire to *continue* talking – many people talk only to fill up uncomfortable silence. (Especially if they know you're not going to help fill the silence!) Additionally, just because someone is talking doesn't mean you have to sit in the passenger seat and let them drive you all over town. In fact, most people don't want to feel as if they are in a one-sided therapy session. Most people would prefer a balanced conversation so while you are talking, they have time to formulate their next thoughts. On the contrary, if you feel you're talking too much, make an effort to get the other person more involved.

Are your conversations usually balanced and seamless like the first of the following diagrams? Or are they more unbalanced and choppy like the second diagram?

Diagram 1.

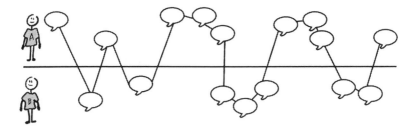

Diagram 2.

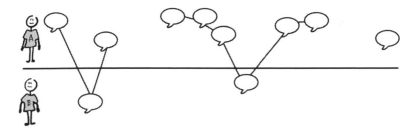

CHAPTER 18: USE IT OR LOSE IT

This exercise is a bit different. Up until this point, most of the examples have been isolated from the contexts of larger conversations. I have included bonus conversations to study because seeing the entire conversation in action should provide additional insights. These are lengthy, but exceptional samples, hand-picked to enrich your understanding of exceptional conversations. Through careful analysis, you will notice many of the techniques covered in this book. Look out for exceptional initiating, feelers, disclosing, angles, support, post comments, rephrases, questions, opinions, observations, action statements, drivers, fillers, and more! Besides reading them to yourself, try to read them aloud. The more you rehearse each conversation, the more your brain will internalize the flow and structure of many of the statements.

Exercises like these help promote *long term* behavior change. It's important to build effective mental schemas for how exceptional conversations proceed. You probably have encoded many ineffective scripts over your life time, and exercises like these go a long way toward re-coding and improving them!

If you're feeling extra ambitious, treat the examples like scenes in a play and try to memorize some lines! Can you re-enact the scene? Can you play both characters differently?

Like a professional athlete, the work you put in when no one is around pays dividends when it really matters.

CHAPTER 18: REVIEW

Before this chapter:

- ✓ The four primary PATs: Comments, Knowledge, Opinions, and Autobiographical stuff
- ✓ The TAPP topics: Things, Activities, People, and Places
- ✓ Initiate with Feeler statements (You, Environment, and Them) and Problem Feelers
- ✓ FOOFAAE: Feelings, Observations, Opinions, Facts, Actions, Autobiographical, and Events
- ✓ Be proactive and consider a second question or comment
- ✓ The Golden Ratio (ISPC): Initial comment, Support, Post comment, and Connection
- ✓ Observations pair well with personal statements, actions, or examples
- ✓ Post comments are usually summaries, realizations, conclusions, or hypothetical conclusions
- ✓ Angles and contrasts are crucial for sounding more interesting
- ✓ Connectable opinions are relatable and encourage multiple ways to respond
- ✓ Free Information will help direct your responses in the right direction
- ✓ Don't be a connection blocker

From this chapter:
- ✓ Remember the Seven Steps of Exceptional Listening: Pay Attention, Echo Their Message, Encourage Sharing, Be the Source of Positivity, Grow Their Topic with Them, Add Hypothetical Statements, and Maintain Balance
- ✓ Half of exceptional listening comes down to effort and desire

Key takeaway from this chapter:

The ultimate goal of the exceptional listener is to help grow the conversation topic into something better than what the person could do on their own.

Coming up next:

What comes next is up to you!

Conversation Study 1

Four work acquaintances (Person A, B, C, and D) all engage in lively small talk at lunch. First, notice how each initial statement triggers a handful of comments, eventually transitioning to a related topic. Second, pay attention to how a majority of the comments involve sharing information about the chosen topic.

Person A initiates with the first topic about their soda habits.

> A: I thought I'd break my streak and have a Coke today. I used to be addicted to soda. Basically every day - even for breakfast. But now I'm down to one a week. I'm very proud of myself. It's probably my greatest accomplishment in life so far.
>
> B: I used to love drinking soda, but I'm completely off it now. I tried it a while ago and didn't even like it - it's like my body rejects it as a foreign substance now.
>
> C: Ever had McDonald's Coke? It's the best. I don't know what magic they use, but it's better than buying Coke itself from the store.
>
> D: Maybe they add extra sugar or something.

Person C introduces a new topic within the food/beverage category.

> C: I saw a commercial for Taco Bell breakfast recently. I'm not sure how I feel about that.
>
> D: Never tried it.
>
> A: It's actually surprisingly good.
>
> B: Their coffee too...and that's no easy feat.

Person A transitions to a sub topic of the previous topic.

D: The Taco Bell menu confuses me. I feel like I need to speak Spanish just to understand the difference between burrito, cheeserito, fajito...

B: Have you tried the new Quesarito? The first time I had it, it blew my mind. A quesadilla wrapped around a burrito...so good...It made me so happy.

C: Taco bell is the best junk food. And I consider it in the healthy junk food class. Not like real junk food places like Greasy Joe's down on 5th Avenue.

Person D takes the food category in a new direction.

D: Ever had Conrad's on 4th? Now they have some good burgers. I always get the Godfather. It's so good.

B: Which one has the cheesy barbeque sauce and a side of deep fried Mac and cheese? That's what I'm talking about.

C: Oh that sounds *really* healthy. Do they actually serve any vegetables at that place?

A: If you count the French fries, then yes, they serve a ton of vegetables!

D: It's very healthy!

Person B introduces a related food topic.

B: I just saw a coupon for Burger King while I was cleaning. I was like 'Oh I forgot about Burger King!' I haven't been there in so long!

D: I like Burger King better than McDonalds.

A: What about Wendy's? Don't forget about the Frosty!

C: That's all I like there.

B: If Taco Bell could serve Frostys, it would be the ultimate fast food chain. It would literally take over the world.

Conversation Study 2

One thing you may notice about the following conversation is the lack of questions. When two friends are actively sharing, commenting, and contributing to the conversation, *asking questions* isn't always necessary to maintain the flow. (From now on the names have been removed so you focus on the flow rather than who said what.)

I could use a double bacon burger and fries from XYZ Burger.

You're giving me a craving for XYZ burgers now.

Sorry!

I love their fries too. And there's always a bonus fry. It's always at the bottom of the bag. It waits for you and gets all cold and hard. But just when you thought there were none left, you get a bonus.

I know, they're great. And I don't even care if it's all black and burned - I'll still eat it!

Yeah I love their greasy food. Your arteries might get clogged for two weeks but it's worth it!

They have good olive burgers too.

I know, and those are so hard to find anywhere. I've looked all over.

I was hanging out with some friends a while ago and it turned out one of the guys owns a XYZ burger place.

Wow. That would be so much fun. Oh my gosh, I'd weigh at least 300 pounds. If I knew him I'd be like 'Can I come in and buy your XYZ ABC in bulk and take it home?'

Yeah those are so good. They're just so flavorful. They don't taste cheap. I don't know how they do it. And I'm not even a big guacamole fan except for their ABC. They put X and Z on it too...it' so good.

I tried to do that at home once and it didn't turn out like that at all! I don't know how they do it, it's like magic.

They must have Harry Potter working in the kitchen back there or something.

Froger's sells something similar. I remember I could find them all over the place when I was a kid.

You'll always find something similar lying around our house though. My husband is Mexican, and his mom will come over and put a few authentic shells on the pan and fry them up and serve them as snacks. Those kind aren't in the stores, but there's a lady who sells them out of a cart at Bostco down on Main Street.

I'll have to go there some time!

Yeah you should, she's great.

Anyway I should get back to doing my work.

Okay, same here, catch ya later.

See ya.

Conversation Study 3

Our house actually just sold.

Wow, that was fast! Didn't you just have it listed?

Yeah, it sold in two days, we couldn't believe it.

That's great for you guys. Did it sell for what you wanted?

Yeah, exactly what we asked for. They said they want it but we have to agree to fixing the back door first - we were like, 'Heck yeah, we'll fix that right away!' So we took the offer and haven't looked back.

That's great. Yeah, fixing a door is a small price to pay in order to sell your house.

Yeah, so now we just have the big pieces of furniture left to move and we'll be done - I'm so excited.

Are you moving it yourself or hiring someone?

We actually found this great non-profit moving company that donates to inner city kids...

So you can move and give to charity at the same time, you can't beat that! And moving to XYZ will give you a much shorter drive to work right?

Yeah, like 30 minutes shorter. I'll actually get to watch the six o'clock news when I get home now.

I used to drive that way all the time to visit my parents...I could do it in my sleep probably.

Yeah, I've nearly fallen asleep a few times driving that way.

There's absolutely nothing out there! It's like all corn fields.

It's the one place where I actually wouldn't mind a few billboards to look at.

Conversation Study 4

Hey, how are you?

Good, and you?

I'm good, I'm just trying to get everything wrapped up before I'm gone next week.

Oh yeah, where are you going again?

Well, we *were* going to the Bahamas, but we decided to use the money for siding on the house instead. The siding is partly ripped off so we figured we might as well do it now.

I don't blame you, that's a big job. You don't want someone to mess that up and accidentally put up purple siding when you wanted blue!

Exactly! You know the perfectionist in me couldn't stand to let someone work on my house without me there! Yeah, so we'll just go next year.

Well, maybe you could rent a movie where they go on a tropical vacation, it's basically the same thing right?

Yeah, right!

Like that XYZ movie, that was really good.

I never saw it, maybe I will rent it. I'll definitely have the time, that's for sure.

Or maybe you shouldn't, maybe it will just make you more depressed.

You're right.

I have a trip planned soon too actually - for that conference I
was telling you about.

Oh yeah, that's right, you're going to that ABC conference in
Vegas aren't you? I'm jealous, I wish I could go.

Yeah, I'm pretty excited. Actually I'm really excited, but I don't
want to show it. I don't want everyone hating me. Plus I'm
just nervous about something going wrong. That always seems
to happen to me. Last time I had a vacation planned, my wife
got really sick the night before the flight.

Oh no, that's not fun.

Yeah it was horrible. She got that kind of sickness that only
happens once every ten years. And we're really tough about
sickness, we always try to keep working. But she couldn't
even get out of bed. So we ended up not being able to get
refunds on a bunch of our reservations and losing like $1,000
- it sucked!

Oh no, that's horrible.

So that's why I'm excited this time. I haven't been on vacation in
a long time.

Where are you staying?

In a little place called the *Bellagio* or something, I don't know if
you've heard of it.

Oh yeah, I may have...

I think it has some fountains or something.

Yeah, like the coolest fountains ever - those ones?

Yeah. I'm excited.

I'm so jealous. I love going to Vegas. And I love to gamble, but I
think my favorite part is the food. I love eating there. The
last time my husband and I went, we made it a goal to only
spend money on food. So we would go to casinos and spend like
a single quarter on a slot machine and then spend the rest of
the time eating. It was great.

That's funny. Where do you recommend?

There is this great Italian place owned by John Smith, and I had
the chicken linguine, and oh my gosh, each bite was like the

best food experience I've ever had. I go there every time
now.

You're making me want to get on a plane right now!

You'll have to tell me how it goes.

Definitely!

Okay, we should probably talk about work.

Yeah, so the XYZ project...

Conversation Study 5

We finally got rid of cable.

Oh yeah?

Yeah, we just do streaming only now.

Do you miss it at all?

Not one bit.

We got rid of ours about six months ago and we don't miss it at
all either.

We've become spoiled now though, because when we find a show
we like we just binge on it for the entire week until we're
done.

I know, it's so hard to resist! Our kids will never appreciate the
days of having to wait for something.

When we have to watch network TV, our kids are so
confused...they're always like 'why can't you pause it Daddy?'

That's so funny.

Yeah, they're so cute.

Hey, I forgot to ask, how was your Thanksgiving?

Good, yours?

We only had one major incident...our turkey exploded, so that
was weird.

Oh no, really? How?

Yeah it must have had too much water in it. We just heard a loud
popping sound - it looked like someone dropped a tiny bomb
inside it. It wasn't the prettiest thing.

That's not good - did it still taste good?

Yeah, it was actually really moist - which probably isn't surprising.

Hey, as long as it's not over-dry, that's probably the best you can hope for, right?

Yeah, my mom was so embarrassed though! In 35 years she has never messed up a turkey before.

Ours wasn't as crazy, but it's strange because everyone has kids and babies now. We used to all talk and stay up late playing board games, but now everyone just wants to sleep! And if we do stay up, we end up waking a baby so our games never last long.

That's too bad. Yeah, silent Pictionary wouldn't be very fun! Anyway, I've gotta go.

Yeah, me too, I'm trying to finish this really great book.

Oh yeah? What's it called?

The Conversation Code.

I've read that too! I loved it.

Yeah, isn't it great?

It's probably the best social skills book ever written.

Most definitely. The author is some kind of genius.

I know. Anyway, it was nice chatting with you!

Thanks for listening.
Now it's your turn to talk!

Notes

Preface

Zimbardo, Philip G., Margaret Esther Marnell, Paul Anthony Pilkonis. *Shyness: What It Is, What To Do About It.* Reading, Mass.: Addison-Wesley Pub. Co., 1990.

Introduction

Maslow, A.H. "A Theory of Human Motivation." *Psychological Review*, 50 no. 4, (1943): 370-396.

Lopes, P.N., D. Grewal, J. Kadis, M. Gall, and P. Salovey. "Evidence that emotional intelligence is related to job performance and affect and attitudes at work." *Psicothema* 18 (2006b): 132 – 138.

Chapter 1: First, Listen to Yourself

Kramer, E. "The judgment of personal characteristics and emotions from nonverbal properties of speech." *Psychological Bulletin*, 60, (1963): 408-420.

Mehrebian, A. *Silent messages: Implicit communication of emotions and attitudes.* Belmont, CA: Wadsworth, 1981.

Glass, Lillian J. *The Complete Idiot's Guide to Verbal Self-Defense.* New York, NY: Penguin Group, 1999.

Chapter 2: Watch Yourself

Morsella, Ezequiel, and Robert M. Krauss. "The role of gestures in spatial working memory and speech." *The American Journal of Psychology* 117, no. 3 (Fall 2004): 411-424.

Chapter 3: Increase Your Conversational Awareness

"ELIZA." *Wikipedia: The Free Encyclopedia.* Wikimedia Foundation, Inc. July 22, 2004. Web. August 19, 2014.

Baldwin, Mark B. "Relational Schemas and the Processing of Social Information." *Psychological Bulletin* 112 no. 3 (1992): 461-484.

Rumelhart, D.E., "Schemata: The Building Blocks of Cognition," in *Theoretical Issues in Reading Comprehension*, ed. R.J. Spiro et al. (Hillsdale, NJ: Lawrence Erlbaum, 1980).

Chapter 5: Fill Up Your Conversation Storage Tank

Churchill, Winston. *My Early Life: 1874 - 1904*. New York, NY: Charles Scribner's Sons, 1930.

Tzu, Sun. *The Art of War*. New York, NY: Delacorte Press, 1983.

Chapter 7: Expand Your Word Choices

Keating, N.H. *Dead Poets Society*. New York, NY: Starfire, Bantum Books, 1989.

Chapter 8: Adapt the Active Mindset and Initiate with Anyone

Carnegie, Dale. *How to Win Friends and Influence People*. New York, NY: Simon and Schuster, 1981.

Chapter 12: Paint Your Portrait with Effective Self-Disclosing

Collins, N.L., and L.C. Miller. "Self-disclosure and Liking: A Meta-analytic Review." *Psychological Bulletin* 116, no. 3 (1994): 457-475.

Chapter 17: Be Connectable and Maintain the Conversation

Kim, Larry. "Why Ambiverts Are More Successful and Influential Than Extroverts." *Inc.com*. October 1, 2014. Web. June 12, 2015.

P 10 — It's time to move away from a victim role

& 18 — energy, enthusiasm, conviction, feeling, concern

22 — deliberately pausing

26 — your movie is always playing

37 — I can prepare for any conversation

62 — TAPP TOPICS

Made in the USA
Lexington, KY
11 February 2018